SCIENCE FICTION AND EMPIRE

Liverpool Science Fiction Texts and Studies

1. Robert Crossley *Olaf Stapledon: Speaking for the Future*
2. David Seed (ed.) *Anticipations: Essays on Early Science Fiction and its Precursors*
3. Jane L. Donawerth and Carol A. Kolmerten (eds) *Utopian and Science Fiction by Women: Worlds of Difference*
4. Brian W. Aldiss *The Detached Retina: Aspects of SF and Fantasy*
5. Carol Farley Kessler *Charlotte Perkins Gilman: Her Progress Toward Utopia, with Selected Writings*
6. Patrick Parrinder *Shadows of the Future: H. G. Wells, Science Fiction and Prophecy*
7. I. F. Clarke (ed.) *The Tale of the Next Great War, 1871–1914: Fictions of Future Warfare and of Battles Still-to-come*
8. Joseph Conrad and Ford Madox Ford *The Inheritors*
9. Qingyun Wu *Female Rule in Chinese and English Literary Utopias*
10. John Clute *Look at the Evidence: Essays and Reviews*
11. Roger Luckhurst *'The Angle Between Two Walls': The Fiction of J. G. Ballard*
12. I. F. Clarke (ed.) *The Great War with Germany, 1980–1914: Fiction and Fantasies of the War-to-come*
13. Franz Rottensteiner (ed.) *View from Another Shore: European Science Fiction*
14. Val Gough and Jill Rudd (eds) *A Very Different Story: Studies in the Fiction of Charlotte Perkins Gilman*
15. Gary Westfahl *The Mechanics of Wonder: The Creation of the Idea of Science Fiction*
16. Gwyneth Jones *Deconstructing the Starships: Science, Fiction and Reality*
17. Patrick Parrinder (ed.) *Learning from Other Worlds: Estrangement, Cognition and the Politics of Science Fiction and Utopia*
18. Jeanne Cortiel *Demand My Writing: Joanna Russ/Feminism/Science Fiction*
19. Chris Ferns *Narrating Utopia: Ideology, Gender, Form in Utopian Literature*
20. E. J. Smith (ed.) *Jules Verne: New Directions*
21. Andy Sawyer and David Seed (eds) *Speaking Science Fiction: Dialogues and Interpretations*
22. Inez van der Spek *Alien Plots: Female Subjectivity and the Divine*
23. S. T. Joshi *Ramsey Campbell and Modern Horror Fiction*
24. Mike Ashley *The Time Machines: The Story of the Science-Fiction Pulp Magazines from the Beginning to 1950*
25. Warren G. Rochelle *Communities of the Heart: The Rhetoric of Myth in the Fiction of Ursula K. Le Guin*
26. S. T. Joshi *A Dreamer and a Visionary: H. P. Lovecraft in his Time*
27. Christopher Palmer *Philip K. Dick: Exhilaration and Terror of the Postmodern*
28. Charles E. Gannon *Rumors of War and Infernal Machines: Technomilitary Agenda-Setting in American and British Speculative Fiction*
29. Peter Wright *Attending Daedalus: Gene Wolfe, Artifice and the Reader*
30. Mike Ashley *Transformations: The Story of the Science-Fiction Magazine from 1950–1970*
31. Joanna Russ *The Country You Have Never Seen: Essays and Reviews*
32. Robert Philmus *Visions and Revisions: (Re)constructing Science Fiction*
33. Gene Wolfe (edited and introduced by Peter Wright) *Shadows of the New Sun: Wolfe on Writing/Writers on Wolfe*
34. Mike Ashley *Gateways to Forever: The Story of the Science-Fiction Magazine from 1970–1980*

SCIENCE FICTION AND EMPIRE

PATRICIA KERSLAKE

LIVERPOOL UNIVERSITY PRESS

First published 2007 by
LIVERPOOL UNIVERSITY PRESS
4 Cambridge Street
Liverpool L69 7ZU

This paperback edition published 2010

British Library Cataloguing-in-Publication Data
A British Library CIP record is available.

ISBN 978–1–84631–024–9 hardback
ISBN 978–1–84631–504–6 paperback

Typeset in Meridien by
R. J. Footring Ltd, Derby
Printed and bound by CPI Group (UK) Ltd, Croydon, CR0 4YY

Contents

Introduction   1

1. The Self and Representations of the Other in Science Fiction   8

2. Resistance Is Futile: Silencing and Cultural Appropriation   25

3. The Word for World Is Forest: Metaphor and Empire
   in Science Fiction   43

4. Things Fall Apart: Relativity, Distance and the Periphery   63

5. Moments of Empire: Perceptions of Lasswitz and Wells   83

6. Exoticising the Future: American Greats   105

7. The Shape of Things to Come: *Homo futuris* and
   the Imperial Project   127

8. A Postcolonial Imagination: Kim Stanley Robinson's *Mars*   146

9. Beyond Empire: Meta-empire and Postcoloniality   168

   Conclusion   188

   Notes   193

   Bibliography   206

   Index   214

Introduction

Science fiction (SF) has historically been perceived as a genre of the fabulous, a form of writing far outside the canon of 'literature', one that lacks boundaries, connections with reality or formal precedent. To some, that perception may be a vital attraction or a critical downfall. What is the purpose of a genre which deals with the extremes of our imagination? Indeed, is there a purpose? Does SF exist as a socially acceptable method of expressing those wild ideas for which there are few other public forums?

Admittedly, many SF narratives are romantic fantasy: that is, they present caricatures from the human imagination, and are derivative and quick to resort to a *deus ex machina*. Yet the SF genre cannot so easily be reduced to an assembly of remnants from other styles of writing mingled with exciting gadgets and exotic backgrounds, nor can its appeal and longevity be dismissed as the lure of scientific romance. Beneath a sometimes superficial appeal, SF is responsible for opening a variety of legitimate and strategic cultural discourses. It is in these cultural disquisitions that we discover the fundamental power and rationale of a genre that ultimately contributes to the knowledge and awareness humanity has of itself.

But an attempt to analyse all the disparate elements of such a massive genre is problematic. It is too broad and ambitious in its enthusiasms to examine as a whole. Therefore it is expedient to examine one of the most important and revealing foundations of SF, that of the function and manipulation of political power, of empire and its abuses within the genre, and to explore the great houses of fiction built upon such an informative substructure. This examination not only reveals the deeply considered purposes of the various texts but also exposes one of the master themes of SF: the human desire to experiment with its own future. It is a literature of the *agent provocateur*.

Despite its ambience of fantasy, SF is not the literature of ageing children. It is frequently brutal and condemning as it examines our today and our tomorrow through the microscope of the future and, equally as often, through the lens of the past. It permits us to see more clearly what we have been and what we may become. Through all the good that we are now or could produce, or the evil that we may consciously or unconsciously tolerate, humanity yearns for revelations of itself. With the curiosity of the sentient, we are always fascinated by our reflection and SF provides mirrors that stretch to either end of our existence.[1]

Since seeing ourselves directly in the mirror of the future is impossible, SF produces instead an unending succession of literary experiments, each one examining a small part of a much larger image and each equally necessary to the greater vision. In order to analyse such experiments properly we need to reason in the manner of scientists and to use contemporary theory, both literary and social, as a tool in the investigation; for each analysis it is necessary to set out the objective and the conclusions of our deliberation. Given that SF texts explore a variety of subjects in multiple environments, in order to test our cultural assumptions we use a crucible of critical analysis to isolate and explore specific behaviours so that we may reach conclusions. And when the experiments are complete, we will possess more knowledge of ourselves, of the human potential and of our willingness to accept the strengths and weaknesses that combine to make us as we are. If we are sensible, we may even learn to avoid some of the more dangerous results as we translate the theoretical into the applied.

But at what point should we begin the analysis? Though modern SF is more comfortable in the company of technology and science, earlier and perhaps more philosophical works, such as Jonathan Swift's *Gulliver's Travels* (1726) or Voltaire's *Micromégas* (1752), escaped with only lip service to any scientific body of knowledge and the occasional nod to literature. Yet even in the earliest of works, SF demonstrated a constancy of non-conformist thinking and a desire to experiment with the accepted standards of cultural thought. Since the close of the nineteenth century, writings in the newly formed genre moved steadily into the future and away from narrative tradition, while providing us with strange though highly perceptive reflections of the time. In the preface to an anthology of his own works, H. G. Wells commented on the function of looking forward in order to see today: 'the fantastic, the strange property or strange world, is only used to throw up and intensify our natural reactions of wonder, fear or perplexity.... The thing that makes such imaginations interesting is their translation into commonplace terms.'[2] Similarly, Terry Eagleton remarks upon the retrospection of understanding in saying that our knowledge of history travels backwards in time, so that we are always 'meeting ourselves coming the other way'.[3]

Just as a blue light is not visible in a blue room, the extraordinary can be seen only against a backdrop of the mundane. If our cultural *Weltanschauung* lies in the contrast between what we know today compared with what we knew yesterday, then how much more potentially enlightening is a genre which focuses itself explicitly upon the future? The usefulness of SF does not depend solely on machines and frontiers but is located in its capacity to place the known here and now beside an endless series of possibilities, of thought experiments, both historical and futuristic. Yet however wild the speculation of SF, it still requires some form of context, otherwise, without a legitimate point of reference, texts might appear so abstract and surreal that not even Samuel Taylor Coleridge's 'willing suspension of disbelief'[4] could guarantee to produce a meaningful narrative. Therefore SF usually provides us with a codified framework of reality, a backdrop of the customary, manifesting not a genre of anarchic fantasy but rather one of infinite and deliberate contrast.

And at what nexus of cultural development should the analysis begin? By the incorporation of alienation techniques which Bertolt Brecht would have recognised, and through an implicit comprehension of cultural, political and historical forces, SF has become an experiment in the quasi-predictive. And nowhere has that experiment been more enlightening than in the exploration of the notion of power formed within the construct of empire, especially when interrogated by the general theories of postcoloniality. Though an experiment to test the extent of the theory is productive, there are also theoretical limitations that require us to step beyond the current hypothesis and instead use related terms and concepts. Since the SF matrix is so complex, it is important for any functional discourse to move freely between contemporary thought and links between human nature and humanity's urge to growth. Though this may sometimes diverge from orthodox criticism and its implications, there is sufficient evidence to argue that a more elastic approach to postcolonialism enables us better to understand SF's dealings with empire.

This text explores experiments in the practice of power and empire in SF as it connects the imperial project from our past with the potential neo-empires of our future. Why does an archaic imperialism still seem to hold sway in a genre which claims the future as its present? How does the fictional combination of science and power affect contemporary cultural expectations? Will humanity ever outgrow its urge to expand and conquer, or are fictional galactic empires more important to the socio-political health of our race than we can possibly imagine? Are the terraforming and exploitation of a planet a human right? Do we, as a species in constant growth and development, have a right to expand and settle beyond our solar system? Since it is impossible for us to enact all of our ideas in 'real' life, we have devised SF as a testing ground for new thought, activities and philosophy. As a modern culture we have adopted the scientific approach and, in lieu of a field test, we probe our hypotheses in SF's theoretical environment.

While conventional postcolonial theory engages with specific historical references and geo-political situations, this text looks at and beyond the constructs of history, to extrapolate postcolonial paradigms and to examine new values of centre and periphery as humanity begins seriously to look at the colonisation of our Sun's planets. The earlier silencing and marginalisation of the Other in SF become the ultimate exercise in self-knowing as we turn to experiments of hybridity and polyvalency when cultures meet and coalesce. An investigation of the contemporaneity of H. G. Wells and Kurd Lasswitz connects us with extraterrestrial beings of an imperial imagination and contrasts them against the metaphor of Stanislaw Lem's *Solaris*, the humanistic visions of Philip K. Dick and Ursula K. Le Guin, and the genuinely postimperial 'Culture' of Iain M. Banks, each of these thought experiments pursuing positions impossible elsewhere in our reality.

Because this text deals with concepts located outside conventional theory, it is useful to examine the existing theoretical platform prior to subsequent discussion. Therefore in Chapter 1 Edward Said's academised notion of the Other and the crucial concept of centre and periphery are extrapolated beyond the conventions of orientalism and into the regions of human exploration as discussed in SF. The marginalisation of earlier cultures is explored and read against the persisting need in contemporary narratives to define humanity as different and elite, where the demand for the Other remains just as strong today, since it is through *Othering* that we may most clearly define ourselves. Probing the role of the Other as both adversarial and friendly, Gayatri Spivak's question of the subaltern is posed and SF tropes of communication and the power of the Western narrative are analysed as human societies seem set to expand and colonise.

A reading of John Wyndham's *The Midwich Cuckoos* and Philip K. Dick's *Do Androids Dream of Electric Sheep?* is the basis of Chapter 2, which considers the continuing inhumanity of the human race as it engages with silencing and marginalisation. In the former narrative, the transgression of British convention is discussed as the women of an entire village become unwilling host-mothers to alien children and Wyndham dissects the agonising process of the imposition of one culture's power upon another. In the latter, Dick uses androids to highlight the uncertainties and inequalities of difference in an environment of cultural disparity. Though both texts attempt to remove stereotypical paradigms and view their protagonists as 'human' despite the limitations placed upon them by the narrative, there is almost a sense of Shakespearean tragedy at the fate of these Others, which is still that of repression and eventual destruction. Is there a possibility that SF is consciously or unconsciously imperialist, or are these texts supreme examples of 'experimentation', narratives capable of objectively testing and examining imperialism?

George Lakoff and Mark Turner consider the grip of complex metaphor in fiction as economics and the elitism of science, both metaphors as a basis for a modern oppression, take their place in SF narratives beside other highly complex organisational models. Chapter 3 builds on this in a discussion of Le Guin's *The Dispossessed*, which relates the repression of an entire world, and begins by observing the simple metaphor of *wall*. Like much of SF, the wall does not appear immediately important, especially when any adult can look over it and it may be climbed by a child. Yet Le Guin's wall signifies much that is relevant to modern SF, as the transposition of importance between reality and concept is comparable to Lem's surreal vision in *Solaris*. Just as Le Guin takes the wall as an expression of imperial containment and exclusion, so Lem is inspired by the divine and the monstrous as human science imposes itself, with disastrous results, upon an inimical intelligence. Lem is particularly useful in this discussion because, while he works by metaphor, his narrative explicitly discusses and critiques science and scientific reasoning.

Chapter 4 turns to a discussion of how practical science affects experiments in the narrative. We see how current explanations of our physical universe render intergalactic travel intrinsically unlikely. Real scientific theory is extrapolated and located side by side with its fictional counterpart as both explore the lure of galactic space. The imperial production is critiqued in such terms as *distance*, discussed in the three essential dimensions of physical space, relative time and as an intellectual notion. Four models of empire are examined; each one is tested for its feasibility and its fictional attraction as the involvement of Said's Other becomes more apparent. And though humankind may yearn for the stars, the desire for an iconic centre – the ideal of 'home' – remains constant. Through a reading of Arthur C. Clarke's *Imperial Earth* against histories of the British Raj, we look at spatial history and the rhetoric of realities.

At the close of the nineteenth century, Lasswitz and Wells wrote almost simultaneously about a Martian invasion of Earth, yet both narratives are unique and display distinctly opposing images. Through a dissection of these texts in Chapter 5, traditional forms of imperialism are examined and questioned: why was one narrative a tragedy of colonial failure and the other a direct condemnation of enforced imperialism? While the differences between Lasswitz's 'Nume' and the Wellsian monsters are immediately apparent, the motivation and ultimate goal of both invading forces are not so obvious. As the texts diverge, we see two quite separate views from the imperial pathway, even though both reflect images of Western behaviour – one brutal and violent, the other benevolent and generous. Lasswitz and Wells each use SF to conduct a social experiment based on an external invasion in order to articulate and highlight the evils of the imperial project. Employing SF as a medium of critique, both authors make direct comment upon the cultural mood of their day. Since neither narrative had Clarke's problem of distance, the discussion of these two European texts reveals the ease with which nineteenth-century authors, lacking modern scientific knowledge, based their experiments on the fantasy of imperialism.

These works may be contrasted with the novels of two important US authors of the 'golden age' of SF, as science and fiction achieved a much closer collaboration. The late 1940s and early 1950s was a time of unusual activity in SF, especially in the United States, where two authors, Isaac Asimov and Robert A. Heinlein, established themselves as foremost in the genre. In Chapter 6, through a reading of Heinlein's *The Moon Is a Harsh Mistress*, we look at the historical connections between this golden age and earlier episodes of the imperial project, with a specific examination of the analogies Heinlein draws between the colonisation of the Moon and the American War of Independence. Asimov's *The Caves of Steel* and *The Naked Sun* provide a fascinating perspective on neo-colonisation and the effect of a roboticised society, as the author explores the radical differences between 'Earthers' and 'Spacers' and the human fear of replacement by automation. Are these texts experimenting with or condoning the various forms of power they discuss?

And where is SF actually going? As historical SF meets up with humanity's present scientific location, an important classical work of SF describes the tragic repetition of human experimentation and leaves us to examine our next step. Walter M. Miller's text *A Canticle for Leibowitz* is an appropriate bridge between the fictions of the past and those of the future. Where Asimov and Heinlein imagine progress and successful revolution, Miller reviews disintegrating cycles of religious power, his narrative of the Catholic Church anticipating the SF of later decades in a more dystopian and politically critical sense. Which experiment is likely to be more accurate as intertextuality increases and authors of SF become far more aware of literary critical theory? Darko Suvin's concept of 'novum' is read against Walter M. Miller's saga of religious empire as Chapter 7 examines the cycles of human power and an apparent manipulation of cultures into a continuation of imperialism and neo-imperialism.

We head to the red planet in Chapter 8. Kim Stanley Robinson's massive *Mars* trilogy observes a more conventional aspect of the manipulation of power and imperialism as we examine a contemporary view of science, politics and economics at work. Ostensibly a postcolonial text, the extended narrative again demonstrates the circular nature of imperial development, while it explores the politics of terraforming as well as the emergent political situations of neo-empire. Cultural hybridity emerges as the new Martians declare their independence from Earth's centre and we follow Robinson's meticulous reportage and extrapolation of developing planetary sciences and economic turmoil. What will it be like to feel divorced not only from the country of your birth but also from the planet on which your species evolved? How will the old bindings of nationalism and religion continue to tic and restrict authentic postcoloniality? The thoughts and memories of earlier European migrants are contrasted with those of Robinson's 'First Hundred' pioneers as it becomes clear that he speaks not only of a physical return when his characters admit 'we can never go back'.

And what will happen when our race is so old and widespread that it no longer remembers the first planet? In Chapter 9, 'meta-empire' and postcoloniality engage with the fall of empire and the development of replacement organisations. Many SF texts deal with the fall of empire, but this is usually to allow them to introduce a new, preferred design. Since so much of SF depends upon the exploration and settlement of our own and other galaxies, what form of central government or general control would need to exist in order that humanity might have the ability to continue a peaceful expansion? Banks dispenses completely with the social laboratory and constructs a sequence of narratives where all historical and cultural constraint is removed. His novels, based around a vast and interstellar body known only as the Culture, offer the clearest concept yet of a postcolonial future as he takes us beyond traditional imperialism and into meta-empire. Will humanity be able to dispense with ancient political and cultural prejudices only by dispensing with almost all else which currently represents the image we have of ourselves?

Let us enter the laboratory and see.

1. The Self and Representations of the Other in Science Fiction

In his work *Orientalism: Western Conceptions of the Orient* (1978), Edward W. Said first academised the postcolonial notion of the Other. For there to be an 'us', he stated, there has to be a 'not-us', an Other, as both subjects define themselves through a mutual process of exclusion. In the demarcation of a place or centre for one culture or individual, there is an automatic displacement and marginalisation of all who stand outside or apart from that place. The opposition between 'us' and 'them', or between man and not-man (or 'Un-man' as C. S. Lewis called his malignant villain in *Perelandra*, 1943), achieves a central structural tension which inspires the very idea of 'alien'. This notion holds true in all domains of SF, and is especially notable in those texts that invoke images of an imposed colonialisation. Said supported this, saying 'we look for things described by the books so that we (in the end) do not see what is real, but what we choose to see as real',[1] a thought originally discussed by Francis Bacon in *Novum Organum* (1620). When we see what we think we ought to be seeing and extrapolate assumptions of behaviour based upon such fallacy, a form of 'representation' is produced. When one culture imposes its perceptions on another, in that it begins to see the Other not as they are but as, in Said's words, 'they ought to be',[2] then the process of representation becomes inevitable: a choice is made to see a 'preferred' real. It is in the combination of these two ideas – *the self* and *representations of the Other* – that we are first able to locate the fundamentally important function of the Other in SF.

The location of the Other in SF is an excellent place to begin the identification and explanation of experiments in the use of power and politics, since it possesses an affinity to both the concepts of postcolonialism and the focus of SF texts discussed in works such as Mark Rose's *Alien Encounters* (1981). However, before we can comprehend the nature of the genre's manipulation of the various forms of political, economic and cultural imperialism, it is important that we see exactly what is being manipulated and why.

The role of empire in SF is a massive form of cultural inculcation, with different factional stances taken at different periods by different authors and for widely differing reasons. Yet all factions, every period and each author share a comparative and basic unit of currency – people. Whether these people are humans from our historical past, monsters of the Victorian imagination or a sublime post-human from our extreme future, each unit is given a place in the structure of the preferred social vision we hold of ourselves. As individuals are selected to meet certain literary and cultural criteria, they are also subjected to a variety of pressures and circumstances in order that we might see, in the clearest mirror possible, potential future images of ourselves. And right beside these images are reflections of those considered 'not-us'. What might we do when we meet the Other?

Whether alienated and excluded by physical distinction, as is Victor Frankenstein's terrible creation, or by less obvious cultural mores, the Other has always been and must always be perceived as different and as the 'outsider'. For the Other to possess narrative power, it is vital that their position outside cultural convention is made manifest, since such a role is relatively weak unless it clearly represents difference. To successfully position a character as the Other demands the *a priori* binary construct of centre and periphery, as discussion of the Other is impossible without a primary definition of the self, which, in turn, rests upon where we see ourselves located. If we inhabit the centre of our existence (our world, life, knowledge), then the Other, who cannot inhabit the same place, becomes marginalised by definition: they cannot be us. They are different and apart from us. They are *outside*. The idiosyncrasies usually applied to those who inhabit this external limbo fall characteristically – and conveniently – into those spaces we choose not to recognise in ourselves, the 'half-imagined, half-known; monsters, devils, heroes, terrors, pleasures, desires'[3] of Said's 'Orient'. In *The Outsider* (*L'Étranger*, 1942), Albert Camus's main protagonist, Meursault, dwells in just such a place, deriving much of his narrative potency through his resulting detachment. It is not unusual for a reader to experience an antagonism towards Meursault because his behaviour appears 'unnatural' and 'different'.

Said's postcolonial contentions, though applicable to the corpus of creative narratives, are particularly useful tools in the analysis of SF. His academic recognition of the Other as a fictional being did not develop from a solely personal hypothesis. The Other has been an essential element of literature since the concept of self first became a specifically acknowledged theme in the Attic dramas. Plainly, no such concept could have arisen outside a definitive bipolar paradigm, as neither form is able to exist in isolation. In meditations on the opposition of the Other, Bernhard Waldenfels comments that 'If we reflect on the fact that the known is what it is only in contrast to the alien, we see that both originate from a common process of *differentiation*, and that this process, opening a social field, takes different forms and achieves different degrees'.[4] This observation suggests that the door of differentiation not only opens both ways, but is possessed of an arbitrary swing and, indeed, depending on which side the observer stands, is sometimes a different door. How we see the Other depends on where we stand, on the social angle at which we learn and on the way our personal paradigms allow us to perceive. The paradoxical connection between these variables is that it is the observer alone who decides what is 'seen'. Since all things outside the self must be Other, then the degree of 'Otherness' rests in the ego and consciousness of the observer. How you perceive the Other depends very much on how you see yourself. Just as Earth's diurnality exacts night and day, where light cannot be seen without darkness, so too does the advanced ego demand the notion of a complementary Other: the illuminated self cannot be seen except in a dark mirror. And our obsession with fundamental self-identification is such that we will go to almost any length to elicit the desired response. As Ted Krulik notes, 'We want to meet the alien so we may say, "Here we are. What do you think of us?"'[5] It seems we cannot fix the limits of ourselves except through the eyes of an external observer. If we accept that the Other is as necessary in literature as is any protagonist, the examination of this construct and a careful dissection of the issue of 'Othering' are vital steps in the comprehension of many themes central to SF.

This recurrent definition and location of self is a pervasive leitmotif in SF, the fascination of 'outside' only partially explained by the allure of the unknown and the expansionist imperative. It is with the possibility of gaining a new perspective on ourselves that the prospect of an encounter with the Other, the alien, takes hold. Humanity's endless dissatisfaction with the status quo ensures that the question of self is an unanswerable binary. As we are never to realise what we are in the absence of alterity, the role taken by the Other is not only crucial but is as important to our well-being as the notion of self. The greater the possible difference between 'us' and 'them', the greater becomes humanity's potential to develop, and many major works of SF have focused upon this philosophical desire to discover the ultimate condition of humankind. It is interesting that a significant number of these works depict the future of the human species as languishing in relative dystopia. It is also of interest to note that some of the most critically acclaimed narratives which deal with the 'future' were not originally viewed as SF texts but as political commentaries. Indeed, George Orwell's *Nineteen Eighty-Four* (1949) and Aldous Huxley's satirical dystopia *Brave New World* (1932) will never be considered simply as SF or fantasy. Yet it is in the spaces between the philosophical iconography of self and the latter-day idealism of such writers as Huxley and Orwell that the Other in SF has evolved.

The link between the Other in SF and the Other in postcolonial theory may seem an obvious one, but there are important distinctions. In the heyday of expansionist Europe's digestion of the East, the indigenous Other was already a known, and therefore, in Western terms, a dismissible factor.

The peoples of India, Africa and the South Americas had been 'discovered' and assimilated into a Western *Weltanschauung* years before an incessant capitalism demanded the full-scale deconstruction and mutation of non-Western cultures. It was not until colonialism was perceived in the light of *post*colonialism that the existence and the erratic acknowledgement of the Other were clearly delineated. However, it required the arousal of Western academe to the possibility that the West was *not* the only centre for the previously subaltern cultures to begin to establish a collective voice. The difference between the words of historic fact and the narration of SF rests in the impossibility for SF to perceive the Other in any complete sense. Any such acceptance denies SF speculative power over humanity's continued development and growth: once all Others were clearly defined, humanity would have lost the opportunity to gain further insight into itself. Postcolonial thought accepts and embraces the concept of the Other, as it enables polyvalency and hybridity, but in SF the Other must forever remain a figure apart: poised somewhere between angel and demon, an existence hovering on the imaginary boundaries of the known.

In a similar vein, where postcolonial theory challenges the silencing and marginalisation of the Other, SF takes the stance that such marginalisation is a key element of self-identification. If something is unusual or different, we treat it cautiously and limit our interactions. Deliberate obstructions to communication or, as Konstanze Streese considers them, 'discursive strategies that denigrate the Other linguistically'[6] are common in SF but often receive only superficial reception: it is not in the interest of the genre to permit the Other to speak too clearly, at least not at first. Just as silencing the Other is an imperialist colonial technique of repression, so too is the Other prevented from speech in SF, but for different reasons. If the Other is permitted to accuse colonial authority in a comprehensible manner, the Hegelian master–slave relationship begins to disintegrate. Although the same relationship may not be overtly sought, the need for a similar *expression* of power ensures that in a confrontation with the Other in SF, humankind must usually be the superior. It is not enough that humanity insists upon the perception of itself only by means of its external reflection: the preferred counterpart is often likely to be the weaker of the two images, as exampled not only by the eventual defeat of invading Martians but also in many other SF encounters, such as with the 'Black Hats'[7] in Robert Heinlein's *The Number of the Beast* (1980).

If silencing the Other provides SF with an indirect ability to define the potential of humankind, we see how humankind's universalistic pretensions to claim the Earth as the only significant centre supports this intent. Humanity's centre is the only one known to us and, as such, requires the same reflection of its Others, though on a much larger scale. For every

Earth, there is a 'not-Earth'. For this reason, the majority of SF narratives dealing with extra-planetary colonisation perceive the exotic 'new' centre through a limited comparison with our mother planet. Again, it is a cultural preference for this comparison to be weighted towards the negative, to be satisfied only with those aspects of the planet that are *not* Earthly, that are *less* than those on Earth: the red of a Martian sky is compared unfavourably with the blues of Earth; planets are too dry or too hot; they have too much gravity or insufficient gravity; they are too biospherically dissimilar to nurture human life; *ad infinitum*. The list of negatives is a long one and is usually more prominent than one of apparent positives. Even those planets which seem initially to offer an Edenic location in comparison with Earth usually declare their hostility at some point – such as Larry Niven's planet Mount LookItThat (arrived at on the ship *We Made It*).[8] It seems that only by a negative measurement of any new planet against a Terran template can the original centre – the Earth – maintain its status. Through Maya, a Martian colonist, Kim Stanley Robinson observes and identifies this habit: 'the negotiators and interviewers revealed what she called their "terracentricity". Nothing mattered to them, really, but things Earthly. Mars was interesting in some ways, but not actually important.'[9] The power of the original 'centre' is maintained by devaluing the competition.

Pervasive anthropomorphism is another technique through which the slight of 'terracentrism' in SF may be detected. Comparison of the self against the Other is relatively simple if the Other is discernibly different. When that difference is not so obvious, or if circumstances dictate that the difference cannot be easily addressed, there is always the option of an anthropomorphic bequest. As used countless times in popular children's images of the unknowable (the 1940–57 Hanna–Barbera 'Tom and Jerry' cartoons, for example, or the 2002 and 2004 *Scooby-Doo* and *Scooby-Doo 2* films), the being of the Other may be diminished to the point where difference becomes 'companionable'. In Heinlein's *Red Planet* (1949), Martians are first seen as 'Bouncers', small spheres of a 'warm furry mass, faintly pulsating'.[10] Here, misrepresentation of the Other denies them even the status of Otherness. Perceived in terms of a cuddly animal, there is little of Heinlein's Bouncer that appears different (to the Terran mindset) from a domestic pet. Heinlein's Other is small and does not threaten; it is warm and furry, therefore easily aligned with a terrestrial animal. It likes to be petted. Only when the discovery is made that the Bouncer is in fact the juvenile stage of the Martian life form, and that the full adult is very large, highly evolved and incomprehensibly powerful, does the representation begin to change. In the passage from the concept of 'known' into the shadows of 'different', Heinlein's Martian returns properly to the SF arena of 'not-self' and resumes its role of comparison provider.

At a tangent to the anthropomorphised Other is the Other as monster. As Gary K. Wolfe suggests in *The Known and the Unknown: The Iconography of Science Fiction*, 'Since monsters symbolise the unknown, the encounter with the monster is often caused either by humans breaching the barriers that separate them from the monster's realm, or vice versa'.[11] Unlike Heinlein's companionable little Martians, the monster illustrates difference as threat. Usually markedly non-human in appearance, the monster Other reminds humanity of its terrestriality and its physical limitations. In the same way that Beowulf overcame great adversity to achieve the destruction of Grendel, so the monsters of SF provide yet another measure against which humanity may constantly redefine itself. The more 'monstrous' the being, the more significant is the power required to defeat it. But, as Wolfe adds, 'Ideally, the monster is not simply annihilated, it is appropriated'.[12] The death of the adversarial monster is an insufficient mark of human superiority, since mortality and death are also measures of humanity. To be rendered totally powerless, the ideological menace supplied by the Other must be absorbed into the body politic of the centre. It becomes clear that any being signified as Other through physical appearance alone is paradoxically an inappropriate reflection of the preferred self-image of humankind. The most 'challenging' monster cannot be distinguished by sight; indeed, its menace is generated by that very fact. Dick adopts this idea in *Do Androids Dream of Electric Sheep?*,[13] where the 'replicant', an android creation in exact human image, becomes the chilling and binary representation of and for the society in which they exist.

Since Said's initial foray into the nature of orientalism and the inherent exoticising of the 'not-us', postmodern and postcolonial claims of universalism and marginalisation have directed a spotlight upon Western writings which indulge in such imperialist fantasies. It is important to note, however, that the technique of Othering is not restricted to Western texts. From an analysis of both Western and non-Western SF, we see that the nature of the Other transcends the idea of culture in its broadest sense. The power obtained by the 'insider' over his or her opposite becomes visible even within the satirical, though occasionally Marxist works of the Strugatsky brothers, Arkady and Boris, whose novellas of 'future history' reflect the teachings of Marxism–Leninism and revolve around the 'centre' of communism.[14] The Strugatskys, whose narratives parallel many aspects of Western SF, incorporate perceptions of the West that question a Soviet ideology. While these texts display a general partiality towards unknown aliens, there are many and various allusions to the hedonism, selfishness and *meshchanstvo* ('philistinism') of the capitalist nations. To the Soviet readers of the Strugatskys, the natives of the West were more Other than any native of Mars, as their texts engaged with the social concerns that surrounded capitalism in the

Khrushchev era. Considered by many of their peers to be the greatest of 'Iron Curtain' SF writers, the two brothers were more interested in how the future might affect people, rather than how people might change the future. Following the Russian narrative traditions of fables and great heroic tales, Arkady and Boris wrote initially of far-future romances where humanity conquers the forces of nature in a search for the ultimate utopia, in such collective works as *Space Apprentice* (1962, translated in 1981) and *Noon: 22nd Century* (1961, translated in 1978). Where the enthusiasms of contemporary Western SF writers related to the fall into dystopia, or moral collapse brought about by automation and technology, the Strugatskys wrote mainly of the soaring spirit of a race concerned to create a better future for itself – where we are all Pinocchios looking for a better life. From such a perspective, the avaricious and predatory expansionists of the West were more to be wondered at than the conventional bug-eyed monster.

These differences in the perceptions humans have of and between themselves provide a further aspect to the notion of the Other. How many images of the future have been created as a result of current political tension, both internal and external to an author's political and moral location? The urge to make political comment has generated numerous narratives, from Jonathan Swift and Voltaire, through to the socialist H. G. Wells's *When the Sleeper Wakes* (1899), to Victor Rousseau's *The Messiah of the Cylinder* (1917) and onward. But at what point does our neighbour become our Other? In *The Chrysalids* (1955), John Wyndham writes of Otherness within an immediate family as physical mutations appear in the generations following an atomic war. Yet as physical 'monsters', these Others inspire less fear than those who look like 'us', yet who are inimical to us, a situation explored in another of Wyndham's novels, *The Midwich Cuckoos* (1957). But while Wyndham's golden-eyed alien children in the latter title are not initially different to their mothers, it is in the process of their becoming different that an Otherness appears. The development of difference, and particularly the known devolving away into an unknown – often forms the basis of the fear of political Othering. A difference in political motivation can produce an increasing sense of estrangement, a situation which the Strugatsky narratives illustrated more and more strongly, and which has been reflected in their latter works of irresolvable ethical tension.

The use of the Other, and the use of a fundamental ability *to* Other, are methods by which SF has evolved into a legitimate cultural discourse. The desire for there to be a recognisable difference between humanity and humanity's Other has taken SF into serious social expositions of contemporary society, in that a social form cannot be constructed without acknowledgement of its opposite. As in Chinua Achebe's *Things Fall Apart* (1958), the centre cannot hold when the periphery becomes indistinguishable. When

Onkonko, a tribal chief and Achebe's main protagonist, becomes assimilated into the fringes of Western culture, his tribal role grows less definite.
Following the reduction of his ancient authority, Onkonko is rejected by his
clan, who can 're-centre' only after the expurgation of his transgression,
the atonement of which requires Onkonko's suicide. This theme of transgression is relatively common in SF, where images of 'going native' carry a
far greater cultural danger than that offered to nineteenth-century imperialists.[15] The choice to embrace the society of the Other (the alien) means that
the individual, of necessity, rejects his or her own centre (Earth). Such an
action, if repeated by a sufficient number of individuals, would result in the
degeneration of the original centre in favour of its opposite – quite literally
the end of civilisation as they had come to know it! It may be argued that
without the clear demarcation provided by such an artificial binary, without
the deliberate externalities created by the concept and the ability to enforce
a cultural loyalty, the inherent value of the Other would lessen. In these
instances, the Other is often seen in the quasi-religious aspect of a satanic
temptation,[16] an attempt to lure the unwary from the true centre into an
alien oblivion. How individuals react to such a temptation depends on the
strength of their link to their centre and on the power of the centre itself.
The redefinition of 'centre' that necessarily results from this type of moral
quandary also redefines the nature of the society under threat, a painful
self-examination that inspects weaknesses as well as strengths. In this way,
the Other plays an integral part in humanity's willingness to know itself.

Given a residual academic reluctance to engage with SF, it is necessary to
extrapolate certain contemporary theories and exchange the term 'East' for
'extraterrestrial', so that the principles thus debated become productive in a
genre which in itself has been marginalised. In his introduction to cultural
and literary theory, Peter Barry reflects on Said's notion of Eurocentrism. The
East, Barry suggests, became the repository and projection of unpalatable
Western attributes, and he cites cruelty, sensuality, decadence and laziness
as prime examples. At the same time, and paradoxically:

> The East is seen as a fascinating realm of the exotic, the mysterious and
> the seductive. It also tends to be homogenous, the people there being
> anonymous masses, rather than individuals, their actions determined
> by instinctive emotions (lust, terror, fury, etc) rather than by conscious
> choices or decisions.[17]

The extrapolation of current argument is perfectly acceptable when the
nature of the principle under discussion remains the same. Yet the substitu-
tion of one term for another fails to accurately portray the essential nature
of SF. Similar to a *Bildungsroman*, the genre charts the growth of a collective
mindset (rather than of an individual). The place of the Other provides a

vast mirror, against which no single parochial culture is large enough to offer a reflectable substance. The appeal of using the Earth itself as a centre for comparison becomes understandable in a debate that discusses the more absolute forms of difference common in a genre that accidentally shoulders various cultural positions on the very definition of life.

And if the Other is no more than a projected reflection of ourselves, how is this image affected by the suppositions of contemporary science and technology? Wolfe writes: 'Technology not only creates new environments for humanity, it also creates new images of humanity itself. We see ourselves reflected in science fiction's visions of robots and monsters and aliens.'[18] This vulnerability of form is one of SF's more constant features, as the trope of 'human' strives to maintain itself against the transience of its narratives. In the same way that we require an external Other to affirm our own humanity, so too does 'humanity' need to reassure itself that it is not monstrous. As with Said's rhetorical figures of 'half-imagined, half-known', SF narratives often go to great lengths to divide the human from the not-human. Wolfe notes that descriptions of the alien frequently incorporate repellent imagery and metaphor, as with Wells's invading Martians in *The War of the Worlds*, which are described in terms of 'snakes, bears, Gorgons, fungi and octopi ... slavering, bearlike mouths that drip saliva ... of a sickly grey colour like "wet leather"'.[19] While the presence of the Other is essential to a human self-perception, it is equally important that the Other is distinctly non-human, so that we may more easily see our differences.[20] Waldenfels's principle of differentiation ensures that, where possible, the Other will be described in a manner that is recognisably *less* than human or, as in Wells's narrative, suggestive of disease and decay. In these instances, the Other revolts rather than threatens us. It is only when the Other is so different as to be indescribable, or too similar to be seen as Other, that true fear results.

In SF, the Other traditionally takes the aspect of the unknown. There is no requirement for this unknown to be overtly different or even antagonistic, though mainstream authors rarely dismiss the entertainment of potential misunderstanding or conflict. The Other is often portrayed as a disassociated humanity, as in Robinson's *Mars* trilogy (discussed in Chapter 8), where Martian colonists come to the realisation that 'we were out on our own; and so we became fundamentally different beings'.[21] But Robinson's texts do not follow the traditional SF theme of 'Other as monster' presented by, for example, Mary Shelley and Wells. His *Mars* narratives offer one of many variations on the possibility of the Other, in this instance a demonstration of the inevitability of change through extremities of isolation by distance. Robinson's colonists are neither superhuman nor outwardly different. Mostly scientists – often seen as a stereotypical and traditional Other – they are tangible individuals, prone to every fallibility, who become Other through the common process of migration. In letters describing the mass migration of German Jews to Bolivia in the late 1930s, Leo Spitzer speaks of a similar phenomenon: 'Bewilderment. Nostalgia. Yearning. Difference. An alien world – a world of Others.'[22] Whether we consider the colonisation of Mars or Bolivia, by desire or compulsion, the nexus of fiction and history provides further evidence of the human nostalgia for the centre and uneasiness with the unknown.

Isolation by distance is a significant aspect of the Other. As artificial and as arbitrarily imposed as a national frontier, the border between the physically known and unknown plays as major a part in the protocols of SF as it does in the definition of the Other. Before the value of the Other can be assessed in terms of fictional impact, it is necessary, as in the process of determining the centre, to ascertain who or what has marginalised the Other. With the implicit realism of contemporary SF, it is a recent convention that the process of extreme travel must render the traveller into a different form. Robinson suggests, similar to Heisenberg's 'uncertainty principle' where the observed is altered through the process of observation, that the act of the interplanetary journey is a component of Othering. Travellers who complete a journey of several years are significantly altered from the beings they were at the outset, and those who measure travel by means of time rather than distance must be perceived from the outset as Other. The extended motion of the venture, the transition from 'within' to 'without' – as in the journey to Mars of the 'First Hundred' (the initial colonising party of scientists and engineers) on the *Ares* – is enough to metamorphose the cultural value of the individual or group.

If distance travelled from the centre is a trope of Otherness, we must consider the extension of that trope in the light of interplanetary magnitudes. Waldenfels identifies three concentric rings of alterity by isolation, with the proposal that 'There is the "alien" that belongs to the Other; there is the "foreign" that comes from the outside; and there is the "strange", which looks or sounds curious'.[23] From the status of being a known quantity, the traveller, through the convention of an extended journey, has stepped from the culturally 'acceptable' into the dubious land of the Other. Distance from the centre, therefore, is directly related to Othering. In this respect, SF has extrapolated a social trend that began with the domestication of the horse and that later saw the arrival of the steam engine and aeroplane. The invention of the railway and the internal combustion engine irrevocably altered a society's perception of distance and what was previously an extended journey became lessened, until global travel now depends on the convenience of the airport. SF takes the perception of distance to the next logical level, with the assumption that travel throughout our solar system will eventually be unremarkable. If we accept that the place of departure is

the traveller's cultural 'centre', it is of interest, given the ongoing exploration of the planets, to question how far a person must now proceed before
he or she reaches the indefinable edge of a nebulous periphery. At what
point do we become Other?

Said offers 'imaginative geography' as an answer. As a physical artificiality, neither specific nor constant, it is rather a motile policy through which
expansionist Western cultures, the self-perceived 'home' of science and SF,
have set up theatrical representations of centre and periphery. After deliberation on the presence of the Other in such artificiality, Said notes that 'On
this stage will appear figures whose role it is to represent the larger whole
from which they emanate'.[24] The entire notion of 'out there' is a fabrication
essential in the self-identification by Western writers of the West as the
centre. Likewise, the historical exoticism of the East maintains its grip on
the imagination of the West. Within this Western centre, the Other is either
adored or despised but rarely accepted on the middle ground; the contemporary Eurocentrism of the technologically advanced northern hemisphere
has, quite simply, been extrapolated into SF. Angelika Bammer calls for an
end to such extremes, with the comment that 'between xenophobia and
xenophilia there is no place to rest: both constitute the place of fear and
denial from which we must, for all our sakes, move on'.[25] If science and
technology are still viewed as a monopoly of the fortunate few, the Other
in SF cannot help but be seen through the eyes of Western positivism. The
boundary between *periphery* and *outside* has been, and continues to be, drawn
by the conflict between the Western compulsions of fear and desire.

Pertinent to this paranoiac Western conception of the outsider, Stephen
David Ross asks 'Can we measure the other at the limits of who we are except
as danger, a threat to our otherness?'[26] The mock bravado of the scientific-
ally advanced West is patently revealed in SF through its obsessions. If the
genre would falter without the construct of the Other to reflect ourselves,
it would be similarly handicapped without the ability to consider the Other
as a threat. SF has traditionally projected human differences upon the
outsider, not the least of which has been an alacrity to perceive a potential
for opposition and conflict. The universal appeal of the hero is lost unless
the hero is situated within an appropriate context, and the unknown Other
constitutes the perfect adversarial foil. Historical Western oppositions in SF
are considered by Brian Ash, who nicely observes that:

> The treatment of alien life forms in the early 'space operas' was reminis-
> cent of the attitude of the American settlers to the native Red Indians.
> It was identical, in fact, to the arrogance of a supposedly superior race
> typified by Wells' Martians. If an alien stood in the way, it was blasted
> into the ground – and how should it have been otherwise?[27]

This aspect of the Other as adversary is only a partial picture and simplifies a complex historical relationship. It is also necessary for the antithetic Other to meet a number of conventional requirements in order for it to become a *suitable* adversary. The ability to appropriate and manipulate the representation of another being into a misrepresented form of threat is requisite in the transformation of science itself into a heroic form. The human desire to be perceived as worthy would be threatened by any opponent able to dismember a superficial morality. Therefore 'suitable' aliens must possess several qualities: they must embody an exoticism of form that renders them easily recognisable as Other; they must be dominated by at least one characteristic that can be portrayed as a negative from the human perspective; and they must, in some manner, menace the human ability to survive (this menace may take several forms, not the least of which is the imperilment of the Earth, the human centre). Once clearly identified as aggressive, or implacable, or too 'different' to coexist peacefully with an enlightened humanity, then the Other becomes a legitimate target. It is at this point that the process of stereotypical manipulation in SF, when faced with the Other, often defeats its own attempts at heroism. To create a resourceful enemy, the alien is endowed with a varied and heterogeneous degree of intelligence. However, it is rarely an intelligence that humans would find incomprehensible and, most significantly, it is hardly ever an intelligence superior to humankind's. From a postcolonial perspective, the misrepresentation of the Other is almost complete. The alien first exoticised and distant, then identifiably different, has now become a quantifiable and dangerous known, sufficiently intelligent to pose a danger but never sufficiently superior to overcome the wiles of *Homo sapiens*.

To meet an ancient measure of heroism, great odds had to be faced and overcome for the hero demonstrate his or her capacity to rise above the norm. Unlike the Babylonian story of the Gilgamesh, who in his magnificent struggles risked the anger of the gods and died, SF has been sometimes weakened by a desire to confront only its own restrained representations, which enables the superior 'us' to defeat the inferior 'them'. While there is nothing wrong in the ability to trounce an enemy, the enemy who is clearly 'not-us' (i.e. clearly inferior) is a soft target and hardly the stuff of legend. Historically, the infinite contrast of SF ensured that aliens were sufficiently different so that SF would not be accused of persecuting its own. Once the alien is separated from 'our' centre by enough distance, its inability to respond in kind limited the threat of reprisal. Best of all, the distant alien provided an opportunity to indulge in the worst kind of violence in the name of human survival or even progress. This image of the Other as a malignant but defeatable enemy is less popular in contemporary texts than in those of the nineteenth and early twentieth centuries, but remains a great favourite with the moguls of Hollywood.[28] For example, the sixth (or third) episode of the *Star Wars* saga, *Revenge of the Sith* (2005), offers a spectacular vision of revivification as the longed-for Jedi saviour mutates into the darkly evil Darth Vader.

An alternative to the Other as 'enemy' is the Other as 'friend', or *same*. Similar in principle to the perception of Robinson's Martian colonists, the outsider is increasingly the subject of a human empathy. From a postcolonial stance, this area is a complex one, rife with circular arguments. At the outset, it is important to acknowledge that SF has established the Earth as its centre: all things beyond are alien and Other. In the same way that Rudyard Kipling developed a deep sympathy with the colonised subjects of the British Raj, so too has SF attempted to represent the extraterrestrial subject as a being compatible with human society. Regardless of worthy intent, any text that attempts to relegate the Other to the position of 'friend' is guilty of the very crime it strives to prevent. Whether the alien is portrayed as aggressive and troublesome or friendly and sociable is academic. The issue is not the approachability (or otherwise) of the Other, but that the myth of the alien as the noble savage has been perpetuated.

In this respect, the notion of a 'friendly' Other is simply another construct of the genre. That the SF authors expound an aspiration for the Other to become as they would have them be does not alter the implied representation and marginalisation of the subject. The issue of 'the Other as same' is a problematic extension of this construct. For humanity to perceive the Other as friendly requires the SF text to produce an appropriate image. To see the Other as we see ourselves necessitates the complete absorption of the subaltern culture, in effect, to direct the change of an external society into its opposite. Therefore the desire to render the Other 'more like us' is a solecism. Once the external society is absorbed, the Other ceases to be, or, as Waldenfels observes, 'a determined, explained or understood alien would cease to be alien. The alien would simply vanish'.[29] According to Said's idea of 'us' and 'them', one group's knowledge of another is of necessity self-limited. The moment either group is aligned too closely with its alternative is the moment difference becomes similarity and when the Other merges into 'us'.

Closely linked to this coalescence of disparate centres is the issue of language and linguistics. Language tells us a great deal about the culture that uses it and the manner in which it perceives itself and its Others. Since the West dominates the SF genre, it is usual for mainstream texts to be written in English. Given that the Other, once known, becomes a lesser threat, it is inevitable that the English language, with all its associated values and sub-sets, plays a large part in the (mis)representation of the alien. Certainly, some authors have challenged this problem and have the alien communicate only haltingly or through some understandable but non-verbal technique, or contrive some device which defeats speech. Non-verbal communication in itself, however, reinforces the image of the Other as that which is *less* than human or, at best, child-like and insufficiently mature to express itself through adult forms. Terry Carr made a significant departure from this trope in his short story 'The Dance of the Changer and the Three' (1968), where the alien Others have no corporeal presence but are a form of energy. Their language is expressed through dance and communication depends upon the correct interpretation of the motion.

While Carr's text is important for its singular approach, the crux of the problem is unchanged. No matter how sophisticated the Other's method of communication, it is always compared with the human skill of verbalisation. As Emmanuel Levinas argues, 'Literary representations of the Other in colonialist writing are more often than not characterized by means of attributing restricted and deficient capability of language to the colonised'.[30] If two centres cannot communicate through a shared language, then the Other remains problematic and unapproachable. Yet a certain approachability is mandatory if the Other is to elicit sympathy and human interest. Arthur C. Clarke made this inability to communicate a central issue when he wrote of the mysterious black obelisk in *2001: A Space Odyssey* (1968). Clarke's resolution was to arrange the convenient assimilation of a human astronaut into the 'mind' of an entity which was then able to act as go-between and interpreter. In his *Out of the Silent Planet* (1938), C. S. Lewis underscored a personal dislike for the arrogance of humanistic scientists through his narrative's main protagonist – ironically, given the problems he faced – a philologist.

It is difficult to explore the deeper values of the Other if a reliable and relatively safe form of communication cannot be established: witness the SF cliché of a universal translation device. For the same reason, the alien cannot be permitted to speak with too obviously a Western accent if the necessary sense of difference is to be maintained. In his discussion of the power of Western narratives, Said observed: 'In the system of education designed for India, students were taught not only English literature, but also the inherent superiority of the English race'.[31] This observation argues that with the ability to use words, to comprehend a set of codified responses, come authority and power. From this, it is plain that the Other is doubly damned: unable to speak because of difference and, 'lacking' speech (and therefore power), unable to defend that difference. If this principle is viewed through the paradigms of SF, we can argue that narratives in the genre that deal with the Other are motivated by an identical rationale. The Other will always be silenced for the purpose of the narrative. Caught in the conflict between the requirements of 'different' and 'similar', the alien, as suggested by Bammer, has 'no place to rest': 'Xenophobia calls for a politics of repression; xenophilia tries to deny this repression'.[32] This entrapment of the Other, through both discursive repression and an inability to supply authentic communication, illustrates the power of narration in the imperialism of SF. Many texts have simply ignored the entire paradox and ascribe the Other's uncanny ability to speak English to part of an alien mystique.

Similarly, the Other is viewed as different (and secondary) when there is a conflict of biologies. Even Robinson, one of the most 'politically correct' of SF writers, admits that:

> No one wanted to live in a bath of mutagenic radiation, and the practical desire to make the planet safe for humans was stronger in most people than the desire to preserve the lifeless landscape already there, or to protect a postulated indigenous life.[33]

With no obvious life on Mars, Robinson concedes, in the form of Ann Clayborne, a willingness to preserve the planet from human impulsiveness. Ann, 'a geologist with strong views, difficult in argument',[34] offers the only opposition to the opinion that 'God gave us this planet to make in our image, to create a new Eden'.[35] However, as already discussed, the human requirement for an identifiable Other is so ideologically overwhelming that, in the absence of such a being, one will be created. With the abandonment of their centre (Earth), Robinson's Martian colonists begin to construct 'Others' from among their own number. Subject to enormous social pressure from Earth, the 'First Hundred' of Mars feel justified in their search for the smallest signs of disunity within the group. Such scrutiny inevitably discloses an entire range of political, moral and ethical schisms. As the group continues to disintegrate, it appears that the colony may founder under the weight of traditional antagonisms. Only when the colonists agree that the greatest danger stems from their 'home' planet do they form a cohesive unit against this newly revealed Other. Analogous to the American War of Independence, the First Hundred attempt to cast off obligations to the Old World and they rebel against the very authorities that sent them to Mars.

Through a series of 'revolutions', which begins with an event reminiscent of the Boston Tea Party (the destruction of the 'elevator', a massive device facilitating access to the planet), the new Martians attempt to establish a legitimate centre. The attachment formed to their new home is such that they virtually abandon the Earth, and they choose instead to be seen as Other and to suffer the consequences of this choice, rather than have a despoiled Mars relegated to the status of an Earth colony. This decision is not an easy one and Robinson's texts productively explore the nuances of a marginalised humanity in conflict with its traditional centre. Earth, for a variety of reasons, which include a global disaster, cannot permit the development of a second centre, since that would detract from its cultural and physical dominance. It is only when the new Martian scientists discover a gerontological treatment offering humans near immortality that Earth realises it has no option but to bargain from a position of equality. In the uneasy peace that follows the *rapprochement*, and as the two centres develop a balance, Ann Clayborne, forever the watchdog, warns that:

> Mars is free now. We're on our own. No one tells us what to do.... But it's so easy to backslide into old patterns of behaviour. Break one hierarchy and another springs up to take its place. We will have to be on guard for that, because there will always be people trying to make another Earth.[36]

Of all Robinson's characters, Ann is the most isolated and therefore the most able to view the situation with an estranged eye. Hers is the voice of Cassandra, whose unbelieved prophecies inevitably happen. Mars becomes not the marginalised colony but the *edge* of an expanded centre. Though free, Mars becomes more firmly entrenched within Earth's culture than ever.

Yet a willingness to push the centre outwards, to absorb the periphery, and thus create newer and greater peripheries, is a central and time-honoured theme within SF. The exploration of uncharted space, the discovery of new planets and the ambiguous desire to find intelligent alien life form one of the core doctrines of the genre. But what is this urge to explore? Can it be explained away as the pursuit of trade opportunities? Can the global exploits of Marco Polo, Christopher Columbus and Richard Burton be reduced to territorial gain? It is possible to answer *yes*, a response that finds its most recent critique in Robinson's *Mars* series, where, despite a significant departure from the norm by the character of William Fort, the excesses of contemporary international business are continued into the next millennium. Yet without the ability to constantly enlarge the centre, it stagnates. Stagnation, in a world already poised at the edge of a Malthusian decline, is little short of disastrous. Therefore exploration outside the centre is both logical and a Darwinian move towards survival. However, as Ash questions:

> would the 'missionary' elements which had ruined the finely-balanced social structures of so many 'uncivilized' tribes on earth, manifest themselves even more damagingly against the greater backdrop of the stars? Would man seek, in other respects, to dominate and exploit every less truculent race than his own which he might come upon? Would he become, at last, notorious down the light years as the rampaging child-hooligan of the Milky Way? And how might he react to the alternative – to contact with superior intelligences and cultures? And what might they think of him?[37]

At this point, postcolonial theory and the development of the Other in SF become divergent: though the place of the postcolonial Other appears to be reprising the mentality of nineteenth-century imperialism, this is clearly not the case in SF, as is made evident in the socialist works of Ken MacLeod and Iain M. Banks. While this does not mean the theory is incorrect, it does suggest that the theory needs to be extrapolated into a less rigid structure.

SF has developed beyond orthodox theory, and while it may still clarify the notion of the place of self and the necessity of difference, it is now possible to credit the Other with an additional, more abstract purpose: that of a model or paradigm. If a society cannot exist without the ability to locate itself in relation to other societies, then the Other becomes an integral element in the identification of development and growth of that society. As we alter our perceptions of what we are and how we perceive our place, the Other becomes a new entity in its own right, adapting and shifting its function to match the new expectations we have of ourselves. We cannot continue to look for our reflection in a nineteenth-century mirror. And therein lies the constant power of the alien in SF. Since we cannot know what we may become in the future, neither can we see the shape of the people we will consider Other, and yet we need an alterity if only to judge the distance we have come in cultural development. The Other is no longer a thing of pity or fear, but the beginning of a thought experiment which accompanies us to the planets and beyond. Postcolonialism has identified the being of the Other. We now look at how this being continues to transcend theory and is taken into the future.

2. Resistance Is Futile:
Silencing and Cultural Appropriation

Before we examine specific treatments of the Other, it is valuable first to consider certain influences upon and within SF. To what degree is the genre intertextual within itself? That is, do narratives often borrow or assume various devices common within SF sub-genres? How important is a rational extrapolation that permits the reader to judge a narrative's plausibility? The isolated narrative which creates completely new worlds, new cultures and even new life forms offers only a single interpretation to the reader, yet, through intertextuality or, as Damien Broderick suggests, self-referentiality via a 'mega-text',[1] a greater range of explanations may be discerned. If there are no alternatives or subtexts to the narrative, no additional means by which the author/reader partnership may expand, the reader must accept the narrative and ideas of the author without recourse to the outside world. This in itself is a form of restraint, a *silencing*. In SF, these restraints may be deliberately imposed, in order to guide the reader in a specific direction, enabling the text to explore without hindrance both the vast possibilities of the totally alien and the microscopic detail of the slightly known, as in the works of Iain M. Banks. Alternatively, an SF text which embraces earlier works, such as the recursive SF of Brian Aldiss's *Frankenstein Unbound* (1973) or David Dvorkin's *Time for Sherlock Holmes* (1983), immediately widens the net of association, from which the reader may gather far more insight than solely from the text contained within the book's covers. By the use of either a general or a specific intertextuality, or a deliberate narrative isolation, the author may produce different responses in the reader, and each technique is perfectly legitimate in the course of a thought experiment.

Because it is able to create both the exquisitely unique and the broadly derived, SF is simultaneously capable of being more focused and more diverse than most other styles of writing. This, in turn, permits its experiments either to achieve pinpoint accuracy or to generate a blanketing awareness. However, this is only one aspect of the genre's potential. It is entirely possible to read a number of similar SF narratives and glean a different perspective from each one, depending on the nature of the frame within which the narrative is established. Further, if a text extols the pursuit of scientific and techno-logical knowledge in, for example, the discovery and settlement of a distant planet, is it, by implication, supporting the application of such knowledge, in suggesting that the discoverer has the right to settle anywhere? If so, do all narratives about planetary settlement share in Broderick's postmodern mega-text and ask the same (or very similar) questions? It is important at this point to note that there is a space between the possibility that SF is inherently imperialistic and the possibility that SF writers are simply incorporating imperialism into their works as a means of testing such inherency. Sometimes the space, the gap, is a very small one, especially in older works written during imperial times, such as those of H. G. Wells and George T. Chesney. These texts, which appear to accept imperialism, are, rather, anti-imperial propaganda but worded so cleverly that it is only through irony and satire that the narrative's intent becomes visible. Likewise, there sometimes seems to be a lack of clarity surrounding what looks like a state of imperialism but what is actually an expression of the use of power, a point made most acutely by John Wyndham and Robert A. Heinlein.

An excellent example of the 'testing' of intertextual imperialism in SF is the notion of 'terraforming': creating an Earth-like environment out of one unsympathetic to human needs. Narratives of terraforming can be read – depending on the depiction – either as a cultural collusion with a semi-fascist mindset where 'might makes right' or as a logical step for a race of explorers. Even though the technology of terraforming an alien landscape is currently under investigation, it is not yet extant, which renders it a speculative and provocative notion, a perfect example of the nature of the genre that employs the reader as both a focal point and, often, its guinea pig. To accept the terraforming narrative, the reader must willingly allow that because something may not be 'true' (i.e. demonstrably factual) this does not reduce its value to or in a futuristic narrative when it may become true. The assumption that a narrative can be read at face value reinforces the difference between SF and non-speculative genres, and adds further weight to the attraction of *what might be* as opposed to *what is*.

If we assume the right to terraform, we place ourselves in the path of a new Other. What will this future Other be like? How will they react if we change a world – possibly their world? Such a divisive moral question may never be fully resolved in the courts of reality, yet such issues are responsible for the legitimacy of the SF genre as a commentary on contemporary social and cultural perspectives. These are the experiments, places where we have not yet gone but which we might consider as a destination. And readers seem fascinated by these old questions of right and wrong, for while there is still an academic resistance to the SF genre, it remains one of the fastest-growing styles of writing in the Western world, a fact which suggests readers are generally more intrigued by the narratives than repelled by them. This in itself raises several questions about the reader's passive acceptance of a narrative and asks that we examine not only the reasons behind such passivity but also the potential impact of the ideologies and philosophies so casually absorbed.

It must be conceded that viewing SF as the combination of intertextuality and thought experimentation is only one method of interpreting the genre. There are others. Many eighteenth- and nineteenth-century scientists began their work in isolation and it was only after the development of the community of scientists that information was more widely shared. It is not surprising therefore that SF, and certainly early SF, works in a similar seclusion. The sciences are considered by many as the backbone of modern civilisation yet, since its inception, SF, the fictional reflection of science, is often perceived as a lesser movement of the grander fictions because of its early leaning towards the fabulous and the fantastic. However, as science and its fictive representations became more informed, SF offered less theatricality and much greater meaning, though this sometimes suggested a governance by forces beyond our control (the advances of science). Contemporary commentaries offered by insightful SF texts clearly demand attention over and above the entertaining.

To examine whether a genre that extrapolates the movement of science is as rooted in determinism as it occasionally appears, it is useful to analyse two texts noted for the fact that their perspectives differ significantly from the norm: *The Midwich Cuckoos* (1957), by John Wyndham (1903–69), and *Do Androids Dream of Electric Sheep?* (1968), by Philip K. Dick (1928–82). These two works are therefore considered at some length later in this chapter, Dick's first.

When novels discuss the inhumanity of the human race as it engages with variations of political and cultural traditions, we cannot easily categorise them as fantasy, especially when the silenced Other is not immediately connected with threat. Nor, with such narratives as *The Midwich Cuckoos* and *Do Androids Dream of Electric Sheep?*, are we able to justify a casual displacement into the realm of monsters and home-made rockets. Both these narratives take an unusually open view of the Other and make efforts to engage with them at a level other than of antagonist. In both texts, the authors attempt to remove the stereotypical paradigm of the Other and to view the characters not as having human motivations but for what they are *despite* the human limitations placed upon them. The tragedy, almost Shakespearean in its magnitude, is that, in both novels, the ultimate fate of these Others is still repression and eventual destruction.

Dick's text requires the reader to engage with the authorial perspective that the human view of life and living beings is hostile to its manifested ideals. His overtly human protagonists become the ultimate hypocrites as they judge Others but repudiate judgement of themselves, and his androids are cruelly banished into a nether world of constraint and antipathy. His sense of the silenced minority is alarming and pointed as he conveys the image of a world where the demarcation between human and non-human is frighteningly arbitrary: his determinism conveys a feeling of deliberate and mocking reproach to those who create the Other within. It is through such marked techniques that Dick compels the reader to engage with the text in a fairly directed manner. Even a resistant reading still ensures an awareness of the fundamental principles of the narrative. Alternatives are silenced by the binary nature of the narrative's function and textual determination. We either accept the concept of an underclass of artificially created slaves or we do not: Dick's experiment allows no other ready option. By questioning the humanity of the main protagonist, Rick Deckard, Dick refuses the reader an easy absolution. Though one may nonetheless read this narrative in a variety of ways, the questions it and the Wyndham text raise are impossible to avoid.[2]

Like Dick, Wyndham deconstructs our most sacred cows and in doing so obliges the reader to acknowledge not the possibility of such a fantastic event but the emotions and responses provoked by the event transpiring, regardless. In the case of Midwich (discussed below), Wyndham cleverly inverts and widens the historical silencing conventionally imposed upon the Other, and suggests the effects of such treatment within the hinterland of a major European power instead of, for example, in Joseph Conrad's colonial Africa. In Midwich, the silencing is not only imposed upon the characters in the narrative but also upon the reader, since the postulated scenario is so unusual that, at the time of publication, the reader had no other frame of reference but colonial history and the narrative itself. It is not the terrifying incursion of an extraterrestrial control that one is designed to contemplate, but the concept that humans could be treated so cavalierly by an external power. The determinism of SF again becomes clear: it is not the ordinary frame of the narrative (Midwich) that is designed to illuminate but the content within the frame. Through Wyndham's pastoral nostalgia, the reader easily identifies with the plight of the Midwich people and readerly objectivity slips away until only a sense of injustice and tragedy remains, at which point the rationale of the turned-tables becomes clear. Though published in 1957, the invasion of Midwich offers the Other as a powerful model in a timeless morality. Not only is Wyndham's experiment insightful but, when read in a global political climate of religious fundamentalism, terrorism and cultural conflict, increasingly relevant.

But with the new relevance of SF, we begin to see more clearly the enormous and central paradox of the genre as it sits within contemporary fiction and impacts upon our cultural tenets. If we are resolved not to repeat the political and cultural errors of our colonial histories, it would seem logical that our most popular fictions should at least attempt to echo that sentiment. But they do not. In fact, so far do the leitmotifs of SF seem to diverge from those sentiments which prevail in other areas of contemporary political and social philosophy that we appear to be faced with a major dichotomy. But it is only problematic if we believe that proposing a thing is propounding that same thing. The ongoing SF fascination with empire and imperialism more accurately reflects the perception that humanity has not resolved its historical nationalistic guilts and responsibilities. Undoubtedly, these literary experiments will continue until it has. Therefore, if we accept that the imperial project is flawed and no longer representative of our allegedly enlightened self-perception, then SF is either generating a political pornography that we, as rational, thinking beings, have forbidden ourselves, or it is becoming increasingly meaningful, though ironic, in its literary experimentation.

Possibly SF's increasing attractiveness arises *because* of its engagement with outlawed sentiments, its motivations and behaviours so apparently at odds with 'accepted' mores that it appeals to our rebellious tendencies. SF narratives may be viewed as the 'new traditional' form of anti-establishment dialogue that simultaneously points out cultural and political errors while positing a more liberal neo-imperialism. This unspoken paradox of SF, supporting, as it apparently does, mutually exclusive and diametrically opposed philosophies, contributes significantly to its interest. The maintenance of the genre has depended upon a clear relationship with the imperial project, in that the vast majority of SF texts involve, in a variety of ways, the exploration and annexation of extraterrestrial habitats. Yet, in the same space, we look to SF to engage in a critique with the very motivations that drive us. Therefore do we embrace SF as an experimental lightning rod that draws our attention to the things that trouble us, or do we cast it off dismissively as a temporary fashion of pseudo-enlightenment? As David Seed observes:

> It may be that these political ideas [of SF writers] are dangerous or foolish. But it is not obvious that we should therefore sweep them aside, or castigate an author brave enough to hold them to the light. If they are dreams we choose to reckon nightmares, we should still examine them – and think it possible that we are ourselves mistaken.[3]

Yet how is it possible for this dichotomy of desire versus understanding not only to exist but to be increasingly extreme? The irony of the situation is ably encapsulated and described in the two selected novels of Wyndham and Dick.

Dick's narrative, set at the close of the twentieth century on Earth, posits a reductive culture where almost all living animals have been exterminated through humanity's affinity with destruction, and where the prevailing society has substituted mechanical simulacra to fill the void. So deep is the cultural guilt over this vast phenocide that the discovery of a small spider becomes a matter of profound analysis and contemplation. The text conveys the impression of a future in which the trends affecting today's cities are continued to the point where humanity, in its incessant expansion across the planet, has squandered its own viability. The remorse over having destroyed so much reveals itself in a desire for, as Brian Stableford calls them, 'agents of illusion',[4] of postmodern replicas and technological *bricolage*. In a depleted, depressive world, unable to offer its inhabitants much more than a bleak, survivalist lifestyle, we become engrossed with Rick Deckard, who acts as a vehicle of investigation into the meaning of humanity through the medium of humanoid machines (as the main character also lives as a bounty hunter, killing things is an essential paradox within the text). In order to exploit the resources of the solar system's outer planets, humanity has designed and built a series of androids, none of whom are produced with a 'life span' of more than four years, a detail more clearly exploited in the film (*Blade Runner*) than in the text. Essentially slaves, these 'andys' are designed for and confined to harsh, off-world environments, where their various functions render them little more than anthropomorphised machines set into stereotypical functions. But the android engineers have been too clever, and now the andys replicate not only the external image of humanity but also its desire for survival at all costs.

Dick's humanity has placed itself in an impossible existential bind. The androids are perfect replicas of humankind yet are viewed at the same level as pets. Even though there is an obsession with the 'real', Deckard's society cannot survive without its mechanised panaceas and yet neither can it bear to be reminded of its dependence upon 'unnatural' things. 'Owning and maintaining a fraud had a way of gradually demoralizing one',[5] Deckard realises as he observes his own mechanised sheep. Notions of ownership encapsulate all that is at fault with his society, yet simultaneously capture those ideologies humanity has neglected. Deckard's underlying impulse to secure a fleeting authenticity, no matter the cost, is expressed as his desire for a living animal. He needs to own a *living* thing, not a fake, since only living things have moral value. But how does this affect the androids, who are very alive (and, moreover, are consciously aware of being alive) but who are reduced to the status of an expensive appliance? What is false here? Is Dick pointing a finger at the deliberate blindfolds of humanity or at our more blatant hypocrisies?

Dick's version of humanity is made to face its worst fears. No longer a powerful and vigorous race, humans have become dissipated and weak, relying upon the 'Penfield Mood Organ' to supply an artificial form of emotion rather than risk a genuine feeling. The narrative focuses upon an addictive opposition of want and hate, where that which is most craved may be obtained only through acceptance of that which is most despised. Deckard's primary motivation throughout the novel is to break this circle of need and fear by securing sufficient money to buy one of the few remaining live animals, something representative of his social place and status. He dreams of a large farm animal, a horse or a cow perhaps. In order to do this, his task is to eradicate artificial humans, the androids brought into being by the same human motivations of need and fear. This might appear to be a most suitable arrangement, in that Deckard is able to pursue his goal for the authentic by removing the unauthentic, yet Dick does not permit us such a simple resolution. The moment it becomes possible for Deckard to see the androids as human, as 'real' as the living animals, the contradiction of killing the former for money with which to purchase the latter becomes clear. During the course of an increasingly reluctant pursuit, Deckard himself is made to question his own biological authenticity, adding yet another dimension to this experiment in ethical morality.

At the outset, Deckard has a mechanised pet that is virtually indistinguishable from the living creatures owned by residents of his apartment building. The narrative's first and immediate conflict is an internalised one, between Deckard's hunger for the 'real thing' and his need to maintain a social image. When he reveals his sheep's mechanical form to a neighbour, the revelation takes on the form of a profound confession, almost a confirmation of guilt. Deckard is ashamed, not of possession, but of possessing a fraud. From a postcolonial perspective, the desire for 'ownership' of the Other is a problematic one, in that it indicates a society that remains unable to see, let alone confront, the nature of its own desires. As in our contemporary materialistic society, possession itself is not taboo – in fact, it is highly approved of – but that which is *possessed* must be appropriate. We may buy baby dolls but we may not buy babies. Dick plays with the idea that in some future society we may do precisely that: purchase customised babies and treat them as no more than dolls. Though Deckard longs to do away with the pretence, he is held back by social pressure and is unaware of the greater evil to which he is unconsciously subscribing. He sees nothing wrong with the ownership of mechanised beings, in his case of a sheep, and, by extension, sees nothing wrong with the ownership and calculated destruction of androids – after all, they are only a different kind of sheep. Through Deckard, Dick hints at a fundamental colonialist justification. As long as that which is owned can be dismissed by the owner as unimportant, there is nothing in it to concern us. But he does not permit Deckard to be unconcerned: Deckard *despises* the false. It is his occupation of bounty hunter which provides him with some respite, as he is required to track and destroy – effectively silencing – those androids who have illegally returned to Earth. By means of this violent catharsis, Deckard is able to vent his hatred of the simulacra in a socially acceptable manner. So complete is his acceptance of the andys as false humans that when his wife accuses him of being 'a murderer hired by the cops', the offended Deckard replies 'I've never killed a human being in my life'.[6]

The dichotomy between living humans and the artificiality of the androids lies at the centre of Dick's novel. It is not that the andys have been created by humankind, but the fact that they have been created so much in the image of humans themselves that disturbs the text's human characters. The androids, though in many ways stronger than humans, are also endowed with weaknesses, the greatest of which is their longing to be 'real': to belong to an idealised version of the humanity from which they have been ejected. It is an emotional appeal to the reader's empathy that permits us to analogise the androids' situation with the story of Pinocchio. This mood is contrasted with Deckard's feelings towards his mechanised sheep. The unauthentic nature of the beast, though problematic to Deckard, does not provide such a serious challenge to his profound biocentricity. The androids, however, are the penultimate strangers, and the most intimate of emotional and physical tests are required to prove their Otherness. Their lack of empathy is an authorial justification which renders them into an adversarial form that in itself is another paradox within the narrative. The human judgement that empathy is something which distinguishes androids from genuine human beings is an important one, since it posits that, lacking empathy, androids lack a basic ingredient of humanity. But it becomes very clear that Deckard, too, lacks empathy, in that he views the killing of an android with a cold and dispassionate objectivity, a point made even more complex when it transpires that Deckard himself might be an android. Ironically, it is Isidore, the naïve and simple 'Chickenhead',[7] who, though 'real' and deemed a flawed and useless creature, displays the most compassion and empathy towards all beings, living or electronic. Isidore is the impartial eye and views all life as equally valuable. Moreover, through his self-deprecation and impartiality we begin to see that the real experiment in the narrative manipulates not an ambiguous authenticity but the various fears of supplantation and self-definition, a theme also carried in the Wyndham text. Dick's androids have become too much like humans themselves, even in their human failings, for them to be considered as anything but alive. In killing them, Deckard finally realises he is guilty of destroying that which he most prizes. Yet Dick does not permit Deckard to take his analysis far enough to achieve enlightenment. For Deckard, there must always be some divide between humans and androids; for things to be otherwise would be an acceptance not only of his own obsolescence but of the fact that humans had become a race of slave traders. For Deckard, an escaped humanoid robot, which had killed its master, which had been equipped with an intelligence greater than that of many human beings, which had no regard for animals, which possessed no ability to feel empathic joy for another life form's success or grief at its defeat – that, for him, epitomized 'the killers'.[8]

Dick has set up confrontations between several contentious issues. First, we have the fact of a human diaspora, a movement away from its home planet after an inconceivably destructive nuclear conflict – World War Terminus. Migrants are induced to leave partly by fear of the latent atmospheric radioactivity and partly because of a government offer of a 'free' android for every family. Then we see that the androids play a significant role in commodity capitalism, as they have an artificially induced lifetime of four years, which supports a constant demand for new models. These points ask us to consider where servitude becomes slavery. We do not, as a rule, feel that the possession of a washing machine makes us slave owners, but what if the machine were sufficiently intelligent to arrive at rational thought? Dick asks his readers to consider that a point may well arrive in the future when the distinction between such mechanisms is no longer moot. In his presentation of intelligent androids, Dick suggests we need to deal with the issue now. In examining the principles behind ascribing life to a machine, we are also forced to examine how we currently regard life in ourselves, a position described with acute irony by Dick through Isidore, the victim of radioactivity forever condemned to the pariah-hood of 'Chickenhead'.

Thus Dick shows us that the perception and definition of life and sentient intelligence is as large a theme within SF as is the acknowledgement of the Other, the two being inextricably bound together and asking the same question: How do we define the Other? Biologically, all humans are alike, albeit external differences evolve from geographical and climactic variance. Yet if there are still ungrounded fears in contemporary cultures based on the superficialities of colour or gender, how much more significant would such fears become if we knew, without question, that we were dealing with a sentient life form of non-human origin? To be faced, quite literally, with a quantifiably physical and intellectual superior would shake the foundations of a person's self-identity. There would be no more room for the fantasy of racial hubris. There would only be the realisation of our worst fears: that we not only have an Other, but that we have *become* the Other – that which we most despise yet simultaneously need. And this is precisely what Dick has sought to accomplish within his text: that we face, without possibility of delusion, the fact that humanity can be a 'lesser creation' by every criterion and standard we have elected to impose upon the Other. This is also why Dick has provided us with a safety valve when discussing this most insidious of enemies. Unlike the 'natural' monstrosities of Wells's invading Martians,[9] Dick's androids, so beautifully and carefully designed and produced, are doomed to a short but perpetual infancy. Dick shows that humanity may still safely consider itself superior because, in its paranoia, it has assumed godlike powers of life and death.

Thus are we asked to consider our thoughts not only on slavery, and the silenced subaltern, but also on the meaning of how humans perceive and rank themselves within a hierarchical system. Dick is dealing with the issues of demarcation in a deliberately unsubtle manner, advising us through the context of the novel that these levels are arbitrary and terrifyingly subjective. The pointed recognition that, in the future, one person may be deemed less than another by means of a differing genesis offers us cold comfort in our search for cultural enlightenment. Unsatisfied with these demands upon the reader, Dick continues to identify and ask resolution of two additional and related matters directly involving the actions of Deckard and the androids he is paid to kill.

First, Dick's androids are not so much mechanical creatures as enhanced humans, genetically adapted to their given station. The only convincing method of proving their physical genesis is through a bone-marrow examination. And so complex have their thought processes become that android designers have had to install artificial memories to ensure their creations continue to relate to the race of people they have been created to serve. But with the provision of these false memories, the androids are now more fully aware of themselves as different from, but inextricably linked to, the rest of humanity. The androids, especially the latest Nexus-6 models, are not only vitally intelligent but also emotionally vulnerable and utterly defenceless in the face of massive human callousness. This is further evidence of how an SF text may productively engage with the limits of postcolonial theory. In an effort to ease the burdens of life, Dick's human race has, lacking an alternative, created its own subaltern. Not only extraordinarily Other, and not only repressed, marginalised and silenced in the most outrageous of fashions, the androids are forbidden even to aspire to the very thing their designers have been forced to grant them – an awareness of their own humanity. An example of this is seen in Deckard's interrogation of the android Luba Luft, who has taken on the persona of an opera singer. Deckard interprets her coolness as typical android detachment, yet her behaviour under his dehumanising treatment might also be explained as a typical human fear response. Dick is offering us a vicious parody of earlier colonial histories, where native servants were an essential part of the household of their imperial masters, their lives intimately linked to the families they served, but who were expected to have no life of their own. As with the Orwellian inhabitants of *Animal Farm*, the androids' lives are intended to meet only the humans' requirements: 'The truest happiness … lay in working hard and living frugally.'[10] Since the androids' existence is all for the betterment of the humans whom they serve and for whom they expend their fractional life, then their existence is deemed acceptable by those humans. Dick's novel acts as a red flag as he illustrates a possible extrapolation of deliberate contemporary blindness. Are we as a species forever fated to search for the subaltern? 'Do androids dream? Rick asked himself. Evidently, that's why they occasionally kill their employers and flee here. A better life, without servitude.'[11]

Second, the placement of the androids in such an insidious position leads us directly into the confrontations between Deckard's self-perception and his developing recognition of the andys as 'real'. During the course of the novel we witness several occasions when Deckard is forced to consider his own humanity. So clever is the androids' design and so sophisticated the implanted memories that, without the bone-marrow test, no one can be completely sure of their place on the human scale, and Deckard begins to examine his life in these terms. However, while these moments are exquisitely poised on the edge of human self-perception, as with Stanislaw Lem's *Solaris* (considered in Chapter 3), Dick does not provide us with an easy answer. The reader is left in a calculated state of ambivalence, almost, we could imagine, thinking about the same possibilities as the androids themselves. The unasked questions are loud in the text. Who am I? What am I? Where do I belong? What are my rights and freedoms? In Deckard's case, it is little more than a weighted social conditioning that tips the balance, although, after the narrative's revelation that Deckard himself might be an android, we are never entirely sure of the bounty hunter's authentic humanity. So finely has Dick constructed his text that for the latter half of the novel we perceive many indications of the android in Deckard and of the humanity in the androids.

Dick's novel therefore not only highlights aspects of the quasi-imperial oppressor in contemporary fiction but also insists that we explore those elements in our cultures which might ameliorate or in any way soften the idea of an 'acceptable subalternity' in the Other. As each thread of the androids' existence is uncovered, we find them to be less than human in a tiny minority of ways – certainly insufficiently different to merit such callous behaviour from those whom they serve. The essential difference appears to be in their lack of 'empathy', an ironic term used to describe the androids' inability to experience the same forms of caring emotions as do most of humanity. Where a human might respond predictably to the notion of a briefcase manufactured from the skins of human babies, the android feels nothing. The 'Voigt–Kampff Altered Scale' is intended, through a series of psychometric questions and physiological responses, to identify empathy (or the lack of it) in a subject. Considering, however, that Deckard's society depends almost totally upon the emanations of the mood organ for their emotional experiences, it is blackest satire that considers the androids lessened because they lack certain emotions of their own.

Other than the invasive bone-marrow test, Dick places great emphasis upon the Voigt–Kampff assessment technique throughout the text, since it is the only apparently reliable (and relatively easy) method of detecting an android. Through the application and the importance of the test, Dick submits that it is only empathy that separates humankind from the lower-order animals. And it is the establishment of human guilt over the fate of the dispossessed andys that assists the experimentation of this text: guilt at the deliberate creation of the subaltern; guilt at the ongoing desire for 'ownership' of lesser life forms; guilt, in all its myriad shapes, for the inherent weakness of a humanity that discards its cast-offs in an eternal struggle for a supreme state of being. It is impossible to declare a moratorium on human development and progress, but in the light of this progress it is hard to face the fact that the very desires that urge us on are those that seem equally to urge us in domination of the Other. The guilt expressed by Dick is so central to the way global cultures have developed that it cannot be separated from what we are. It is the human paradox to simultaneously need and deny that which makes things Other, as humanity strives always for height on the shoulders of the Other.

Therefore Dick's novel, though superficially a detective thriller set in a time future to its writing, might be better perceived as an exploration and rationalisation of social history. The text asks some very specific questions concerning the nature of the Other and the definition of sentience, as well as the place of the sentient being, especially as expressed in the terms of Jean-François Lyotard, who commented:

> Shorn of speech, incapable of standing upright, hesitating over the objects of its interest, not able to calculate its advantages, not sensitive to common reason, the child is eminently the human because its distress heralds and promises things possible. Its initial delay in humanity, which makes it the hostage of the adult community, is also what manifests to this community the lack of humanity it is suffering from, and which calls on it to become more human.[12]

Dick's androids, their 'delay in humanity' aside, are not even permitted the same functions of childhood.[13] They will never grow up and are designed to be the eternal hostages of a hierarchical society too terrified to contemplate its potential equal. But what might happen in a society that is overtaken and marginalised by the Other in the form of children? Filmed in 1960 as *Village of the Damned* (with a sequel in 1963, *Children of the Damned*, and remade in 1995), Wyndham's *The Midwich Cuckoos* invites us into a small English village, where an imposed somnolence (known later as the 'Dayout') introduces the first undertones of disquiet.

From 10:17 that night, information about Midwich became episodic. Its telephones remained dead. The bus that should have passed through it failed to reach Stouch and a truck that went to look for the bus did not return. Someone in Oppley reported a house on fire in Midwich, with, apparently, nothing being done about it. The Trayne fire appliance turned out – and thereafter failed to make any reports. The Trayne police dispatched a car to find out what had happened to the fire engine and that, too, vanished into silence.[14]

Even though the reader still only suspects the intervention of an external, possibly even alien agency, the text is already preparing the way for a trope of suppression by introducing the postcolonial notion of *silencing* through a physical reality. During periods of historical conflict it has always been a standard military tactic to take immediate control of all sources of communication upon attacking a town, and Wyndham – who acted as a censor during World War II – makes it clear from the outset that Midwich is definitely under an invasive, not colonialist, siege. That Wyndham selected a small, undistinguished hamlet set deep in the English countryside, so similar to dozens of other geographically insignificant villages, sends a message of its own. To a determined invader, no haven, no matter how benevolent or remote, is secure, a thematic tradition in much of British SF. The author has Midwich represent all that is English, with gentle pastoral stereotypes of both the countryside and the characters who live there. He makes certain that we cannot possibly perceive the village to pose any legitimate kind of threat, and renders it utterly defenceless. Therefore the attack, when it takes place, is doubly shocking. It is the last place one would imagine to be in need of defence. Nevertheless, it is the launch site of an invasion and, as with Wells's selection of three small towns in *The War of the Worlds*, the innocents of Midwich are the ones to suffer.

Viewed in the light of postcolonial critique this novel provides a useful and illuminating reframing of the use of power. Wyndham is using an inexplicable yet tangible device which, from the very beginning of the narrative, tells the reader that this is an 'unnatural' situation and allows no other rationale to surface by which to ameliorate the events that follow. We are made to understand, without exception, that all subsequent events in Midwich are a direct result of this initial attack, and that the villagers, no matter how stoically they attempt to maintain their previous lives, are victims of an invasion. Yet, as the narrative continues, the reader is able to see both parties as victims: the Midwich villagers and the alien children foisted upon them. Observation can be made of attempts by Wyndham to justify the actions of both sides, but even so the novel still ends in the destruction of the Other.

Once the initial furore has died down, and the Dayout passes into memory, there seems to be little in the way of an obvious invasion. But every woman of childbearing age who was in the village at the time it went incommunicado falls inexplicably pregnant. Here, too, Wyndham specifically examines a generally accepted Western taboo, the rape and non-consensual impregnation of captive females, often a primary technique in aggressive cultural assimilation and absorption. In his quiet, conventionally understated British manner, Wyndham has cut to the heart of two vital aspects of hostile imperialist precepts: the removal of the victim subaltern's voice, and the appropriation of their most intimate society. On top of the inexplicable nature of the phenomenon, the women of Midwich are also overtaken – understandably so – by enormous fear, as Ferrelyn attempts to explain her pregnancy to her stepmother, Angela:

> 'But – you don't understand, Angela. It wasn't Alan.'
>   The look of sympathy died from Angela's face. Her expression went cold. She started to get up.
>   'No!' exclaimed Ferrelyn, desperately, 'you *don't* understand, Angela. It isn't that. *It wasn't anybody*! *That's* why I'm frightened.'[15]

Wyndham has deliberately inverted the conventional (British) imperialist perception of the world. Instead of the British being the perpetrators of cultural appropriation and silencing, they are now the recipients and must deal with the situation as best they may. It is interesting to observe that, in both the Wells and Wyndham texts, it is an overwhelming extraterrestrial force – something above understanding and commonplace activity – which brings the British down. Clearly, both authors, owing quite possibly to a cultural self-regard, felt more comfortable with the notion that only a force of extraterrestrial genesis would be able to overcome the northern Europeans, a sign of the British sense of superiority even when being invaded. Midwich is subdued by an unspeakable alien force and the village women bring the outsider, the Other, into their sanctuary in the most abominable manner. The Other has now become, because of the strongest social and cultural conventions, a thing to be cherished and nurtured. The Other has become 'the children'. And here Wyndham, with the advent of the golden-eyed, blond-haired babies, offers us an insidious hint of social Darwinism's race theory, or, as Aaron Perkus notes, 'Technology, which was once seen as the domination of the mind over nature, served as another metaphor for race instinct. Whites were seen as the only race to have technology, and thus must be the more advanced. Ad infinitum.'[16] If the white-skinned northern races are hypothetically superior, how much more so might be the children? And just as the cuckoo chick solicits total control over its adoptive nest, so, too, do Wyndham's unearthly children set about securing their future and the future domination of their forcibly adopted parents.

It is also interesting to note that during the late 1940s, 1950s and early 1960s, there were several prominent texts dealing with the topic of children as Other. Stemming partially from the postwar baby boom as well as from the trauma of war itself, children of these decades were frequently seen as different and no longer fitting in with prewar mindsets.[17] Children as Other was a topic much considered in the postwar years, when scares over comics, drugs and juvenile delinquency were all fodder for a variety of uncomfortable SF texts. The anxieties aroused by social change and threats to the new stability seemed to be generated by the young, their differences to their parents literally appearing as 'alien', as the innocence and potentiality of prewar childhood was removed by trauma and replaced with unknowable powers and drives. Children as Other in SF became a less favoured topic in the 1980s and 1990s, possibly because this sense of 'unknowable power' was no longer so alarming to parents who themselves were children in the years after World War II.

Thus the incident at Midwich is kept secret at first, not because of any immediate physical danger or even fear of the unnatural offspring, but because the element of shame hangs heavy over the women. Though they may have been impregnated against their knowledge and will, in Britain of the 1950s there was still a form of criticism attached to a woman who knowingly carried an illegitimate child. This criticism, almost an accusation of complicity, suggests that there was in some way a measure of collusion in the woman's behaviour. In the case of the Midwich women, only the sheer volume of simultaneous pregnancies makes an overt or individualised accusation impossible. The function of shame is an intricate one and much underestimated in its power and complexity. Being ashamed of one's vulnerability can induce the individual to undertake a wide variety of actions in order to disguise or discharge that emotion. The greater the emotional burden, the more extreme can be the reaction. As Salman Rushdie says in his novel *Shame*, 'there are things that cannot be permitted to be true'.[18] Likewise, Marx strenuously upholds shame as being an active element in the suppression of others, saying: 'The actual pressure must be made more pressing by adding to it consciousness of pressure, the shame must be made more shameful by publicising it'.[19]

The women of Midwich are therefore forced to endure shame on two levels: a direct and intimate physical imposition, and a cultural transgression, neither one being their choice. Wyndham has cleverly targeted not only these taboo areas but also those issues that are least easily defined within any society. The subject of women's natal health in most European nations has achieved a great level of public discussion only in the last century, before which it was a fairly private affair. But the coming of the children to Midwich brutally exposes the village people to the public eye on an area of intimate sensitivity. Yet this last century has also been the time of greatest imperial decline, and therefore the idea of shame being used as an overt weapon against a subalternised group would in itself have been a covert strategy used to support a sagging imperialism. Wyndham's text, published in 1957, the year after Soviet troops had marched into Hungary, observes the anti-imperialist Western trend. Had only a single woman been impregnated, the incident might have been rationalised away as some type of mutation, or even as miraculous. Wyndham has elected to involve the entire village and thus, like Dick, forces our observation of an unpalatable truth. However, whereas Dick speaks of things to come, Wyndham's text recalls the past. His narrative of silencing, first involving the women and then the entire village, effectively reflects the hidden aspects of colonialisation, those barely visible shadows which add significance to the more overt political disenfranchising of a people. In Midwich, it is not an individual who is silenced, but a micro-culture. The microcosm of Midwich is intended to reflect the larger vision: to observe in a controllable format that which might have been inflicted upon a much greater scale.

The children are born without major incident. Other than their luminescent golden eyes and fair hair, they are in most respects easily confused with normal human babies. The villagers attempt to integrate the children into their midst and observe all the usual rituals and conventions normally associated with a new baby in rural England. There is a flurry of baptisms, not because the villagers believe that the baptised soul of a child will undoubtedly journey to heaven, but because a baptism is the traditional and conventional thing to do with a newborn child. There is a sense of an attempted return to British propriety as Midwich strives to disregard the unnatural genesis of the children, one mother calling her son Theodore ('gift from God') in an effort to placate ancient cultural mores. Yet, behind the façade of convention, it is already known that the children are Other. As Midwich's Reverend Hubert Leebody observes, 'They are – strangers, you know'[20] and, as with Dick's indistinguishable-from-human androids, the stranger within offers the greatest threat. One of the first indications that cultural and social convention will not accommodate the interlopers is when Mrs Brinkman is compelled (by forces beyond her comprehension) to breastfeed her child in broad daylight in a most public place. In postwar England, even in rural areas, public breastfeeding was not a casual thing. Wyndham trespasses once again on the intimacies of British culture as he grants the invasive cuckoo-child power over the mother's deeply entrenched sensibilities. Not only has the voice of Midwich been silenced, but also British society and customs are now under attack.

The attack is continued as the children grow. There are increasing instances where the mothers are forced to undertake actions that they would not normally consider. The women, and by extension the families and lifestyles of the families, are subverted into activities which more suit the alien children. Those villagers who dare object or fight the control are peremptorily dealt with in brutal and shocking fashion. Not only is the population of Midwich silenced in a literal sense, but also in a figurative and symbolic one. The essential alien-ness of the children does not permit a functional hybridity or polyvalency as might eventuate from a likewise forced merging of two human cultures. In this experiment of Wyndham's, a postcolonial reading of the text lays bare the cruellest forms of power, where the only possible resolution is either abject compliance on the part of the subaltern group or total and complete destruction of the invading Other. In accordance with the conventions of human superiority, it is the children who eventually perish, destroyed, ironically, by the one enlightened human capable of acting as a bridge between the two cultures. The status quo is restored upon the shocking mass extinction of the children. It is as if the invasion never occurred, with all evidence being neatly eradicated along with the offensive aliens. Wyndham's experiment in British subalternity ends with the clear message that such imposition would be an intolerable repression and one that must be removed at whatever cost.

In both the Dick and the Wyndham texts, the reader is offered a differing view of the Other, and both perceptions are different again from most main-stream SF, in that they attempt to paint the Other as much a victim as the offender. Dick's text portrays the android Other as the underdog: unfairly banished, grossly mistreated and denied all hope of a future. It is their suffer-ing which directs the flow of the novel as the human protagonists attempt to justify not only the slave-like marginalisation and repression of the artificial humans but also the callous destiny that the androids are compelled to accept. It is through the authorial design that the reader must engage with these themes and concepts, presented as a series of moral paradoxes which direct the reader along one of two paths: either the androids are human and have been silenced by a neo-imperialistic humanity, or they are not, which asks us then to consider the existing definitions of humanity itself. Neither option is particularly simple or easy to embrace, but the textual determination removes alternatives. Wyndham's alien children seem to follow an equally predestined path, although in Midwich their presence in a powerless village, and their imposition upon equally powerless women, are designed to strike up an immediate opposition to their existence. Yet, even though their continued domination of the villagers and, specifically, their birth mothers is calculated and deliberate, the fact that their presence is sufficiently feared to render them as a collective object of hatred is bitter.

That both novels are experiments with the Other as something apart from the stereotypical monster of nightmares is undeniable. That both novelists saw no way to end the narrative other than in the traditional manner of an eventual Western supremacy and the destruction of the suppressed group is tragic. Is this what should happen to the intruding Other, or is it the authors' way of making us examine the way we might behave in the future? These two texts have made an exceptional effort to engage with the Other in the most human of forms, yet the intruder is still the one to suffer. It seems that no matter how desirable a human–alien *entente* might be, the human drive to secure the safety of the race at all costs is a notion not even the most liberal-minded of authors can successfully overcome.

We see in these novels the ability of the SF narrative to illuminate the paradox of power and imperialism. Experimenting with imperial principles in SF is acceptable because not one of us would be happy to accept these principles in 'real' life. These novels of Wyndham and Dick manipulate the deepest emotional and rational beliefs we accept of ourselves because, though there are consequential issues at stake, humanity seems reluctant to identify and engage with them except through the medium of fiction. As explorations of imagination, they are especially productive when read in the light of postcolonial principles, their incorporation of metaphoric tropes directing the reader to examine assumptions of responsibility. For a closer examination of the influence of metaphor in SF narratives of power and empire and how these metaphors challenge our cultural foundations, we turn in the next chapter to Ursula K. Le Guin and Stanislaw Lem.

3. The Word for World Is Forest: Metaphor and Empire in Science Fiction

Metaphors identify phenomena in a manner that is literally distinct from their realities. This allows a game of chess to become a 'battle of wits', enables the poet U. A. Fanthorpe to 'choke the future back down our throats'[1] and justified Arthur C. Clarke's modelling of his alien 'Overlords' as the 'shepherds' of humankind in *Childhood's End* (1953). Metaphor creates a higher level of understanding by using elements of an older, already exist-ent knowledge and placing it into an unfamiliar space, as with the typical Asimov observation that 'Astronomers were queer ducks'.[2] Both metaphor and metonymy are eloquent in SF, as authors experiment with the human mindset on planets populated with alien life forms and fantastic, unknow-able cultures. As George Lakoff and Mark Turner suggest:

> Complex metaphors grip us partly because they awake in us the experi-ence and knowledge that form the grounding of those metaphors, partly because they make the coherence of that experience and knowl-edge resonate, and partly because they lead us to form new coherences in what we know and experience.[3]

Given that metaphor is traditionally the product of imagination, it is interesting to note as an aside that even in the realm of science, usually the most quantifiable and concrete of disciplines, there is a place for such creative description: a 'black hole', for example, is neither black nor a hole – the term was chosen to communicate the fact that light and matter inevitably fall and are lost into these seemingly endless voids. In a similar fashion, the term 'quantum leap' has taken on the metaphorical value of meaning 'a great stride forward', when in fact it was originally coined to explain the abrupt transition of an atom or molecule from one quantum state to another – a very small transition at that scale. It is understandable, then, why SF, so often the fictional extrapolation of science, has taken both literary and scientific metaphors and romanticised them into an aggregation of tropes and dramatised scenarios. As an aspect of cultural and social struc-ture, metaphor can also reveal many details about us, both as individuals in the metaphors we choose and as a society by the common recognition of the term. The use of a neutral scientific term such as 'parasite' to describe a literary form[4] tells us a great deal about the society that employs such a metaphor. Much of the success of H. G. Wells's *The War of the Worlds* (1898) was due to his uncomfortably apposite metaphors; for example, he perfectly intimated the ascendant possibilities of the violently expansionist and terrifyingly *human* Martians by using such eerily metaphoric phrases as 'minds that are to our minds as ours are to those of the beasts that perish'.[5] With typical subtlety, Wells creates a metaphor where 'thinking' is the mark of superiority and renders humanity into a herd.

While figurative language – the use of metaphor, metonymy, synecdoche and simile – facilitates the comprehension and understanding of difficult points of communication, it may also obscure and distort with over-familiarity.[6] To reduce the game of chess to a 'battle' negates the subtle interactivity of the players. The black hole of science becomes the epitome of absence, but this provides no hint of the phenomenon's effective role within the universe. The 'parasite' metaphor suggests only negative aspects of a relationship. It is easy to view Isaac Asimov's entire *Robot* series as a transparent metaphor of massive proportions, although it may be wiser to invoke a different descriptive term, such as *allegory* or *symbol* as an extension of the metaphoric act. Such large-scale alternatives do not weaken the force of the individual metaphor but rather underpin its essential expression, since it is the shared *likenesses* in the various levels of comparison that provide a metaphor with its power. The anthropomorphisation of Asimov's positronic beings into lesser versions of humanity, as the underlings of a higher species, may also be viewed not as allegory but as a trope that actualises (in this instance) a subconscious social Darwinism. The irony of Asimov's robots, a reductive metaphor in themselves for a 'lost' humanity, and unlike those depicted in Karel Capek's play *R.U.R.* (*Rossumovi Univerzální Roboti, Rossum's Universal Robots*, 1920), is that while Asimov situates his positronic marvels as the creation of humankind, he also credits them with the capacity to become more humane than the race they were designed to serve. Since one of Asimov's basic tenets is that humankind constantly underestimates itself, his texts serve a further metaphorical purpose, in that they illustrate the higher potential of our species. In *Foundation and Earth* (1986), we see the culmination of his *Foundation* series and witness the transformation of robot Daneel Olivaw into something that transcends both the creator and the created. The potential of the robot to become greater than its function, to become greater even than that which created it, is an extended antonomasia of immense structure generated by Asimov over a period of forty-five years.[7] Through his 'Three Laws of Robotics', Asimov perfectly expresses the human need to feel safe and protected from the anxiety of science while seeming to promote an equal need for superiority over others.[8] But this is only the lesser element of his design, the larger aim being human enlightenment.

After the natural science of Victor Frankenstein, the stereotypical scientist of post-World War I SF is aware that he may not lightly transgress the domain of God by the creation of a higher biological life. Metaphor becomes the perfect solution: let there be robots.

Just as the robot may take on physical and moral qualities that surpass those of its human creator, so too may a creative metaphor carry weight beyond its original intent, thus illustrating far more than it was perhaps intended to. It is ironic that, within a metaphorical construct, authors may devise relationships that tap into cultural or personal values of which they are unaware, perhaps into notions that, consciously, they would not even approve. Iain M. Banks uses the term 'the Culture' to denote the central society in many of his narratives (see Chapter 9), a term which signifies not only his vision of a complex future humanity, elite and fascinating, but also the place of this group in relation to all other protagonists or groups in his texts. To be *of* the Culture is to be possessed of desirable qualities, both in the realms of Banks's novels and through the word's contemporary metaphoric connection with a lofty state of existence. To be *outside* of the Culture hints at barbarism and the exotic orientalism diagnosed by Said (see Chapter 1). Banks makes exceptional use of the term in all its connotations, cleverly expressing both a narrative and a metaphorical significance. The application of Banks's metaphoric connotations is remarkably clear throughout all of his 'Culture' texts, and may be seen as sly innuendo in *The Player of Games* (1988), where, in the words of Jernau Morat Gurgeh, that most famed of Culture game-players:

> The very first-rank games acknowledge the element of chance, even if they rightly restrict raw luck. To attempt to construct a game on any other lines, no matter how complicated and subtle the rules are, and regardless of the scale and differentiation of the playing volume and the variety of the powers and attributes of the pieces, is inevitably to shackle oneself to a conspectus which is not merely socially but techno-philosophically lagging several ages behind our own.[9]

Speaking confidentially, almost as a self-conscious narrator to the reader, Banks offers a metaphorical reference to an elitist group. The words of Gurgeh refer not simply to the construction of a game but also, with a much more potent subtlety, to the reader's impression of the society which has such insight and power. The poorer the 'game', the less advanced the players. This is the power of Banks's texts. The Culture does not need to flaunt its ideological superiority over others; it simply exists in such a manner that all competition and all competitors are outranked before they begin. The only way to 'win' in a confrontation with such an ideology is to become one of 'them': to sacrifice individuality for the benefits of assimilation. Thus 'the

Culture' is the metaphorical embodiment of a deep imperialist rationale, in that its very elitism and superiority render it supremely attractive to 'lesser' groups. Moreover, for those resistant to such charms, the Culture has 'Special Circumstances', a semi-secret service that, in contrast to its peace-loving society, possesses the ability to coerce and subvert.

This theme of homogenised superiority has been frankly displayed in the *Star Trek* television series *The Next Generation*, where the notorious Borg (a race of cyborgs – part biological, part mechanical) 'assimilate' all who stand in their path. The main difference between the Culture and the Borg is that the Culture rarely absorbs other races by force, whereas the Borg know no alternative. If the Borg used enticement rather than force they would not be viewed as an enemy to be resisted and destroyed. The use of gratuitous force becomes a metaphor for barbarism, as all reliable heroes avoid needless destruction.

SF does not restrict metaphor to a narrow linguistic sense, but often applies it in a manner that conveys highly complex organisational models. Entire concepts may be mapped out by reference to points of paradigmatic familiarity, making metaphor a fundamental method of structuring conceptual systems. With the single synecdochic act of 'decanting' babies, Aldous Huxley's *Brave New World* (1932) sets the scene for an existence where humanity is ultimately condemned to a reductive scientism and cultural sterility, its very perpetuation dependent upon the precise labelling of bottles. Heralding the rise of fascism in the 1930s, Huxley's seminal dystopia incorporates a metaphoric structure which stabs repeatedly at the underlying ideologies of 'civilised' behaviour, inverting the conventional meanings of such notions as 'savage' and 'stability'. *Brave New World* makes its impact through pointed satirical metaphor as those things once believed to be essential freedoms become the things now most controlled. Sharp irony perverts Western forms of morality into metaphorical immorality. Humanity is evolved into the Other, and, as in George Orwell's *Nineteen Eighty-Four* (1949), the only culture we have succeeded in oppressing is our own.

Nor is metaphor limited to works of pure fiction. For example, literary critics indulge in their own form of creative description, for, as Gerard Steen observes, 'metaphor has come to be defined as a mapping from concepts in one domain to concepts in another domain'.[10] In this manner, Sara Suleri considers the trope of colonialism as rape, 'in which colonized territory is rendered dubiously coterminous with the stereotype of a precultural and female geography',[11] rape or physical violence being a pervasive metaphor in much anti-imperialist rhetoric. Postcolonialist critic Leela Gandhi uses the term 'battleground' to describe the place of postcolonial studies in contemporary theory,[12] and dismisses the mechanism of colonial power as a 'disinterested purveyor of cultural enlightenment'.[13] Denis Judd discusses the British empire in clearly anatomical terms as he subjects the organs, limbs and characteristics of the imperial body to a searching post-mortem examination, just as Asimov writes of the physical decay of empire where 'circulation ceases first at the outer edges'.[14] Thus, even in science and the academic arts, metaphor is treated as an essential ingredient in the conveyance of new ideas, or as George Lakoff and Mark Johnson suggest, 'Novel metaphors can have the power of defining reality'.[15] It is possible to go further and argue that unfamiliar metaphors have the power to make us reflect on the nature of the metaphor itself, prodding us into a sharp awareness of how easily we suppress the sometimes raw unpleasantness of an original experience.

In defining the reality of her narrative *The Dispossessed* (1974), Ursula Le Guin (1929–) begins her metaphoric description of a world's isolation and oppression by discussing a wall, an object that forms the leitmotif of the text. There are many walls within Le Guin's narrative, but this first one is archetypal in both manufacture and placement, and underpins the remainder of her novel, which confronts the reader with barriers of all descriptions. Walls consistently obstruct the hero, Shevek, intentionally or incidentally, as he moves from one environment to the next, each barrier different in nature and complexity. The image of the wall acts as a foundation for Le Guin's story of cultural and economic control, the construction's basic simplicity emphasising the fundamental nature of its role. Her archetypal wall seems innocent enough:

> It did not look important. It was built of uncut rocks roughly mortared. An adult could look right over it, and even a child could climb it. Where it crossed the roadway, instead of having a gate it degenerated into mere geometry, a line, an idea of boundary. But the idea was real. It was important.... Like all walls it was ambiguous, two-faced. What was inside it and what was outside it. It depended upon which side of it you were.[16]

The simple construct of rocks and mortar provides an image of the most elementary separation,[17] but it is a separation so profound that it does not require a functioning barrier, the *notion* of the wall being sufficient for its purposes. On the outside of the barrier lies the world of Annares, 'a great prison camp, cut off from other worlds and other men',[18] while on the other side, the inside, protected, enclosed and made special by its exclusivity, lies a quarantined Urrasti space-port, the territory and sole representation on Annares of the planet Urras, the inhabitants of which are the economic overlords of the Annarestis. As Shevek, the central Annaresti character, realises once he has crossed the 'idea of boundary' to board a Urrasti space-ship, he has now 'yielded himself up to these people; he had given up his birthright of decision'.[19] The nature of the difference between 'inside' and 'outside' is so monumental that the willing movement from one to the other appears treasonous. For an Annaresti to accept the patronage of the Urrasti speaks of the unthinkable, namely, that a member of 'the Solidarity' (the name of the Annaresti collective) wishes to 'defect'. Crossing the division, or, as Le Guin has it, crossing the 'idea', is a metaphorical gesture of great magnitude, rendered all the more significant by the apparent lack of a barrier in the first place. By stepping through the wall, Shevek has passed from the familiar into the unfamiliar, at several levels. Physically he has moved from the land of Annares into the land of the Urrasti, a political comment on the transition of loyalties and allegiance.[20] Emotionally and intellectually, however, Shevek has taken a much larger step (and, interestingly, exhibits an awareness of the metaphoric nature of each hurdle), one that announces his willingness to abdicate his freedom as he steps into what is essentially the realm of a colonial power.

It is significant that Shevek is a brilliant academic and mathematician. That the author did not select a more typical representative of Annares, a farmer or an artisan perhaps, again indicates that the obstacles in her text are more intellectual than physical, as Shevek discovers that only by the power of his intellect is he able to comprehend and transcend the notion of 'barrier'. On Annares, walls are used to hold up buildings and protect from the elements. The idea that some might also be barriers designed to exclude people, or ideas themselves, is as foreign a concept to Shevek as are thoughts of doing things purely for the self. And here, Le Guin's metaphoric structure becomes linked with inevitable irony, for her base philosophical model of the anarchic Annaresti is that there is no 'self', only the group, in total opposition to the Urrasti model. Yet only as an individual can Shevek face the Urrasti, and only through the power of *his* thinking can he 'unbuild walls'.[21] Additionally in Shevek's case, knowledge and *naïveté* appear to walk hand in hand, as his lack of personal fear and total ignorance of foreign custom indicate. He does not 'see' the walls as he faces them at first, and so has to re-learn their function from foreign teachers and through a slow inculcation of Urrasti social mores. Shevek does not fear transgressions of the body or the mind at first, because he has never before experienced either. Only when he has become 'educated' in foreign ways does he understand the presence and power of these invisible barriers. The adjustment of the subaltern into the dominant power of the centre is slow and painful as, in many ways, Shevek's character is as much a metaphoric construct as the walls he confronts. Thus Le Guin's initial metaphor becomes more complex, suggesting not only that barriers of the mind are harder to breach than their physical counterparts, but also that to gain passage from without to within requires a near-biblical innocence to avoid the resulting pitfalls. Shevek's position is uncannily similar to Christian in John Bunyan's *Pilgrim's Progress* (1678, 1684), as, with a book in his hand and a burden on his back, he heads into a pilgrimage that will test his most fundamental beliefs.[22]

Le Guin's text is possessed of other forms of metaphorical meaning, too. The presence of the space-port wall in a society that apparently understands no such thing intimates a fundamental cultural difference between Urras and Annares: the ability to oppress and restrict and the willingness to be oppressed and restricted. Instead of a gate, this wall 'degenerated into mere geometry, a line, an idea of boundary', just as the text takes the subaltern relationship into a minimalist setting. Where another author might have spoken of imperial armies with vast ranks of warships and unlimited physical power, Le Guin's metaphor offers nothing more tangible than the power of the idea. And yet there *are* 'walls' within the Annaresti culture, barriers so faint as to provide the merest trace of an idea threading through the dominant theme of the text, an ironic nod to the blindness of those who will not see.[23] But since an idea cannot be destroyed or lessened by force, it becomes more potent than any material manifestation of dominance. *The Dispossessed* is not so much a narrative which uses metaphor to illustrate meaning as it is a text which bases its rationale on the fundamental place of metaphor in SF, a place where the unpalatable concept and the hidden belief are far more influential than the material realities of a physical construct.

This transposing of importance between reality and concept is a fundamentally important part of many SF texts, where 'reality' cannot be known and where only a metaphorical bridge can effect a useful connection between the fictional universe and our own. Thus the great galactic empires of SF are frequently based on the metaphoric extrapolation of both physical imperial history and the philosophy of imperialism; SF takes the material and intellectual resemblances of the past and experiments with them in new environments. Previously unexplored planets may be portrayed as barren wastelands or as forbidding jungles, both hostile to an expansionist humanity in a very physical and concrete sense. But wastelands have been made fertile and jungles have been controlled, rendering such examples inadequate barriers to the imperial project. Yet when an image is based on an *idea* rather than a concrete thing (as in the case of the utterly irreconcilable political and social structures of Annares and Urras), the force is effectively infinite. The idea of revolution is far more inspirational than the unpleasant realities of the act. This implies that the real location of the unexplored is in the *concept* of the unexplorable. While we know there is a vastness of space surrounding us on Earth, it is the intellectual idea of the vastness of the universe that inspires, rather than the more prosaic and mathematically calculated area. Le Guin takes metaphor to a more intellectual level than Kim Stanley Robinson, who associates the naïve, untouched Martian surface with Navajo sand paintings, or even Arthur C. Clarke, who speaks of the winds of Titan that 'sighed and whispered across a lifeless landscape'.[24]

When the science in SF is realistic, picturesque or ornamental, metaphor may seem redundant. What is more intriguing in the application of new technology and science than to allow readers to formulate their own understanding? 'The truest respect which you can pay to the reader's understanding,' says Laurence Sterne's Tristram Shandy, 'is to halve this matter amicably, and leave him something to imagine, in his turn, as well as yourself.'[25] Clearly, a great part of the enjoyment in SF is to be tantalised by the possibilities of theoretical science, so is there really a need for metaphor to clarify the image further? Writers of 'hard' SF are habitually making an implicit assumption that our science-educated society is sufficiently familiar with the commonly accepted qualities of distant planets and therefore does not require romantic metaphoric representations. We *know* that the Earth's moon has no breathable atmosphere; that the space between planets is usually cold and dark; that organic life cannot exist in a vacuum. What need is there then for additional description of these things, which have already been described a thousand times? Hard SF prefers to focus on those, usually technological, things which are still unknown, still in development, such as the components and construction of Robinson's space elevator,[26] a crystalline umbilical cord of massive proportions. The metaphors of hard SF are designed not to dazzle the *cognoscenti*, but to add a human depth to their technological genesis. Clarke's description of the first space station in *2001: A Space Odyssey* (1968) is elegantly free of metaphor: 'The sunlight glinted and sparkled from the polished metal surfaces of the slowly revolving, three-hundred-yard-diameter disc.'[27] Clarke's technological product is relatively simple, albeit a work of genius, and does not require a sophisticated explanation; he uses simple structures and simple tools to describe it. The station's attributes are tangible and obvious. Similarly, Robert Heinlein's 'continua craft' (a dimension-straddling 'convertible'), and H. G. Wells's 'Time Machine' are fantastic, indeed mesmerising in their fascination, but do not demand any deep explanation.[28] The devices are interesting in themselves but lack an ideological frame, although this lack does not prevent such concepts from being highly attractive in themselves. Complex metaphor is unnecessary here, hence the popularity of technological SF in contemporary films. Metaphors of power are often more easily comprehended in the visual because to be visual they must be overt (though not necessarily obtrusive), such as the presence of the Death Star in the first *Star Wars* film (1977), or the physical containment of the three (human) 'pre-cogs' in the 2002 film *Minority Report*.[29] Examining the list of recent releases makes it obvious that there is a great demand for SF films, especially those that indulge a general clamour for technological fantasy, because the metaphoric meanings are frequently unmistakable. But when the narrative moves not just into deeper space but into those areas of the imagination only slightly supported by the known or the possible, we require metaphors of power and substance as the text, as these areas lack the simplicity of the visual, and an intense effort is required to convey an unclouded representation.

With the production of such narratives as *Solaris* (1961), by Stanislaw Lem (1921–2006), in which a living, sentient ocean covers the surface of a planet larger than Earth, it is no longer sufficient for an author to paint engaging technological word pictures; it becomes necessary for the author to invoke 'the explicit tale, the hidden messages'.[30] In the *Solaris* example, the philosophical metaphors of Lem are drawn by necessity to the concrete and ultra-tangible as he attempts to depict a world of nebulous and theoretical Otherness in practical scientific terms, or, as Rose suggests, 'not so much by making the whole situation of contact metaphorical as by forming his narrative precisely around the problem of anthropomorphization, the problem of coming to grips with or even conceiving something truly nonhuman'.[31] Vivid physical description is enhanced by metaphysical analysis as Lem's main character, psychologist Dr Kris Kelvin, gives the scientific view of the sentient ocean: 'a sort of gigantic entity, a fluid cell, unique and monstrous … surrounding the globe with a colloidal envelope'.[32] One can almost hear Kelvin's clinical scientific dictation as he speaks into his recorder during attempts to rationalise the events following his arrival at the base. Lem's technique describes the enigmatic ocean through minimalised metaphors, as brief strokes of insight against the vast canvas of the narrative. This austerity of description moves Lem away from the often conventional tech-fest of contemporary SF, as he gives us an image of the world ocean and the mindset of his characters in the simplest of terms. In accordance with Sterne's philosophy, we are not provided with lavish imagery, but rather with an overall suggestion, one which offers us a hinted outline of what Kelvin and the others are experiencing. This has the dual effect of providing a flexible perception of the narrative's substructural image while simultaneously enabling it to appear even more monstrous and unearthly.

Just as Le Guin chooses the image of wall as the leitmotif in her novel, so Lem associates his essential imagery with the divine and the monstrous. Kelvin arrives at the station orbiting Solaris in the *Prometheus*, a ship named after the hero of legend who brought contraband sparks of fire to humankind. For this crime, Zeus punished humanity by sending them Pandora and her box, and Prometheus by chaining him to a rock and having an eagle daily consume his liver, which renewed itself. The name Prometheus means 'foresight', a gift of prophecy supposedly possessed by the heroic thief. With this unmistakable metaphor, Lem begins his narrative by appealing to the reader's existing knowledge of myth. The assumption that the legend of Prometheus will be known is as valid in this text as it was when Mary Shelley claimed the name in the subtitle of her gothic novel *Frankenstein; or, The Modern Prometheus* (1818). Thus Lem's modern hero arrives on a strange world on the back of ancient legend and presumes to manifest godlike knowledge. Kelvin's *avant-garde* intellectualism correlates with the original stolen fire, 'the cause of our own suffering',[33] both being the essential tools from which space exploration began. Kelvin will be made to suffer similar punishments as the original transgressor, as the psychologist seeks to illuminate the nightmarish *mise en scène* that awaits him.

Lem seems determined to have everything about the Solaris station appear hellish. Kelvin's approach to the space habitat is marked by a tumultuous and terrifying descent as he is faced with 'a blinding crimson glare'.[34] As he walks into the station, conventionally a place of extreme order and scientific cleanliness, the scientist observes both the cathedral-like construction and the unusual physical jumble of the base, where 'a nauseating smell hung in the air; footprints, in a series of glutinous smears, went off in all directions'.[35] Nor is Kelvin's first sighting of his fellow scientists a promising one, for Snow, a cybernetics expert and great academic, slumps in a chair, 'his face burnt by the sun, the skin on his nose and face coming away in great flakes'.[36] Snow also greets Kelvin with a look of horror; the scientist's initial awareness of Kelvin suggests the older man is in terrible dread of something. His face pales, his hands shake and he cringes as the newcomer steps towards him. It is only after a brief and cryptic conversation with Snow that Kelvin realises the older man's hands are covered in dried blood. In these opening moments of the text, Lem has set the stage for a performance of infernal metaphors: not quite the entrance to hell, yet more than the merely purgatorial. The contrast between the anticipation of the stereotypical pristine space station and its actuality is significant and calculated. Lem intends to question the right of humankind to meddle with metaphysical mysteries and begins his interrogation of such an imperialist act with the metaphor of the sane man's fall into darkness, horror and destruction.

In combination with the overall imagery of Kelvin's arrival, Lem incorporates a series of vague metaphors revolving around the Other within ourselves, our subconscious, and draws on well established archetypal fears to do so. We have no idea whether the blood on Snow's hands is his own or someone else's. Since the man is in a semi-drunken stupor when Kelvin arrives, and though dishevelled and dirty appears unharmed, the implication is that Snow has severely injured another. This small but pointed aside confronts one of humankind's essential fears – the threat to life. Is Snow a murderer? Has some knowledge of the Other driven him to the ultimate crime? Snow does not immediately recognise Kelvin as either a fellow scientist or even a human: 'I don't know you',[37] he says. Snow is terrified because of the horrors he has seen. He is no longer able to make the differentiation between friend and foe or between reality and hallucination. Lem removes the boundaries between reality and possibility to such an extent that he creates a third realm, a place where possibilities and realities mesh, and where different forms of power and control synthesise into a metaphysical limbo. No longer is *Solaris* adequately quantified by Said's vision of 'us' and 'them', but it is now a homogeneous domain where such subjectivities are blended and incorporated into a fluid movement of awarenesses, a 'pooling of information'.[38] The surreal elements of Lem's vision – not only the thinking ocean but also a giant black woman and the ghosts of ideals – form a new Other: a shifting place where the division *between* is unclear and rational demarcation an impossibility. The Other changes and morphs in both meaning and form as the text explores and experiments with physical and intellectual metaphor.

The image and metaphor of the monster is prevalent in *Solaris*. As his primary protagonist unravels the mystery facing him upon reaching the distant planet, Lem institutes a series of metaphorical questions that are focused not on the sentient ocean, as one might expect, but rather on the perceptions of the scientists who are engaged in the study of the ocean. The questions are similar, in that they all probe the behaviour of the human scientists as they strive for knowledge under the incessant provocation of the unknowable. To be constantly aware that you are observing something totally outside the bounds of human familiarity, and to be equally aware that nothing you are able to do is likely to increase your knowledge, must place an incredible strain on intelligent, thinking beings. Such pressure is made clear when, shortly after arriving, Kelvin considers that the scientific crew may have gone mad. Yet even here, the psychologist asks only the leading question 'Could madness attain such a degree of reality?'[39] Lem does not elaborate and neglects to offer us images of 'typically' insane behaviour. And he very carefully does not provide an answer. Further, when Kelvin considers that human existence on the planet was 'not simply a question of penetrating Solarist civilization, it was essentially a test of ourselves, of the limitations of human knowledge',[40] Lem holds the psychologist back from providing an exegesis. The text in turn does not attempt to 'penetrate' the ocean (although the scientists do undertake some fairly invasive activities, such as a bombardment of the ocean's surface with dense X-rays) as much as it seems to validate the actions and reasoning of the main characters. That Lem considers madness a genuine threat to those deconstructing scientific mysteries is clear, as the text proceeds to encompass nightmarish dreams where individuals analyse their intrusion of Solaris through the metaphorical construct of conversations with the dead.

As discussed in Chapter 2, a taxing issue with the creation of SF narrative is that, since each unique authorial voyage is by its nature definitive, it is possible to see the imaginary world only in the way the author has created it. This determinism in SF arises because there is often absolutely no avenue from which the reader may glean an alternative viewpoint. Historical novels are based in some portion of the recorded (or at least acknowledged) past, but future narratives have no references except from within themselves and possibly intertextually within the SF genre. Therefore, while we may try to imagine alternative views to that provided by the text, we are required to accept the narrative as being the only version, the authorial perspective as being the only one. Yet even here, a reader familiar with the tropes of SF may infer subtleties. For example, just as the Solaris station is dirty and run down, the reader is able to contrast Lem's image with the more traditional one, where such a space station would be gleaming and sanitised. Thus, by making use of an implied intertextuality, Lem's imagery reaches far beyond his words. This is a problematic stance at times, especially when the text deals with non-human culture, for, as Said argues: 'The power to narrate, or to block other narratives from forming and emerging, is very important to culture and imperialism, and constitutes one of the main connections between them'.[41] In this respect, we are able to see Solaris only as the problem Lem wishes us to see – an unsolvable and enigmatic riddle of a clash between different forms of awareness. It is through the power of his metaphysical metaphors that Lem permits us to question the authorial stance. Lem's minimalist style of metaphor enables readers at least to imagine 'in between' the imagery of his perspective and their own, a vital facility when dealing with such a non-conventional setting such as Solaris.[42]

By cleverly instituting a multidimensional textual construct, Lem gives us three versions of the narrative simultaneously: an adventure of technology and the future; a pragmatic model of human expansion and absorption of the Other; and the intellectual and questioning analysis of human motivations. The search for knowledge about the mysterious sentience of the ocean is interwoven with an identical search for answers from within the scientists themselves. As Snow observes, 'We think of ourselves as Knights of the Holy Contact. This is another lie. We are only seeking man. We have no need of other worlds. We need mirrors.'[43] Through imagery of dreaming and scientific procedures tinged with a trace of the neo-gothic, Lem raises the notion that all knowledge is internal, suggesting that we cannot know another until we are able to know ourselves. In this respect, the giant fluid brain that covers the planet is a grand metaphor for the human reflection and projection of our desires onto others. Lem has us see the ocean as unambiguous, in contrast to the human mind, which is clouded and forced into ambiguity as a response to an impossible desire to know and apportion knowledge of all things according to conventional human values. The intellectual imperialism depicted by Lem's text is far more vigorous than the material model, as the very concept of life is considered something that humankind must understand and add to its repository of knowledge. Not only do the scientists (and, by association, human sciences) seek themselves, but also the search is possessed of an impossible circularity. In the attempt to interrogate the life that is the ocean, Kelvin and the others must first realise that the ocean is a mirror. Lem's unique manner of exposing human fears and deeply hidden yearnings using the concept of the Other as a reflection is often disturbing. Kelvin's tragic interaction with the ghost of his wife, Rheya, is only one of the ways in which the novel argues the impossibility of separating the observer from the observation.

Every author has different metaphoric techniques. Whereas Lem seeks the metaphysical at the boundaries of science, Le Guin suggests the realities of Annares and Urras in small increments, allowing us to establish a connection with the unseen world through everyday familiarities. She describes Shevek's first step onto Urras as follows:

> He looked up, and as he stepped off the ramp onto the level ground he stumbled and nearly fell. He thought of death, in that gap between the beginning of a step and its completion, and at the end of the step he stood on a new earth.[44]

For Shevek, his old life ends as a new one begins but, in a split second of interval, he stumbles. This brief physical hiatus, a hint of death and rebirth, introduces a further motif, which echoes throughout the text and tells us not so much of the physical as it does of the ideology of the Annares and Urras cultures. In contrast to the sophistication of the Urrasti, Shevek is provincial and unpolished in society. As with Le Guin's concept of the wall as barrier, so Shevek's falterings take on an education-by-metaphor aspect as he learns by his 'mistakes'. Each time he bumps into another wall, he must re-evaluate his situation before continuing. With the first mis-step from the ramp we do not see Shevek fall, but Le Guin prepares us – metaphorically – for the event.

The narrative of Urras and Annares does not in itself contain spectacular drama or scenes of intergalactic struggle. It does not involve the passage of vast distances, or an encounter with an exotic, multi-tentacled Other. Nor does it rely heavily upon incredible technology (other than Shevek's theoretical physics, which leads to the invention of the 'ansible', an instantaneous communications device). Instead, it describes the effort and struggles of a small group of people breaking away from the essentially capitalistic and paternalistic society of Urras in order to colonise the Urrasti moon and to form a new culture. Urras, an Earth clone planet, orbits around the star Tau Ceti with its moon, Annares. As it was the larger of the two and as it had a greater abundance of water, Urras was the first to be colonised; only a small mining settlement was placed on the less fertile Annares. A group of Annaresti – 'the Solidarity', who follow the egalitarian teachings of the anarchic philosopher Odo – decide to migrate in search of a refuge from general Urrasti intolerance. But the new Annaresti are trapped by economic circumstance into accepting an exploitive relationship with Urras to supply raw materials to maintain the mother planet's lavish lifestyle. The Solidarity are forced by a poor climate into maintaining trade links with Urras; this evolves into a basic dependency of Annaresti on Urrasti, an essentially subaltern position. Urras is lush, fertile and easy to inhabit; Annares is bleak and arid. Interest in the narrative stems not only from the ideological likenesses between Urras and Western societies, but also from partial political metaphors of East and West, one society embracing comfort and personal wealth without intellectual freedom, the other striving for equality in all things at the cost of great physical deprivation. The rich textures of the narrative are evoked by difference, difference which Le Guin describes through the intensive action of metaphor.

The Urrasti are initially depicted as hedonistic and decadent, with marvellous clothing, ornate standards of living and, as Shevek observes, a certain 'splendour'.[45] The immediate contrast between essential survival on Annares and the luxuries of Urras is brought home to him when he experiences 'the springy feeling of live grass underfoot; he recognised it from having walked in the Triangle Park in Abbernay'.[46] On Annares, there is insufficient spare water for something as impractical as grass to be cultivated outside of a special place, a park. Le Guin uses the commonplace as an element in her growing structural metaphor of the binary opposition of the two societies. The Urrasti have an abundance of material wealth – in this case, unrestricted water; so much, in fact, that they think nothing of wasting it on useless but decorative plant life. Because the Annaresti must hoard every drop of water for times of great drought, the swathes of grass Shevek walks casually across must seem an enormous extravagance. The essential metaphor at work here is the conversion of Shevek's initial interpretation of grass as a luxury item into other images of luxury. The nature of the difference between the two societies is so very basic that the only way Shevek can begin to connect to his new life is by metaphor. He cannot easily or immediately comprehend the reality of Urras, and therefore must absorb new information in stages. The first stage is one of contrasted metaphor, where his presence as the first Annaresti scientist on Urras is linked by a metaphorical admiration for a piece of glassware:

> Shevek drank off the water thirstily and sat looking down at the glass
> in his hand, a fragile, finely shaped piece that caught the gleam of the

fire on its rim of gold. He was aware of the three men, of their attitudes as they sat or stood around him, protective, respectful, proprietary.[47]

Shevek realises that he may not be as elegant as the glass he holds, but his relationship to the Urrasti is perceived in the same way as an item of usefulness. The Urrasti are equally protective, respectful and proprietary about their world, their culture and their way of doing things, and have now added the dissident scientist to their inventory. The colonial relationship may not be precisely comparable with historical record, but there are enough similarities to make the narrative assume a familiar pattern. This familiarity in itself adds to Le Guin's metaphorical structure, as we contrast known history with the events of Shevek's attempted assimilation by the Urrasti intelligentsia. The same feeling of proprietary interest and power is evoked when the narrative examines the concept of *prison*, which, like 'wall', is an alien notion to the Annarasti. By exploring the idea as an abstract rather than a specific model, we are able to see how such notions become part of a larger metaphoric organism. In this instance, Le Guin takes us back to a youthful game in which Shevek and four friends decide to 'play' at 'jailer'. But the play takes on an ominous tone when there is a disagreement among the boys and what was play now becomes reality. Instead of re-enacting an event learned in a history class, the boys imprison Kadagv, one of their number, and force him into a small dark space by means of violence and threat. Upon Kadagv's release, Shevek is violently ill as he comprehends what has been done, especially as the incident suggests something in himself and the others of an instinct to imprison. By enacting the role of jailer, he has taken on the historical values of the society the Annaresti believed intolerable. Even in play, a metaphor in itself for the ignorance of innocence, Shevek cannot tolerate the tenets of an imperial central authority.

Just as Shevek feels himself to be an anomaly on Urras, so too does Kelvin on the Solaris station. While Le Guin uses metaphor to expound the relationship between a subaltern and imperial ideology, Lem's text invites us to engage with the imperialistic desire to possess ultimate knowledge of (and therefore power over) the Other. In addition to metaphor, Lem invokes the power of stereotypes. That such a senior and acclaimed scientist as Snow desires sanctuary in thought-blurring alcohol points to an uncomfortable repositioning of accepted representations. Is Snow demented? The possible subversion of the higher-thinking scientist into the mindless animal attacks another Western archetype, where the rational being is separated from the beast within through the power of the intellect. Whether the Other is sage or monster, Kelvin confronts it in terms of possible madness – both his own and that of the other scientists – as the narrative dreams become reality and people gain the ability to interact with the dead. Each of the scientists now living on the station hovering above the sentient ocean is plagued with visitations of the monsters of the id and the ego. In Kelvin's case, his 'visitor' is Rheya, the wife he was divorcing but who chose suicide rather than live without him. Through the poignant interaction between Kelvin and versions of Rheya,[48] Lem identifies and highlights several issues where the expansionist ambitions of humanity and the unknowable powers of the sentient sea form an inversion of the scientists' objective. While they are there to study and quantify the ocean, it is the ocean that is, in fact, observing them, both sets of 'observations' releasing repressed material in an autonomous form. The theme of symbiosis and mutuality pervades each encounter between the scientists and the ocean – each contributing an element to possible self-discovery. As Kelvin admits to Rheya in a moment of intellectual helplessness:

> You may have been sent to torment me, or make my life happier, or as an instrument ignorant of its function, used like a microscope with me on the slide. Possibly you are here as a token of friendship, or a subtle punishment, or even as a joke.[49]

Kelvin, the sanest of all the humans on Solaris station, is himself doubting the values of sanity. The heat rises in the station, a further intimation of the increasingly diabolical conditions, and the unreal becomes more significant than the real. As in Shakespearean plays, the ghostly visitations provide a greater focal point than the interplay between the narrative's living personnel, as Kelvin and the others concentrate on how they deal with the ocean's ability to reject their physical investigations. In scenes reminiscent of James Whale's neo-gothic 1930s film interpretation of Shelley's *Frankenstein*, fantastic machines and experiments are brought into play, and the issues of causality are flung open. However, even here, meaning is elusive and tantalising. The challenge of comprehending and understanding what Solaris is doing to them still eludes Kelvin until he realises that the ocean is an emotional reflection of that which is hidden inside himself. It is only when he makes the correlation between his desires and his fears that he achieves some form of enlightenment. The ocean Other cannot be known until the self is known. He wonders whether the ocean will remove Rheya to save him further distress if both are cognisant of the fact that her removal will also cause him pain. As he admits to himself:

> I am a murderer unawares. Man has gone out to explore other worlds and other civilizations without having explored his own labyrinth of dark passages and secret chambers, and without finding what lies behind doorways that he himself has sealed.[50]

While Kelvin is attempting to unravel the metaphysical knots of humanity's fear, the ocean is subjected to massive doses of hard X-rays and fed concentrated replays of Kelvin's own brain waves. The harder and more invasive the scientific experiment, the fiercer and more tenacious become the apparitions, although it appears the ocean is making greater inroads into the psyches of the Solarists than they are into that of the ocean. The reader understands that the scientists have themselves become objects of an experiment, peered at through the wrong end of a telescope, where everything 'looked meaningless, trivial and slightly ridiculous'.[51] With the imposed exoticism perceived through the eyes of the interloper, the world ocean becomes not only a secret the human scientists must uncover but also the ominous outsider, whose threat cannot be clearly ascertained. We see the scientists' dominating need to expose the essential nature of the Other and assimilate it into human knowledge. The metaphor here is exquisitely subtle, as it inverts Shelley's account of natural science. Instead of assembling elements to construct life, the Solarists attempt to deconstruct life down into its integral factors. The drive to 'own' the knowledge of the Other has taken precedent over all else and the mysterious sentience below renders the Solaris scientists into archetypal explorers in the Western mould. Since the ocean's response appears ambiguous at best, Lem satirises the stereotypical Western academic trend whereby esoteric knowledge becomes trapped by its own theories and concepts. The ocean becomes a silent witness to the machinations of the power mongers. Simultaneously, Lem's vision of science and the upholders of the scientific method transposes the experiment until it is one of rats in an infernal maze. Either some form of mutually acceptable compromise will occur, or one faction stands in danger of destroying the other. However, as Kelvin admits, many years of space exploration have sanctified the nature and purpose of contact; the act of human expansion has become 'the heaven of eternity'.[52] And few among us would willingly give up heaven.

On Solaris, Kelvin, contemplating an eventual return to Earth, reaches his own plateau of awareness. The experiences on the station have produced a problematic self-knowledge, but it is a knowledge formed through the externalisation of the internal rather than the influence of purely external factors. The posited mirror ocean seemingly reflects only that which is already there, just as the ghosts, which Lem calls 'phi-creatures', are reflections of each scientist's inner fears. Events aboard the station take on the air of a continuous illusion, produced by the scientists' compulsion to superimpose analogies of the safely 'known' upon the unknown. Through a combination of inductive and deductive reasoning, Kelvin now realises that the ocean is indeed sentient, but speculates that it is a childlike or vastly uninterested intelligence. It is not that the Other has taught him a great deal, but rather the lack of information from external inquiry has forced Kelvin to look inside himself for the rationale of discovery. The most significant change has been effected not through increased scientific data but through the realisation that so much cannot be known, at least not in a quantitative sense. In his final analysis of the Solaris Other, Kelvin feels himself 'somehow changed':

> The contrast was inexpressible between that lively curiosity [of the ocean] and the shimmering immensity of the ocean that stretched away out of sight ... I had never felt its gigantic presence so strongly, or its powerless, changeless silence, or the secret forces that gave the waves their regular rise and fall. I sat unseeing, and sank into a universe of inertia, glided down an irresistible slope and identified myself with the dumb fluid colossus; it was as if I had forgiven it everything, without the slightest effort of word or thought.[53]

Regardless of whether he has the right to forgive the ocean anything, Kelvin has come to think of it as an evolving ego and moral agency and not as a potential enemy; there is no longer the urge to transcend the power of the rival life form. The parable told here by Lem offers Solaris as a metaphor of the Earth, with the narrative providing some insight into the nature of human imagination. Only by yielding to its influence is Kelvin able to understand the monumental Otherness of the ocean. Lem's text is simultaneously a lesson on the limits of metaphor as well as of science and, paradoxically, a grand metaphor of Otherness.

On the return journey to Annares, Shevek, too, is contemplative about his new awareness, but his is a closure, as opposed to Kelvin's opening. Shevek is aware now only of his destination, of 'going home', of walls finally behind him: 'He was aware of hope deceived and of the promise kept; of failure; and of the sources within his spirit, unsealed at last, of joy. He was a man released from jail.'[54] Having travelled the same roads as Odo, full circle from innocent idealist to weary political dissident, Shevek has explored the gamut of experience outside his normal environment and found it less than satisfying. Le Guin has confronted her main protagonist with metaphorical walls, upon which he has beaten out his doubts and ethical anxieties. Just as Shevek triumphs by discovering the inner context of barriers in his life, so too does Kelvin reach inside to uncover the monsters which plague him. Both novels offer an insight into SF's ability (self-reflexively and self-critically) to ride metaphor across imaginative bridges from the known into that which is unknowable. In the experiments of Lem and Le Guin, we engage with specific explorations of the Other, which in itself is a key to postcolonial consciousness.

Where Le Guin offers the rigidity of a wall as an external metaphor of resistance against which her protagonists prove themselves, Lem offers the yielding fluidity and elusive qualities of the untouchable psyche as an unfathomable ocean. Where one resists through obstruction, the other does not resist at all, but slips further away at the reach of a hand. The only conclusions the protagonists of either novel may draw are subjective and unique – a comment from both authors on the fallibility of 'hard' science as the only basis for human certainty. In the search for knowledge and therefore 'possession' of the Other, Kelvin is forced, though lack of alternatives, to peer inside, into the mirror of 'self'. The gigantic ocean also mirrors all the fears and hidden miseries of the imperial desire. In the search for monsters, Lem's hero realises that the only real monstrosity is the arrogance of those who cling to a self-imposed blindness. In Shevek's case, he has mirrors to spare as each barrier reflects back to him some of the things he most fears. They both see that the Other is an aspect of the self we have not yet met.

While descriptive metaphor – images of lunar sands and exotic off-world expanses – is essential to the general flavour and background of any SF narrative, it is the ideological metaphor, the fundamental images of existence and conflict, of superiority and exclusivity, which underpin and wield the most power in a great majority of SF texts. There is rich contrast between the desperate aridity of Annares and the lush benevolence of Urras, and between an austere people, on the one hand, and a culture of hedonistic lotus eaters, on the other. These images, though in themselves stereotypical paradigmatic representations of shifting binary differences on our own planet, do not produce the essential weight of Le Guin's text. Such contrasts are clever and productive, but act only as a backdrop to the main conflict, the struggle of one man forced to choose between fundamental principles. Shevek is a Jesus figure on the mountaintop tempted by Satan with all the kingdoms of the world. Without the presence of the various walls in his struggle to accomplish his goal (which in the end become one wall, the ultimate decision to set himself free of his knowledge), Shevek cannot reach an awareness of the meaning of his people's bravery and resolution. Le Guin takes the image of 'wall' and fashions it into a metaphorical rock against which her hero tests his ideological and moral convictions. The wall becomes the embodiment of all that threatens an enlightened humanity, the metaphor made even more insightful because of its utter simplicity and ubiquitousness. In *The Dispossessed*, we are also seemingly presented with another basic metaphor: two aspects of the Other, one shadowed and inward facing, the other self-indulgent and obvious. However, this second sequence is in itself a wall: the hard and unforgiving despair of Shevek contrasted against his childlike innocence and hopeful idealism.

As many representations in SF are so clearly drawn from that which is already known, the conventional style of the corpus frequently stands accused of popularist weaknesses, a fairly applied charge in many instances.

However, not all SF texts are the equivalent of *Star Trek*'s 'Wagon-train to the stars', and the enduring fascination and development of the genre cannot be reduced to a simple reproduction of the human condition in space. For those texts that take the reader beyond the comfort of the known, into areas that engage and experiment with internalised aspects of human relationships, with past and future anxieties, there is a freedom of expression unparalleled by any other mode of writing, bar the purest fantasy. Once narrative steps away from the conventions of other writing styles and into SF, it embraces a freedom of expression, the successful rendition of which demands extraordinary insight from the author. Such insight uses whatever writerly tools are most effective, metaphor being one of the most potent. The Other is vital to imperialism and to a postcolonial analysis of it; of its nature it is best explored by metaphor, and we see this in two very different cases in *The Dispossessed* and *Solaris*. The use of metaphor in these texts is far from non-consensual, as it depends upon the reader's willingness to engage with the writing process as one scenario describes another, involving not only individual words but whole fields of association. Metaphor in SF has become the tool that describes the indescribable, and with which new superstructure is laid upon old foundations. And the entirety of metaphor is often needed in a genre linked so closely to 'hard' science, where, to be true to that science, the fictions must often work in the confined space between fantasy and fact. One of the greatest exponents of 'hard' SF is Arthur C. Clarke, often known as the 'prophet' of science. And with Clarke, we turn next to an examination of why a galactic empire, the great experiment of social expansion, will probably never happen.

4. Things Fall Apart:
Relativity, Distance and the Periphery

It lay only three seconds away, yet that was enough. He had travelled a mere million kilometres in less than half a day; but the sense of separation was already almost complete. It was intolerable to wait six seconds for every reaction and every answer; by the time a reply came, he had forgotten the original question.[1]

Travelling from Titan to 'Imperial Earth' for the first time, Duncan Makenzie begins to understand one of the problems posed to communications by interplanetary distances. In a universe that conforms to the principles of relativity, nothing comprised of matter can move faster than the speed of light.[2] Arthur C. Clarke (1917–) thereby has Makenzie experience, at first hand, the primary hurdle faced by any imperial authority seeking to control colonies that are located beyond its physical grasp: distance as time. And imagining or dealing with distance, the crossing of massive spans of empty space, is a significant form of experiment within the skilful creations of future empire and the colonising of planets, both of our own solar system and of remote stars.

However, before considering the theoretical connections between empire and the application of science, either as a movement in itself or through the medium of SF, it should be understood that the relationship between empire and the technological problem of overcoming distance has been extant since the early 1800s.[3] Authorial experiments based on real science, which extrapolate what we already know and accept into areas that we might consider fantasy, have long been an integral part of the genre. The connection between the rampant progress of eighteenth-century imperialism and the sudden ascent of technology was due, in the main part, to the Western ideology of 'development', which supported both spheres. Aaron Perkus acknowledges that 'Technology was seen as a racial progression across time … the possession and exploitation of technology guaranteed superiority along an evolutionary continuum'.[4] Once explored, this interconnection also reflects the complexity of imperialist and postimperialist issues as they affect and are affected by SF. Is SF designed as the handmaiden, the smoking gun or the nemesis of the imperial project?

Knowledges change. Societies change. The constant influx of knowledge into a society acts as a tide that cannot permit stagnation. Just as there has been movement towards or away from certain social and political vogues, certain theories and beliefs, so too have there been 'fashions' in SF credibility. What is exciting in the genre and draws the mind at one moment becomes *passé* in the next, each action and reaction leading inevitably towards a new level of awareness. This process was never more acutely observed than during the rapid technological advances made in and since the twentieth century, a scientific *accelerando* which in turn supported a fast-growing literary genre. Moreover, just as science sometimes moves in intuitive leaps rather than in a plodding linearity, so too does its symbiotic genre, which speculates upon its fantastic possibilities. There are times when SF sits shrewdly on its scientific plausibility, especially during those moments when science seems limitless and fresh. Then there are times when SF extends itself beyond the plausible, when it becomes dissatisfied with even the most extreme of new developments and seeks to construct pathways based on tenuous quasi-scientific structures. During its moments of introspection, we also see SF engage productively with a variety of critical literary theories, including postcolonialism, when it creates, by its ingenuity, an intriguing blend of the synthetic and the real. In the postmodern world, we often see only the extremes of SF, its playful moods or its apocalyptic warnings, but this ignores the many fundamental issues upon which the genre is based. SF's ongoing commentary on the imperial project asks skilful and earnest questions, for which there have been too few considered responses. Just as Gulliver's travels once probed the social dilemmas of eighteenth-century Europe, so too does SF's experimental thinking highlight a broad range of cultural and political topics. In a text such as Isaac Asimov's *Foundation and Empire* (1952), an authorial jump into hyperspace signifies far more than an innovative method of transportation.

The links between social shifts, imperial expansion and SF are illustrated, as are all developing constructs, in a continuous sine wave of contraction and expansion, of plausibility and diverse creativity. In the earliest forms, before modern science was able to conceive of lunar vehicles and space shuttles, these links produced the fantastic spacecraft of Jules Verne and H. G. Wells. In the absence of 'known' scientific limits, SF was itself without limit or division. Cyrano de Bergerac's *Histoire comique des états et empires de la lune* (1656) and Voltaire's *Micromégas* (1752) are but two texts which hypothesised in realms of empire and SF centuries before the possibility of space exploration. Following a flourishing of research, contemporary science has considered the increasingly likely exploration of planets within our solar system. The sinuous progressions of social development, science and SF cross and interweave, linking one to the other as each is pressured and strained by a variety of external forces.

Given the magnitude of the genre, it may be helpful to imagine SF as a series of terraces, each sub-genre partially overlapping and connected to its neighbours, each providing a platform from which the newest flying buttress of writing may be launched. When considering those areas of 'hard' SF (traditionally the most technologically plausible), we examine texts based within the framework of a physically bound universe, where the extrapolation of science is an exercise in rationality and logical thought. These offer us terraces of dense 'not-yet' fiction, but representative of short-lived knowledge, as real science supersedes that which is defined by the text.[5] Separate from these are extensions of remote and alien probabilities, of places where even the most theoretical science has been either removed or transcended in some form. These are the places of faster-than-light (FTL) travel, of matter transportation and of endless possibility.[6]

Thus when we examine the foci of SF (in its imperial mode) and technology, we see they have become interlinked to such a degree that the one has often apparently spawned movement in the other, or, as Daniel R. Headrick notes:

> connections between technology and imperialism must be approached from both sides: from the history of technology as well as that of imperialism.... Given a particular historical phenomenon – for example, the new imperialism – how did technological forces shape its development?[7]

With this in mind, it becomes useful to consider the possibilities of a future human empire without the benefits of space science and technology. Could it happen? The answer is most likely 'no'; however, this does not detract in the smallest sense from the thought experiments which consider the possibilities. If people lack the ability to colonise off Earth, the likelihood of the imperial project continuing in any of its historically accepted forms becomes increasingly remote.

Wylie Sypher observes that 'Knowledge in scientific form is coherent disillusion, organised disappointment, a loss of epiphany'.[8] But where science is bounded by fact, and therefore 'knowable' and able to be demystified into an 'organised disappointment', SF is restrained by nothing except the ability to imagine. While science is limited to tangible places, the genre also has the intangible ones.

Though distance has always been a governing element in the notion of colonisation – distance from the centre providing the very rationale for the concept of 'colony' – never has its impact been so unqualified as in SF. Throughout recorded history, imperial nations have always had to consider the physical outward movement of their citizens and values as much as the inward absorption of the colonised societies, a cultural translocation possessed as much of a concrete aspect as of an ideological one. However, all movement before the twenty-first century was based on the presupposition that the distances under consideration were humanly navigable. Whether by sailing ships or route marches, it was essential for the centre to be able to reach out in a physical manner and present a solid, corporeal presence of itself in the colony. From the expansion of Rome with the First Punic War in 264–241 BC until global imperialism achieved its fullest geographical hegemonies in the early twentieth century, the matter of empire has been one of gathering in and holding ground. Any serious consideration of a future empire in SF must engage with the element of distance: at what point do we take that leap into hyperspace and cross from the platform of hard SF into the realm of optimistic imagination?

As with the link between technology and imperialism, imperial expansion and the expression of physical force are also historically indivisible from one another. Any colony set in an extrapolated future would be affected by, and would need to demonstrate an awareness of, the power of a physical imperial presence, in both its aggressive and its passive forms; Larry Niven's *A Gift From Earth* (1968) offers a particularly fertile expression of this awareness. And while the notion of employing force may no longer be a predominant one in the initial stages of (interplanetary) colonisation, its implicit power is always there – a source of comfort perhaps, suggesting a protection of the vulnerable periphery by the centre. Whether the colony is located on an inhabited or uninhabited planet, a need would remain for a constant resourcing and reaffirmation of the imperial power from the centre, as the 'First Hundred' discover in Kim Stanley Robinson's *Mars* series. This *knowledge* of the power that a physical presence can bring is vital in the empires of SF, where only the solidity of material form gives function to any of the myriad concepts of the genre. It is precisely this desire for the tangible aspect of power that conflicts most openly with Albert Einstein's theory of relativity, and it is at this nexus of extrapolated science and the experiential political forum of the known past that SF's projection of an imperial future appears to waver.

If we assess imperialism in SF by how it conforms to our existing parameters of empire, then there is either a discrepancy in terms of physical possibilities or we need to broaden our concept of 'empire'. To entertain the possibility of interplanetary empire in a future society we need to consider three main aspects of SF: first, the palpable constraints placed upon an imperial expansionism, if it is to remain in line with accepted physics; secondly, the removal of such constraints, and how such a removal has affected the growth and style of potential future empires; and finally, the potential meaning of the intellectual notion of 'empire'. If a society is to consider the future of empire in a pragmatic manner, it cannot easily look beyond accepted theories of physics, although many texts involved with galactic dominions do precisely this. Can we indulge ourselves and contemplate empire in more philosophical terms, or must we be cognisant of our movement between the sub-genre terraces, where a defined notion in one is merely the suggested framework in another? Realising that science itself is often the first place where absolutes are written with an eye to later amendment, perhaps it is more proper to consider SF as a continuous form of *Bildungsroman*: the development of a work in progress, where what we learn tomorrow may change the validity of the facts we hold today. If this is so, SF might be more properly regarded not as fiction but as experiments with undiscovered fact.

Two of the most concrete hurdles when considering the restraints placed upon physical expansion in the future are Einstein's general and special theories of relativity. Both arrive at the conclusion that, in our universe, nothing comprised of matter may travel faster than the speed of light, and for anything macroscopic probably not at speeds even approaching that velocity. This being the case, interplanetary travel would seem to possess an uncertain future, and interstellar travel becomes nothing more than a dream of extended, deep-sleep voyages. As we have seen in the case of Duncan Makenzie's journey from Titan, and even allowing for the advanced speeds suggested by Clarke, Makenzie's intolerance of limitations of distance is already visible at a mere three-second removal. Imagine how travellers might feel as distance becomes 'time' and when weeks and months divide them from ready communication. Accepting that science and technology will continue their exponential progress, providing us with better and faster methods of transportation, we are still faced with the inevitability of a speed beyond which we cannot physically travel. According to Einstein's theories, there will always be a finite limit to the velocity at which physical matter may be thrust through space. If so, conventional practices of colonialism would be stretched to their utmost practical limits, even within the bounds of our own solar system, making the hypothesis that imperial conventions might be continued beyond interplanetary distances an increasingly dubious one. It is precisely because of current science that SF seeks to occupy those terraces of imagination adjacent to the contemporary obstacle and to move directly into a more productive field of inquiry. Where factual science is too limiting, extrapolation and metaphor may be of greater effect. Beyond both lie spaces of imagination.

Whether it is feasible for the Earth to someday control a traditional imperium among the worlds orbiting Sol is important only at the most academic of levels. Colonisation, actually assuming an ability to settle planets such as Mercury and Jupiter, would be a slow and tortuous process, and vastly expensive, and the resulting colony would require enormous effort in constant maintenance by the imperial centre. Although NASA and various international space organisations are in the throes of planning manned journeys to the Moon and Mars, the notion of solar colonisation is ancient history in SF terms. Rapid interplanetary travel is a fairly commonplace assumption in the genre, yet at some point in an expanding empire distance as time would still present an insoluble problem. But such an empire *is* conceivable; as Headrick remarks, 'the appearance of a new technology can trigger or reinforce a motive by making the desired end possible or acceptably inexpensive'.[9] If the encumbrance of distance is the only problematic issue, it is still possible to envision a historically conventional empire extending from Earth which could dominate and govern human colonies. Where science is forced to deal with the problems of interplanetary travel in a traditional form, SF does not. With a nod to the successors of Einstein, Mars becomes the local bus stop, enabling the text to engage with issues that are more important to the genre than to science itself.

Similar to the difficulties of conquering distance at speed would be the equally vital production of dependable communications. The dislocation of travellers caused by distance would be exacerbated by the complicated business of developing reliable transmission and reception of information. Just as the fictional leap into hyperspace eludes the leash of relativity, so devices such as James Blish's 'Dirac' transmitter, which 'operated instantaneously over any distance',[10] address the logistical problems of basic communications. These tropes of SF are not simple contrivances, although there is a distinct element of convenience about them. While they may not deal with the factual realism of science, they do admit its presence and seek methods of transcendence. When the text is more concerned about the issues of human life on the periphery, of exploring the nature of isolation and the effect of technology at great distances from the centre, certain creative utilities are acceptable.

It is also necessary to consider that the influence of empire is likely to be most strongly pronounced at the centre, at the heart of the imperial authority, and to wane in strength as the distance between the colonial subject and the imperial centre increases. The apparent omnipotence of empire remains so only where it is concentrated and focused, and becomes attenuated and feeble when stretched over significant distance. This attenuation would naturally be heightened unless there was a solid and constant restatement of strength through a physical presence. Control from the centre relies upon an ability to constantly renew and nourish a sense of 'home', of *centre*, at the margin. No imperial authority could afford to allow its remote colonies to become 'disassociated', either in theory or in practice. As soon as the outer margin is extended beyond the capacity of the centralised authority to police, the inherent weaknesses of the imperial project become clear.

We see therefore that the terms of SF are not confined by definition to the physicalities of travel. Although vast expanses of empty space divide even the planets within our own solar system, it is also important to consider the nature of existence at the peripheral destination. What would it be like to live not only billions of miles but also *decades* away from 'home'? How would this affect the individual migrant or the colonised culture? The logistics of regular return to the centre would render that goal impractical if we are forced by Einstein's theories to think in terms of centuries rather than months of travelling. In addition, if an armed imperial force were to be sent on an interplanetary mission, it is highly unlikely that the prevailing situation at the time of departure would have endured without change by the time of arrival. It also would remain to be seen whether even a minimal journey, say of ten years, might not have the reinforcements themselves questioning the reasons behind their dispatch, thus complicating an imperial rupture with subsidiary schisms. Thus there are three governing aspects of the imperial performance affected by the notion of distance: the physical space to be covered; the passage of time during the journey; and the intellectual concept of 'distance'.[11]

As Duncan Makenzie has been taught:

> It might have been different if the velocity of light was infinite; but it was a mere billion kilometres an hour – and therefore, real-time conversation would be forever impossible between Earth and anyone beyond the orbit of the Moon. The global electronic village which had existed for centuries on the mother world could never be extended into space; the political and psychological effects of this were enormous, and still not fully understood.[12]

Without the provision of such technological marvels as the Dirac, the absence of near-instantaneous communication is an obvious cause for the immediate dismissal of an off-Earth empire as a realistic notion. In those texts which otherwise strive for realism, a model where communication and transport take more effective forms than those currently available to science is an absolute necessity. The generation of such a model is not as fanciful as it may sound, since the Advanced Space Propulsion Laboratory at NASA's Johnson Space Center is actually developing a new type of rocket technology, the Variable Specific Impulse Magnetoplasma Rocket.[13] This plasma rocket drive is not powered by conventional chemical reactions, as are today's rockets, but by electrical energy, which heats a propellant. This new type of technology could dramatically shorten human transit times between planets (to about three months for a journey to Mars). So, even within the physical confines of our universe, an interplanetary voyage no longer than it took the huge ships of the East India Company to traverse the distance between Liverpool and Bengal is quite possibly in sight. While not yet close to an 'instantaneous' passage of either people or communications, science already promises both a time when the obstacle of distance will be lessened and when the extrapolation of contemporary technology in SF is viewed as increasingly logical. Humanity may yet live on other planets.

And the idea of an interplanetary concord is an attractive one. If the conventions of traditional empire will not work, then perhaps a more pragmatic but loosely bound alliance might be practicable, a hegemonic-style grouping paying some deference to a centralised parliament on Earth. But this would not be 'empire' in the traditional sense, where the imperial authority holds sway over its dominions. There would be no dominions; the act of domination could not withstand the restrictions of physics. But if empire cannot exist where control by force is rendered impractical, is an empire of any description feasible? One possible answer lies in the definition of the term 'empire', of which there are many. The *Oxford English Reference Dictionary* offers that empire is 'an extensive group of states or countries under a single supreme authority; a large commercial organization owned or directed by one person or group; a type or period of government in which the sovereign is called emperor or empress'.[14] Denis Judd notes that the British empire was a 'trade-driven and settler-based system',[15] whereas Elleke Boehmer takes empire as referring to 'the authority assumed by a state over another territory – authority expressed in pageantry and symbolism, as well as military power.… Colonialism involves the consolidation of imperial power, and is manifested in the settlement of territory.'[16] Perhaps the most politically revealing definition of empire, specifically in SF, comes from Iain M. Banks:

> Empires are synonymous with centralised – if occasionally schismatised – hierarchical power structures in which influence is restricted to an economically privileged class retaining its advantages through – usually – a judicious use of oppression and skilled manipulation.… In short, it's all about dominance.[17]

Although it is unlikely that a future human empire would be bound together by ties of force, it is easy to see, *a priori*, the potential placement in the genre of any number of SF empires based on a simple centralised dominant government. From the extremities of extrapolated realism involving current science, we move quickly through the terraces of imagination to a place where SF is able to envision the possibility of such events. If we waive the science and accept FTL travel as possible (just as we accept the convention that aliens are often and conveniently humanoid, living

on suitably Earth-type planets), do we also place at risk a meaningful discussion of postcolonial issues in empire? In real practical terms there can
be no element of force, for force is redundant in a universe which runs
along Einsteinean laws. There can be no central diktat, for this requires the
support of an underlying basis of physical power. There must be benefit for
both the colony and the centre to abide within the bounds of a neo-imperial
agreement. 'Empire' must become a business arrangement.

Having seen the unlikelihood of an empire that stretches beyond Earth
in a universe that accords with Einstein's theories, we must still consider
those texts that transcend or move laterally from such limitations. In the
experiments of SF, it is invaluable to accompany humanity on journeys that
will take decades to complete, for in these we see some of the new realities
of society. Authors of SF are creating 'mind models' with these voyages,
dramatising ideas and alternatives as the commonly accepted behaviours
of people and societies are constantly intermixed and examined. If we
consider the nature of various types of imperial model, as set out in Table 1,
it becomes easier to see the point at which SF takes leave of the historical
conventions of empire and begins its work as a creative genre. We then see
some of the problems generated by SF if it purports to portray the practices
of empire in the absence of the physical possibility.

As we have seen, in a universe constrained by relativity, an interplanetary
and especially an interstellar empire would be impossible to maintain by
conventional historical methods. However, as Clarke suggests:

> Whatever the Seven Worlds might say about their independence, the
> centre of power was still on Earth. As, two thousand years ago, men
> had once gone to Rome in search of justice, or prestige, or knowledge,
> so in this age the Imperial planet called to its scattered children. No
> man could be taken seriously in the arena of solar politics unless he
> was personally acquainted with the key figures of Terran affairs, and
> had traced his way at least once through the labyrinth of the terrestrial
> bureaucracy. And to do this, one *had* to go to Earth; as in the days of
> the Caesars, there was no alternative. Those who believed – or pre-
> tended to believe – otherwise, risked being tagged with the dreaded
> word 'colonial'.[18]

Though physical dominion as a technique of imperialism is largely absent
in SF, rendered effectively obsolescent through a greater knowledge of
science, the desire for an iconic centre remains constant. For example,
control by brute force has been transmogrified in Clarke's novel into a
dominating but seductive elitism. Since Einstein has made it impossible for
an army to reach an interplanetary point of rebellion in time to make any
effective difference, in Clarke's experiment physical might has given way

Table 1 *The four basic types of imperial model: historical and fictional*

	Location of construct	Nature of construction	Communications	Inter-empire access	Distance from centre	Degree of divergence
Actual historical and contemporary models						
Model 1: Small empire, single nation	Earth	Tightly constructed land-based empire	Good and unlimited two-way communications	Good accessibility to all areas by citizens and officials	Easy transportation. No isolation of the periphery from the centre. Free movement of citizens	No free or independent development or evolution experienced by any area. No differing perception of 'self'. Centre/periphery schisms improbable
Model 2: Large multi-national empire	Earth	Moderately tight hegemony of state colonies	Occasionally erratic communications	Slightly limited/ moderately expensive travel opportunities. Limited movement of citizens	Significant distance between colonies. 'Centralisation' an intellectual concept. Moderate isolationism on the part of colonies, which are ruled by decree from the central authority	Development of 'satellite' centres. Open to individual/sporadic development and evolution of colony. Colonial officials see the centre as 'home'. Introduction of 'them' and 'us' administrative criteria. Occasional schisms. Overt rebellion improbable

Science fiction models

Model 3: Interplanetary empire	Earth, Moon, Mars; near-Earth stations	Colonies connected only by technology	Communications highly complex and erratic at times	Transportation expensive and regulated. Travel between colonies limited to officials or official migrants	Earth is the imperial centre ('mother planet'). Doctrine of sustenance and subalternity inculcated by the centre	Each colony develops its own centre. There are significant individual developments. A general philosophy of 'them' and 'us' is accepted. Political and moral schisms are a reality. Rebellion is probable
Model 4: Interplanetary empire/hegemonic alliance	Solar system and beyond	Colonies connected only by extreme technology	Communications by rote, arrangement, or in emergency	Movement of peoples is negligible. Links to the 'body corporate' are maintained by agreement and trade	Earth's centrality becomes increasingly redundant as extreme distance reduces imperial control to tokenism. Earth's government is reduced to a purely legislative body	Empire of human-habitable colony planets produces its own centres. There is dislocation from the Earth centre. Colonies experience major social developments. Differing versions of empire evolve. Schisms of all types are frequent. There is major potential for violent rebellion

to an intellectual understanding of 'force'. In keeping with this constitutive ideology, other areas and points of contact would be augmented and balanced to maintain the need of the periphery for the centre. Economic and cultural reliances would be expanded. Religion, too, would be an obvious way to maintain the old centre as the primary site of focus. Though unable to dominate by physical power, Earth's new empire would be one of exclusivity by uniqueness, in effect, the practical reversal of traditional imperial thought. Why waste time and energy sending armies to conquer and subdue new colonies? Make yourself sufficiently valued, and they will knock at your door requesting entry. Several of Clarke's other novels echo specific imperial and ostensibly postcolonial stances, including *The Fountains of Paradise* (1979), in which a massive Earth-built space elevator takes humanity onto its next step of development and technical evolution, and *The Songs of Distant Earth* (1986), which examines how an isolated but established colony of humans deals with the cultural problems engendered by a ship full of more recent human evacuees. One of the most interesting of Clarke's 'post-empire' novels is *Childhood's End* (1953), which discusses not simply the evolution of humanity into a postcolonial reality but also a corporeal evolution of the species, which removes children from any physical existence as they merge into a single cosmic 'mind'. Many of Clarke's SF experiments pursue themes of change and of movement on to a higher plane of existence, whether from the perspective of ape descendants who puzzle over the meaning of mysterious black obelisks, or from the vantage point of high technology which facilitates an ever-outwards physical movement, as in *2001: A Space Odyssey*.

However, given that Clarke was noted for his knowledge of technical and technological sciences, the majority of his novels are based upon models of accepted physical and political form. Thus Clarke's practical body politic of *Imperial Earth*, encompassing its extra-Earth colonies, would need to be designed around a federalistic agreement. Duncan Makenzie may travel to Earth because he thinks that is his wish, but in reality it is because of a beguiling reversal of the imperial diaspora. Earth has become an exclusive club, with colonies as 'members'. How then does this *derangement* affect the postcolonial aspects of SF? It would seem that if Earth renounces a dominating physical influence, and opts instead for withdrawal and exclusivity, we are no longer dealing with imperialism, or certainly not a conventional model of imperialism. Nonetheless, while the 'club' form considers those transplanted from Earth, rather than the colonisation of an indigenous people, the same processes of silencing, distancing and marginalisation take place, but, ironically, at the willing behest of the colonies rather than through a dominance of force from the centre. Once the colony has become established, as in Robinson's *Mars* series, the colonists are usually no longer considered Terrans, but a new breed. Robinson's 'First Hundred' become the first *Martians*. Yet even in these circumstances, Earth is just as much the centre of SF as ever England was of the British Raj, but now a reversal of ideology is required. Instead of compelling the periphery to accede to the centre's demands by force, the inducements of power and a desire for economic and cultural inclusion have become the guiding motivations. In Robinson's *Mars* trilogy this was exactly what was needed, but the narrative also required an abortive invasion from Earth, a final demonstration of the uselessness of force before an economic model of cooperative association could rise from the confusion. The *Mars* texts describe the nature of imperialism as it is cleverly inverted in line with Ali Mazrui's basic concept of *counterpenetration*,[19] where the influence is reversed, to flow from the periphery back into the centre. If empire cannot be imposed upon the margin, then the margin draws closer to the centre of its own volition and by doing so adds another level of influence.

While this restatement of conventional domination inverts the placement of the inner and outer elements of empire, we are still faced with the problematic continuance of 'traditional' behaviour at the frontier itself. New colonists, especially those arriving on an inhabited planet, are forced to recreate the original imperial dilemma: do the colonisers take their empire with them, or do they, as did the 'First Hundred', become citizens of their own state? In the end, does the notion of empire depend more upon a physical actuality or upon an indoctrinated ideal? It would seem that although the life of empire may be possessed of a relatively short existence, the intellectual concept of empire is not. The *idea* of expansion has become so inculcated into humanity's self-identification that Neil Armstrong, placing one foot on the barren Moon, inspires our species to look even further outwards, no matter the cost in materials or lives. Thus in SF empire does not deal with the physical, other than on a superficial level. It cannot: the reality of the physical is limited and reductionist. Empire in SF is almost purely of the mind, for even if there were no centre, if the mother world had somehow been destroyed or rendered uninhabitable, an idealised 'Earth empire' of the mind would still exist. By examining the uses of experimental empire in SF texts, we are able to 'alienate' the present in a Brechtian sense: the estranged eye sees much more clearly, or, as Robert Scholes suggests, 'we must use the future in precisely the same way as a probe into the truth of the present'.[20] Such a deliberate estrangement may be seen in Gordon R. Dickson's *Delusion World* (1961), where he writes of two completely different societies – each invisible to the other – sharing the same city.

While the globally broadcast first footprint on the Moon spoke to the latter half of the twentieth century with symbols of power and colonialism, the human obsession with exploration in SF can in part be traced back to the earliest days of the genre, when almost all writers were male, and wrote almost exclusively for a male readership. Setting the action of the future out in space was akin to writing about frontier skirmishes in the Wild West of North America. Predominantly American in genesis, many early SF stories, such as Henry Kuttner's *Fury* (1947) and E. C. Tubb's *Alien Dust* (1955), were deliberately designed to mimic existing frontier adventure. As Susan George argues:

> There are two basic ways the Frontier Myth manifests itself in science fiction narratives. In one version space and other planets are seen as new frontiers to explore, exploit, and if necessary conquer and/or settle. In this case we are the settlers of the myth.... The second version features Earth and its peoples as the new frontier for a variety of usually unfriendly settlers, typically labelled 'invaders'.[21]

However, with the examples of Edmond Hamilton's 'Conquest of Two Worlds' (1932) and Robert Heinlein's 'Logic of Empire' (1941), Jack Williamson internalises this drive:

> The frontier should never lose its allure. We're all of us born freedom-seeking individuals. To survive, we yield when we must to society, to the pressures of family and friends, of school and custom and the law. At best, the constraints sometimes seem oppressive. We all yearn for escape and find it where we can. In imagination if not in actuality. At heart, we're all potential pioneers.[22]

Regardless of perspective, the need to develop fresh frontiers is not a new subject of popular writing, but the ability to extend the frontier across the borders of the fantastic has enabled SF writers to propound a new type of colonialism, one not bound by the intrinsic restrictions of contemporary politics. In effect, empire and colonialism in SF have taken on certain aspects of unsophisticated escapism and adventure first engendered by stories of the frontier. The submission and reduction of other cultures can therefore be viewed in SF not so much as a political statement but more as an imaginative reiteration of a pioneering past – the old myth of the frontier repeated in the new myth of the future. Thus we can still, through texts of the future, regain the thrill of reliving that first step on the Moon. And what if the Moon was inhabited? Through SF, it has also become possible to legitimise, vicariously, through direct comparison to our own histories, the subalternity of the Other: the less probable the notion, the more we feel free to enjoy its incarnation. But this view in itself is complex. Does the placement of the repression of the Other at the remote end of the reality scale provide a buffer of distance and fantasy that renders the idea of sub-alternity less offensive? Is SF, at its basic level, a vehicle for the expression of our most unspeakable desires – including the desire for scope and power, a love of waste and change, and a fascination with the exotic? Alternatively, does it provide insight into our deeper concerns and illuminate the apparent human compulsion for suffering and destruction?

There are at least two ways of examining this plurality in SF. If we consider only a readership that revels in the imaginary conquest of others, valorising the triumph, then SF may be seen as a simple codification of fascist imperialistic behaviours. Richard Wilson speaks of such supposed Earth colonists, who found 'the ancient culture of Mars as possibly interesting anthropologically – but undoubtedly of a low, almost savage order',[23] an observation that humanity would probably carry its ancient values into the future. Wilson continues by suggesting that human dignity is the only thing worth 'working, fighting and dying for,'[24] a rather frightening defence of the old argument by which the end justifies the means. If, however, we take the fantasy element of SF as an exploration *in absentia* both of the world we currently inhabit and of the influence of historical social behaviours, then such infamous activities become experiments which re-reference contemporary cultural mores. With a nod to such authors as Lem and Le Guin, Poul Anderson argues that, in SF, 'The author is free to construct radically strange environments, put people in there, simplify social factors, and thus show us societies, with the individual persons in them that are clearly shaped by their settings'.[25]

Comprehending the role of empire in SF is troublesome. While it facilitates an outpouring of imagination, and permits creative circumvention of the realities of physics, it might also provide the impression that the imperial project has no moral flaw, in that it cannot possibly 'count', given its status as an experiment. Therefore we see yet another element of 'distancing' at work here: a removal of the physical act from the imagined act, distancing the *real* from the *unreal*. This is potentially difficult moral ground, in that SF has, by the very nature of its popularity, already exerted some influence upon the participants of a future society. If empire is truly outdated, a thing distanced from current culture by its political and social inadequacies, then exactly why is it still such a central theme of SF texts? Are stories of imperialism becoming increasingly satirical and therefore more obviously separated from our real lives, or is the use of empire as a metaphor of power becoming so outdated that contemporary readers automatically suspect a hidden authorial agenda at its appearance? The paradox of accepting the precepts of a 'thing' because of the impossibility of that thing is a dangerous one, a main reason why contemporary images of empire, such as those of Ken MacLeod, are displayed as complex, dictatorial and trending towards dystopia.

Given that the fantasy of FTL travel enables a physical interplanetary diaspora, there still remains a question surrounding the motivation for such outgrowth. While the centre of any highly populated interstellar hegemony would need a constancy of economic support from outlying colonies, this is no clear reason in itself to establish those colonies in the first place, unless we all want to live, like Asimov's Solarians, in solitary splendour on great estates of our own. With FTL travel it would be comparatively effortless to visit those planets that offer a supply of primary materials such as mineral ore. Conceding that the desire to explore and increase our knowledge of what is 'out there' will continue to propel us beyond the known, the founding of a colony implies a much deeper objective and purpose. Why would significant numbers of people effectively abandon their society and embrace a life of potential hardship and danger? Once again we return to the knowledge that SF is, in part, a mirror of ourselves and our past, or, as Patrick Parrinder observes:

> These projections of the future in terms of conquest and hegemony, of foundation and empire or 'first contact' and eventual confederation, are indebted to particular ideas of historiography. The history of the future, however much the future is claimed to be novel and different, is inevitably modelled to a great extent on the history that we already know.[26]

One reason to colonise might be the impulse to improve the lot of future generations, as in Poul Anderson's *Orbit Unlimited* (1961), where the Earth has effectively become a totalitarian state. Potential colonists would want their eventual descendants to be successful pioneers, even though their ship might be designed for a one-way journey to the next star system, which the original passengers might never live to see. The human biological imperative of procreation is something so fundamental to our species that we usually ignore it at the conscious level. However, if we accept Abraham Maslow's motivational 'hierarchy of needs', procreation crosses two of the first four basic motivational levels, being expressed in both a physiological and an emotional state.[27] For whatever reason we hold as the most germane, there will always be a drive in some to continue life in whatever form appears most viable. And with FTL travel, the colonisation of a distant planet would seem less daunting if there was a possibility that technology might offer colonists the chance of returning home at some point in the future.

Another significant reason would undoubtedly be commercial gain. As with the machinations of the multinational organisations in Robinson's *Mars* trilogy, profit and the gaining of power on Earth through extraterrestrial resources are easily seen as driving motives for off-planet activities. In Philip K. Dick's cautionary text *Do Androids Dream of Electric Sheep?* (1968), the creation of physically enhanced androids to take the place of humans for off-world exploration has frightening consequences. Numerous novels depict the future of humanity as being driven by an insatiable consumerism in conflict with the inevitable depletion of natural resources. Robert Heinlein's often satirical economic theorising in this area led him to produce works concerning the financing of colonisation, such as *The Man Who Sold the Moon* (1950) and in a similar vein *The Moon Is a Harsh Mistress* (1966).

Possibly the most compelling reason for humanity to seek a foothold on another world would be if the Earth became unable to support life in its current form, presumably following some natural cataclysmic event or the often suggested holocaust of World War III.[28] As World Wars I and II wracked the globe and the great Western empires fell, texts submitting that humanity might destroy itself grew steadily in frequency. After the bombing of Hiroshima, the potential for global atomic destruction gave new meaning to such texts as Judith Merril's *Shadow on the Hearth* (1950), and *Level 7* (1959) by Mordecai Roshwald. Likewise, images of 'entropy' or the eventual heat-death of our own Sun have been significantly used in British SF, especially in works as *Mother London* (1988) by Michael Moorcock, as well as in the dystopian fiction of such authors as J. G. Ballard and Brian Aldiss. Entropy itself has also taken on overtones of metaphor as the fate of worlds is echoed in the demise of societies and individuals.

Whatever the motivation, SF will likely continue its urge to colonise, the style of such colonisation depending on authorial decisions regarding the relevance and application of Einstein's work. If the text remains in our 'real' universe, then it will be considered a more technical (i.e. realistic) text, dwelling as it must upon the limitations and restrictions of real science. Such novels and stories will be focused more on the near future and, as such, may offer a clearer insight into contemporary moods of postcoloniality. As Paul Carter observes of such technical accounts of foundation and settlement: 'They are not like novels: their narratives do not conform to the rules of cause-and-effect empirical history. Rather they are analogous to unfinished maps and should be read accordingly as records of travelling.'[29]

Focusing on the practicalities of actual travel requires consideration of the physical endurance of the people who may be called upon to undertake such extensive journeys, especially those classed as 'first colonists'. Though not necessarily examined in detail in SF texts, this is a productive place to ask some pertinent questions. Would males be a necessary part of the crew in space? While most generational voyages at least begin with a maintenance of the social status quo,[30] frozen sperm and artificial insemination would fill the only physical need for males. A larger gene pool could be maintained this way and the colony would be much more diverse[31] and thereby give rise to newer 'traditions' for even more futuristic voyages. Likewise, would a crew of females be of any greater value, especially since life may exist almost as well *in vitro* as *in vivo*? Then we are faced with the dilemma of whether to have an artificial crew – robots or androids (or possibly cyborgs) – or a human one. It seems unlikely any ship would be sent off with a freezer full of embryos, regardless of whatever technological nannies might accompany them.

And once the problems of crew selection were resolved, what kind of a society would we want for our future generations? Given how young some of our social conventions are even in the twenty-first century, a 'realistic' voyage of 1,000 years would provide ample time for the development of an utterly new onboard culture. It is also likely the passengers and crew of any such ship would require some enormous project to keep them from fomenting revolution – the sheer uselessness of an entire life lived only for the purpose of generating the next crop of children would be exquisitely self-destructive. And how would the command of such a voyage be structured? Once the first command group had died or been forcibly retired, what then? The various British colonies in the Americas started with either a military or a religious basis and evolved into systems that mimicked the Westminster model of government to a greater or lesser extent. Would this same evolution happen (planned or not) on a spaceship or would it begin with a civil command structure in place? Or perhaps the situation would be similar to the voyages made by upper-class Edwardian civil servants to India at the turn of the nineteenth century. For some it was as if they had never left the homeland, and upon arrival that attitude was reinforced by the maintenance of tradition and convention, and the avoidance of anything tainted with the prospect of 'going native'. Thus, while the complexities of a 'real' voyage are daunting, the *concepts* of such voyages are perfect material for interrogation by SF.

Should the text define itself as being outside the reality of our universe, then we enter the realm of the truly fantastic, where experiments with the morality of empire are as legitimate as the manner in which humanity achieves the stars. The indexing of SF into the *probable* and the *unlikely* provides some insight into the relayed values of the imperial project. Where the advent of colonisation is deemed possible and probable, the text moves more slowly away from the realism of contemporary thought, extrapolation becoming a delicate task, involving the definition and placement of each social article into an appropriate and logical niche. If an event seems logically likely, then authors of realistic SF such as Clarke, Robinson and Aldiss explore not only the scientific grounds for it but also those elements affecting the social aspects of the narrative, for what use is a practicable starship if the colony is not equally functional?

At this point of textual awareness, it is easy to sense a form of literary nihilism, or at least a nostalgia for the days when SF could be considered simply fantastic. By peering too closely at an author's experiments, it is possible for the results to seem prosaic without the smoke and mirrors. Yet the author's forays into the fantastic provide a necessary vehicle for such important underlying themes. The reality of the *possible* is located firmly in the science and technology of the contemporary and the near future: a reality that locates itself inside the boundaries of known and evident theoretical science. This reality will be more slow moving than its fictional counterpart, for it is tied and linked to the present and previous time, and may progress only along accepted lines of 'proper' science. In doing so, it will avoid such technological marvels as FTL travel and matter transportation until there comes a time – if any – when science is able to expand on determined scientific theory. The relationship between science and SF will continue to be mutually, if conditionally, supportive and will maintain the convention begun by such authors as Wells, whose earliest fictions gave depth to the students' magazine of the Royal College of Science, and Clarke, considered by many to be the last prophet of scientific enlightenment.

In the current understanding of our real universe and corporeal existence, we will never reach the furthest stars of this galaxy, let alone set our footprint in the cold dust of some exotic and mystical galaxy. No matter how advanced our science and technology become in the near future, our space voyages will remain parochial. The entirety of SF, though, is located *between* the imaginary and the real. Duncan Makenzie may continue to fume at his six-second delay but, equally, he will never be able to disregard his connection to the past, where the social and cultural affairs of humankind have developed in conjunction with an eye to the future.

Complementary to this, there is the SF reality of the impossible, where we are free to travel in our minds to those spaces and across distances to which we are unable to commit our bodies. This is the province of the purest, most undiluted SF, where science and technology exist primarily as an experimental vehicle for stimulating depictions of exploration and colonisation. It is in this realm that we hypothesise our fears and allow a postmodern sense of playfulness to present us with an assortment of imaginary worlds. Here, the vast distances that keep us pinned to our own Sun are unimportant. We may bypass and dismiss the limitations of the real because in these experiments of the far future, the farthest suns are available, without restriction. It is also a place of potential disquiet, since a disregard of all rules leaves the door wide open to all that is monstrous and utterly unknown. If fantasy permits the expression of the unreal, it is accompanied by the threat of unlimited power and unspeakable licence, a position often used to great effect in such early SF dramas as Alex Raymond's *Flash Gordon* comic strip. To see this experimental mode more clearly, we look in the next chapter at two early SF experiments, one British, one German, produced in a colonial environment and unrestricted by knowledge of contemporary physics. While these texts do not illustrate problems of distance, they do examine issues of fantasy contrasted against scientific extrapolation. These European examples are followed in Chapter 6 by an examination of two American works of the non-imperial 'golden age' of SF which engage with problems of both distance and extrapolation.

5. Moments of Empire:
Perceptions of Lasswitz and Wells

From the perspective of history, empire is a recorded process. Its fact cannot be removed or altered, but the possible and far-reaching consequences may be sharply examined by moving away from the imperial pathway proper and into the arena of fiction. Countless interstellar conquests have begun from the third planet. Not one of Earth's solar siblings has escaped the fictional grasp of Earth's incessantly expanded centre. Imperialism, it seems, is not a thing of the past: it never left, but moved its narration into SF. As Jane M. Jacobs observes, 'imperialism may also be reactivated in the present through various nostalgias which seek to memorialise the period of imperial might',[1] a concept clearly illustrated by the culturally and politically inspired conflicts in Afghanistan and the Balkans during the late twentieth century. Early SF texts were more often about an imminent future rather than the 'far future'. Although the latter narratives have become more common in recent times, the principles of nostalgia, or a desire to look backwards, are still evident. While authors of SF stand with one foot in tomorrow and one in today, there sometimes seems to be an unwillingness to cut their narratives entirely free from precedent. Even in the supposed *avant-garde* of fictional texts, the empires of humankind do not step completely away from the historical past. Issues that were of import to both the coloniser and the colonised remain starkly visible in the narratives of the postulated future, where 'the weight of antiquity continues to dominate cultural production in much of the post-colonial world'.[2] Empire cannot be relegated to history when its monuments are still so clearly among us.

To nineteenth-century imperialists, empire was a fine thing. It facilitated further European expansion, increased trade and nourished Western economic and social prosperity. Empire built railways, bridges and roads, constructed massive navies, commissioned works of art and brought the Christian religion and the great European languages to those unfortunate enough to be without such things. For the peoples who now lived in a land no longer theirs by the law of the imperialists, empire was not so glorious, nor such deeds of accomplishment so great. The colonised of empire were usually without choice and often the most basic of freedoms, their power of self-determination replaced by the imposition of an extrinsic power.

Views from the imperial pathway were available only through the singular focus of conditioned knowledge: things were perceived only as they had been learned, or taught, to be seen. The irony of Westernised education of the subaltern bourgeoisie meant that they saw, as Said notes, 'truths about history, science, and culture … millions grasped the fundamentals of modern life, yet remained subordinate dependants of an authority based elsewhere than in their lives'.[3] The merit of empire was, and is, an impossible and endlessly subjective binary.

The experimental nature of SF permits us, with subjective limitations, to view the imperial project from aspects other than that of the coloniser. One of the eternal strengths of this genre is that it enables the reader to explore, in vicarious configurations, the possibilities of the Other. The reader *becomes* the isolated colonist threatened by the insatiable centre, as in Kim Stanley Robinson's *Mars* series; or experiences, like Matthew in John Wyndham's *Chocky* (1968), an alterity of perception through eyes other than human. It is even possible to extrapolate the act of invasion of the human centre, the Earth itself, and analyse the consequences of 'our' existence under the imperial Other, as in the insightful works of H. G. Wells (1866–1946) and Kurd Lasswitz (1848–1910).

Lasswitz, who sometimes wrote under the pseudonym 'Velatus', was a German mathematics teacher, noted philosopher and science historian; in 1897 he published the novel *Auf zwei Planeten* (*Two Planets*), which featured a Martian space station that served as a staging point for space travel. Two years before the publication of Lasswitz's book, Konstantin E. Tsiolkovsky, the earliest recognised proponent of spaceflight theory, produced a work of SF entitled (in translation) *Reflections on Earth and Heaven and the Effects of Universal Gravitation* (1895), which discusses the possibility of using artificial satellites as bases for launches into deeper space, and the creation of synthetic gravity on space stations through rotation. The year 1895 also saw the publication of astronomer Percival Lowell's seminal non-fiction work *Mars*, several elements of which seem to have been directly transported into Lasswitz's narrative.

The central components of *Two Planets* form a cautionary drama: a tragedy of colonial failure. Earth has been 'discovered' by the Nume (Martians), whose main intent is to demonstrate the utopia-like benefits of peace and advanced technology to their nearest neighbours, the belligerent humans. Despising violence and any loss of freedoms, the Nume believe that universal education for the common good is the only method by which humanity may rid itself of the plagues of conflict, poverty and famine. In their attempt to inculcate such tenets into the fabric of human society, the Nume discover that these altruistic ideals are inevitably subverted, resulting not in the pacification of Earth's culture but in the brutalisation of their own.

The Wells narrative speaks of colonialism and the imperial drive from the most violent and dystopian of viewpoints. The Earth is attacked by Martians intent upon the eradication of a competing species. At first glance, *The War of the Worlds*, published just one year after *Two Planets*, recounts only the more savage aspects of empire, in that it describes (attempted) assimilation through a template of destruction. Wells's invaders embody entirely negative aspects of a colonising power, their objective being a total and rapid subjugation of all life on Earth. The irony in this narrative is not that the imperial desire is inherently seeded with its own destruction but that the goal, once achieved, is a lethal reward.

Wells, a profound socialist, completed his BSc (majoring in zoology) in 1890. He is more often remembered for his fictions of science than for any serious discussion of scientific theory.[4] Passionately concerned about a wide variety of issues in the Victorian political and social order, Wells's stories, which are complex, ambivalent and changing, looked more at the effects of the scientific world upon his characters rather than advocating science for its own sake. Among his best-known novels, two most reflect his interest with utopian and dystopian society, *The Time Machine* (1895) and *The War of the Worlds* (1898), the truly alarming potential of the latter demonstrated by Orson Welles's radio adaptation in 1938, in which aggressive Martians were reported to have landed in a location Americanised from the original Surrey. Mass panic was reported along the eastern seaboard of the United States.[5]

For both these writers, Mars proved an irresistible topic. Lasswitz examines the political and technological methodologies behind a meeting of the two societies, whereas the hyper-reality of Wells focuses on the emotional, psychological and biological impact of the same possibility. Other than the red planet itself, the main similarity between *Two Planets* and *The War of the Worlds* is the shared theme of invasion of the human centre by the outsider/Other. In both narratives, the Earth falls under the formidable regard of a Martian empire that seeks to expand its own centre through the annexation of the human home world. Lasswitz tells us that 'the Martians were intellectually incomparably more highly developed than civilized man',[6] just as Wells observes 'And we men, the creatures who inhabit this earth, must be to them as least as alien and lowly as are the monkeys and lemurs to us'.[7] Although the style and narrative of each writer are unique, these texts, uncannily synchronous in time and focus, also share an ironic dread of the imposition of an empire on Earth not of human, and more specifically not of European, making. While 'not human' may be read partly as a metaphor for 'non-European' in the Wells text,[8] it is also possible to perceive it as a metaphor for 'inhuman'; this, though, is more true of the Lasswitz text, which simultaneously deals with the suggestion that European colonialism is itself an inhuman imposition.

The formal differences between the two narratives are reasonably clear. Wells involves only two narrators, mostly in the first person, whereas Lasswitz shifts the point of view from scene to scene; he describes much of the Nume's science and technology in exquisite register. Wells focuses upon moments of action and those details that have an immediate and forceful impact on the plot. Lasswitz cultivates the plot slowly, taking the narrative surely towards the tragedy he intends. Wells manipulates his plot around moments of breathless activity, leapfrogging from disaster to casualty. Lasswitz links the diverse aspects of his narrative with a romance between the two humanoid races, whereas Wells tints his narrative with the monochromes of fight and flight. Both authors struggle with the narrative challenge of encapsulating a global experience into the circumscribed linear perspective of narrators.

In the Lasswitz narrative, the Nume are already based on Earth, with stations at both poles. Through a chance discovery by German explorers set on finding the North Pole by balloon, the Nume's existence becomes known. Merely to exist in such difficult conditions heralds the superior science of the Martian intruders, but it is only after an initial contact with the explorers Grunthe and Saltner that the precise nature of the outsiders' abilities become clear. At first sight, there is little visible difference between the two species, other than the Nume's fantastic dwellings and clothing. The Nume resemble their human counterparts, to the extent that Saltner is immediately attracted to one of the Martian females, La, describing her 'large shining eyes' and the fact that he is 'disturbed at this wonderful being'.[9] As the novel progresses, it seems that Saltner enters into an almost *ménage à trois* with two Nume females, an interesting focus from an author who values reason so highly, but who uses the motif of a romance between emotional and intuitive characters to advance the plot.

Yet even before meeting the aliens, Saltner's more pragmatic companion, Grunthe, is already reflecting on the problematic relationships indicated by the unexpected discovery of a non-human settlement:

> There is no doubt that we find ourselves confronted with a completely unknown power.... Perhaps it lies in the interest of these polar inhabit-
> ants not to inform the civilized countries of their existence. We would undoubtedly lose our freedom. And also, we must not consider our-
> selves as conquerors but only as scouts.[10]

Grunthe's comments point to an important and ironic theme within the text, as the Nume value freedom particularly. The Martians awake within Grunthe not only the dread of a physical empire, but also (and clearly of greater issue to Lasswitz) the implications of an immensely superior intellectual empire, far beyond humankind's ability to resist. The German explorers quickly comprehend that, beside the Nume's abilities to travel such a vast distance, to exist on a planet for which they were not biologically designed, and even to flourish under such circumstances, the glories of modern human society fade into a pale shadow. Given Lasswitz's personal affiliations with the world of science and philosophy, it is not difficult to see why he would perceive an intellectual domination to be far more damning than one of simple force, and perhaps Lasswitz anticipates the concern with insidious cultural domination that is so important to modern anticolonial thinking, as illustrated by Fantz Fanon[11] and Edward Said. It is clear, though, that Lasswitz does not permit his protagonists to fear or suspect the Nume simply because they are Other. If anything, his human characters appear unnaturally concerned with their own inability to make the Martian food-dispensers function. The humans are depicted as intellectual children who suddenly discover themselves in a toyshop of technological marvels. The author's own cultural upbringing denies him the ability to abandon the merit of the German explorers totally, and he contrives to bring about their intellectual *rapprochement* with the Nume by means of scholarly understanding:

> But a feeling of humiliation, which was only natural whenever the self-conscious[ness] of the scholar had to capitulate before a higher intellect, tended to make them stubborn in the beginning. But this could not last long in the face of the intellectual and moral superiority of the Martians; almost without opposition it changed to admiration.[12]

In a seemingly hasty acceptance of the Nume's overweening intellectual superiority, it is tempting to consider Lasswitz guilty of collaboration, as he suggests that the higher science and (postulated) higher moral tone of the Martians render human opposition an unworthy ambition. This might be taken as a cold rationalisation of the same ethos that governed and extended European imperialism in Lasswitz's own time, in effect proposing that those with the more advanced technology rightly deserve the submission of others. However, this is not what Lasswitz says. His design is entirely different, and he argues, rather, that the Nume have arrived with *only* the best intent, with *only* the highest motives. The author has anticipated the problematic universalism of cultural domination as well as cultural difference. In the ultimate collapse and defeat of the Nume's higher purposes, the intended tragedy of Lasswitz's text becomes known. It is the Nume's decline into violence and self-betrayal that makes the narrative so enthralling: it becomes an image of imperialism – and imperialism even at its 'best' – going wrong. Lasswitz's narrative steps far beyond any simple fear of the Other and his focus on the inevitability of the degeneration of empire makes us examine this Otherness from a perspective of terrible omniscience, as his text describes the downward arc of moral superiority subsumed by the desire for domination.

In *The War of the Worlds*, the reader is adroitly advised that the Martian invaders are probably aggressive. In the first paragraph of the novel Wells tells us that 'across the gulf of space, [there are] minds that are to our minds as ours are to those of the beasts that perish, intellects vast and cool and unsympathetic'.[13] The unknown narrator, a 'philosophical journalist', makes it clear from the outset that the Martians' presence is menacing. His imperfect observation of the invaders (delivered retrospectively) lends a certain fearfulness to the description of humanity's first contact with the Martians, and hints at a disturbing alien strangeness:

> I think every one of us expected to see a man emerge – possibly something a little unlike us terrestrial men, but in all essentials a man. I know I did. But, looking, I presently saw something stirring within the shadow: greyish billowy movements, one above another, and then two luminous disks – like eyes. Then something resembling a little grey snake, about the thickness of a walking stick, coiled up out of the writhing middle, and wriggled in the air towards me – and then another.
> A sudden chill came over me.[14]

It is interesting to observe the negativity in the narrator's description of the Martians. Expecting something 'in all essentials a man' (unlike Lasswitz's protagonists, who appear to anticipate nothing), Wells's narrator constructs the Martian very much in the image of the Other-as-monster, using a complex series of similes. He sees 'greyish billowy movements', 'luminous disks – like eyes' and 'a little grey snake ... writhing', the grotesque imagery of fancy. His mixture of homely comparison – tentacles being compared to the thickness of a walking stick – and horror succinctly captures the strangeness of the Martians. Wells advises us through his detailed portrait that the Martian is not human, is monstrous (and *ergo* physically inferior); moreover, despite their obvious technological superiority, their subsequent behaviour displays no moral superiority. While Lasswitz concedes that the Other may insidiously resemble the human form, a motif continued much later by Philip K. Dick in *Do Androids Dream of Electric Sheep?* (1968), Wells makes the Other overtly threatening, by physical form alone. If there is little perception of physical difference between the human and the Other, a difference barely sufficient to divide the two without recourse to a mechanism similar to Dick's Voigt–Kampff test, then where does difference lie? The monster, the 'unnatural' by human standards, is to be feared and eliminated, but the Other 'like us' cannot be so simply categorised or dealt with.

The full and subtle rhetorical force of this perception is most clearly highlighted when the Wellsian narrator begins to look beyond the Martians' monstrousness and considers, quite impersonally, the ways in which the Martians are nonetheless human. His deliberations proceed to the point where we understand that this is what humanity itself *may become*, as our species evolves away from the physical, transcending into the realms of higher intellect. Wells's insightfulness provides us with an image of how modern humans may develop into aggressive, calculating and technology-using invaders in their own right.

Contiguous with *fin de siècle* imperial thought, Lasswitz suggests that an invader 'like us' is almost acceptable, at least when compared with the Wellsian alternative, of undeniably non-human (non-European) origin. Readings of any number of contemporary salutations to empire, such as Rudyard Kipling's poem 'The White Man's Burden' (1899), indicate an elite 'fellowship' of racial similars: the 'us' and 'them' of Said's fundamental dichotomy. This is the first indication that the two texts, although sharing multiaxial perspectives, are examining different threats, each perception through the doorway of differentiation uniquely its own. But which illustration is the uneasier? In nineteenth-century Europe, so secure behind its vast and foreign ramparts, Wells's unthinkable chimera would appear the most obvious choice. In the late 1890s, while there were a number of 'invasion' or 'future war' stories,[15] it is also clear that little more than aggressive political manoeuvring was imminent within the continent itself. In these circumstances, an unnatural and invasive outsider becomes a perfect vehicle of horror. Conversely, Lasswitz's vision of the Martians renders them almost as allies, indeed, with their scientific advantages and with their sanctified perception of life, the Nume seem to embody the highest ambitions of humankind. But is this the case?

From a twentieth-century perspective, the visible foe is the more easily defeated. It is the threat from within a society's own ranks that concerns us today, where terrorists are indistinguishable from tourists. To be faced with something visually monstrous may instigate fear and repulsion, but this kind of threat is more readily acceptable as 'the enemy'. To face a being who resembles, in all the important ways, our next-door neighbour is far more unsettling. In SF terms, to engage in conflict with creatures for whom a potential kinship is felt is tantamount to fratricide. The 'physical' monster may be destroyed with impunity, since we feel no affection for it, but the destruction of 'one of us' is usually a less clear-cut consideration. So, the more insidious danger would appear to come not from the monster who is visibly Other but from the Other who remains unseen – the Other within.[16]

Where at first the Nume present themselves as 'higher' versions of humanity, 'intellectually incomparably more highly developed than civilized

man',[17] Wells's fearsome creations are immediately inimical to life on
Earth. There are two distinct images in these texts: one friendly, one not.
Faced with an obvious threat, appropriate responses (whether effective or
not) may be taken immediately; the guard is raised. When that danger is
unseen and unimagined, no defensive stance is taken and vulnerability is so
much greater; consequently the risk of a more fundamental injury is vastly
increased. At first reading, Grunthe's deep suspicions of the Nume seem
unfair, as if he is unable to rise to the great new possibilities offered by the
Martians, but, as we later see, it is equally possible he is right.

Lasswitz raises a series of questions. Where did the 'wrong' of the Nume
come from? From where does the conflict between the two species spring?
Is there something inherently authoritarian in the Nume's attitudes, as
becomes visible in their chauvinistic overreaction to the first battle? Or is
there an underlying flaw in the structure of contact between Earth and
Mars? Is the dreaded scourge of 'Earth fever' (an illness brought on by
moving to the hot, moist climate of Earth) a metaphor for what can go
wrong when one race is put in a position of power in an anomalous or
strange environment? The Nume are a paradox in themselves, since they
have already 'conquered' other (inferior?) races on Mars, and appear to have
some spectacular high-technology weapons for a race that advocates only
peaceful means of development.

From the perspective of both authors, the appearance of the Martians
poses a hazard to the human centre. Yet the suggested perils threaten different elements of society: the physical and the intellectual; or, given the
religious undertones of both texts, the 'heart' and the 'soul' of the human
enterprise. In each narrative, we are shown the 'smoking gun', but only in
the Wells text are the weapons of humanity's enemy clearly portrayed as
such. The Lasswitz and Wells texts discuss not only different threats but
also differing perceptions of threat. It may also be argued that Lasswitz
and Wells are identifying their narratives with different types of empire,
despite their synchronous choice of the Martian Other. The Nume represent
a semi-realistic opposition to humanity which accords with Lasswitz's own
philosophical stance, while the outlandish Wellsian model provokes a more
visceral response. However, imperial thinking at the end of the nineteenth
century was not overly concerned with purely physical threat against the
centre. There was little technological competition to the modern 8 mm
Mauser and Martini–Henry rifles of Europe in the 1890s. Therefore Wells's
violent Martians were not frightening because they represented an evil force
but more because they evoked the terror of the unknown, as well as a hint of
what we might even become. Wells's experiment suggests that humankind
is evolving into a species of technological murderers who would do well to
experience a reversal of conditions. The strong religious sense which creeps

into his writing, in conflict with his scientific and rational views at several points, is very powerful and expressive. Even given Wells's anxieties, it is still Lasswitz's Nume who represented the greater menace to the inhabitants of that period in history: too much like humanity to instantly fear and guard against, their invasion is guileful and covert. Appearing benign but ultimately destructive and self-corrupting, the Nume represent the way Europeans might be perceived by others. In terms political, the coming of the Nume provides not only a wholly unanticipated invasion, but also the more familiar fear of a *coup d'état*.

Wells chooses to provide us with a view of the invader as a physical force. Analogous with the unification and militarisation of Germany in the latter part of the nineteenth century, or as a parallel to the near elimination by the British of the Tasmanian aboriginals in the earlier part, his narrative is one of cultural vandalism. There is little else to fear (though fear of death is surely sufficient for most), even given the monstrous Martian's superior scientific abilities. Their physical form renders them superficially frightening, but this repulsiveness removes their ability to corrupt at the level of the ideal. An interesting aside from this is that Wells's novel *does* discuss the corrupting of ideals, as his protagonists all fall from grace, and through the degenerative behaviour of the mob fleeing London. The essential fear, however, is for the preservation of mortal existence, not the preservation of an ideology. The invaders may threaten the life of the individual but not of fundamental British culture. Such a culture, though ruined and disintegrated, will always continue in some form, as illustrated by the character of the artilleryman, who is able to dismiss the death meted out by the Martians as a form of race purification: 'Life is real again, and the useless and cumbersome and mischievous have to die. They ought to die. They ought to be willing to die. It's a sort of disloyalty, after all, to live and taint the race.'[18] The soldier's Nietszchean social Darwinism is explicit. It is by means of such deeply ironic political contrast that the fundamental danger of the Wellsian Martian is made clear. The individual may perish, but the ideal and purity of the collective regime must be maintained at all costs. Wells permits us to witness the bowing of an empire but not the dismissal of the key ideals behind his concept of an enlightened socialism.

Lasswitz's insightful identification of the deepest fears of the imperialist Europeans raises his narrative far beyond the uncertain confines of SF. As with Aldous Huxley's Brave New World (1932), the author's use of SF permits him to experiment with the potential of a world of unthinkable circumstance and condition. As Frederik Pohl observed in the 1975 'Galaxy Reader':

It isn't really science fiction's business to describe what science is going to find. It is much more science fiction's business to say what the human race will make of it all. In fact, this is the thing – the one thing, maybe the only thing – that science fiction does better than any other tool available ... it gives us a look at consequences. And it does it superbly.[19]

And this is what Lasswitz has done: provided the reader with a glimpse of the consequences of collaboration with an unseen enemy, which enables that enemy to destroy from within. His Nume may bear all the hallmarks of beneficent plausibility but, while they shrink from physical harm of the individual, they have little compunction regarding the well-being of the ideals – mistaken or otherwise – of humankind.

Wells's Martians follow the path first ascribed to Mary Shelley's unnatural Other, Frankenstein's creature. The fear of the monster is pan-cultural and provokes similar apprehensions wherever it is found, but the notion of 'the Other within' produces a set of disturbances along an entirely different axis. And it is at this point that Lasswitz has situated the Nume. The threat they offer is not located so much in the physical plane as in the moral one. Even the sites of the invaders' first contact with humanity indicate the differing intentions and purposes of their respective authors. The Nume are isolationists by choice; they do not seek immediate contact with populated centres, and prefer limited interaction with indigenous life in the polar regions. In contrast, Wells's Martians not only land close by the capital city but also in the middle of a triangle formed by three towns, and in the centre of a communal area of land much used for recreation. The significant difference in contact sites with the Other may be considered in terms of causality and response. These landing sites cannot be assumed accidental, since they define the inherent nature, and the preferred visibility, of the Other. The Nume's covert existence at the Earth's poles enables them to undertake a measured level of infiltration, although this is hastened by the untimely meeting with Grunthe and Saltner. The 'Surrey' Martians, however, could hardly have selected a more propitious spot from which to terrorise the locals.[20]

It becomes clear that while the two texts share an uncanny number of parallels, their warnings of attack against the centre of the human empire are very different. The ultimate goal of both sets of Martians is still one of imperial domination, though brought about by alternative mechanisms of power. As Leela Gandhi points out:

> Power transverses the imponderable chasm between coercion and seduction through a variety of baffling self-representations. While it may manifest itself in a show and application of force, it is equally likely to appear as the disinterested purveyor of cultural enlightenment and reform.[21]

Therefore, while both narratives threaten invasion, they do so from disparate perspectives, involving diametrically opposing tactics, and offer their greatest danger to quite separate horizons of society. Yet the ultimate aims of the narratives appear identical, and conform in part to the historic parabola of the imperial project. From whichever angle the invaders' actions are observed, their progressive motion follows the process whereby one culture attempts, in Gandhi's words, 'systematically to cancel or negate [the] cultural difference and value'[22] of another. The other emergent point in the narratives is how each author indicates the ways in which the Martians are already human. Wells considers them representative of the typical techno-aggression and ruthlessness which Europeans are unwilling to see in themselves, while the Lasswitzean Nume cherish a monolithic version of 'goodness' but imagine they can learn nothing from such a backward race as the Earthlings.

Thus the scene has been set. The first Martians are on Earth and the danger of their coming has begun to be understood. From the Surrey sandpit in which they land, the Wellsian monsters commence their reign of terror and destruction. A deputation of men are destroyed under the banner of a white flag – a horrendous act of infamy in the eyes of the English, whose rules of combat (with other Europeans) usually required a written notification in advance of the onset of hostilities. This act in itself permits Wells to cleverly highlight two distinct aspects of the conflict: that the invading Other cannot or will not perceive physical or semiological gestures as anything other than an attack; and that humanity (specifically the English in this instance) are too naïve or innocent to have considered this point.[23] Bystanders are brutally destroyed by a technologically advanced 'heat ray', the appearance of which substantiates Wells's allusion to the first awareness of Europeans by the Tasmanian aboriginals.

Wells continues his narrative with lurid descriptions of the Martians' fell industry and perverted mechanical endeavour in the pit – biblical undertones permeate the narrator's nervous account of these activities. Ungodly lights and the hiss of steam emanate from the site of the cylindrical craft's landing place, until the Martians at last rise from their self-imposed prison in gigantic tripedal machines. Now the archetypal monster has evolved into a prototype of SF. The Other has become 'other' indeed, a mutation of the known and the unknown; the alien from the pit emerges as the hybrid of nightmare. In keeping with the archetype of evil, nothing in the path of their mechanical advance is spared: people, property, even the land itself is burned and infected by the fire and 'black smoke' of the Martians' destructive technologies. Encased by metal, Wells's Martians transcend the physical and seem intent upon the assumption of near invincibility: all-powerful and driven by a higher purpose. His narrator contemplates such a dire eventuality:

Were they intelligent mechanisms? Such a thing I felt was impossible. Or did a Martian sit within each, ruling, directing, using, much as a man's brain sits and rules in his body? I began to compare the things to human machines, to ask myself for the first time in my life how an iron-clad or a steam engine would seem to an intelligent lower animal.[24]

These shifting perceptions of the invader are typical of the Wells novel, which provides first the image of the horrifying Other then a more reasoned contemplation, but are also visible in Lasswitz's text. However, Lasswitz appears determined that the presence of the Nume is seen to offer only benefits to humankind, especially to Grunthe, who comments, 'I feel like a savage in an institute of physics'.[25] Gandhi is able to rationalise the differences between these perceptions and modes of reaction, suggesting that:

The humanist valorisation of man is almost always accompanied by a barely discernible corollary which suggests that some human beings are more human than others – either on account of their access to superior learning, or on account of their cognitive facilities.[26]

Gandhi's observations raise the question of the role of the reader in each of the narratives. For whom does each author write? Is there an analogy between the type and level of threat posed by each of the dissimilar Martians, and a specifically targeted section of the social order in each case? If Wells's mechanical invaders threaten only the physical, then those truly at risk (the individual, 'the man in the street') are the most likely to be immediately aware of it and act defensively. But is the danger greater if it directly affects not the individual but rather the underlying society and culture of that individual? At which point does the menace of these (fictional) imperial narratives become truly threatening? If a single life is lost, it is tragic, but not necessarily a tragedy. Lasswitz's postulation of a slow subhumation of an entire culture by the superior Other transcends tragedy and enters into the realm of grand narrative as the story of the Nume becomes the discourse of a fictional social Darwinism. Where Wells examines the individual hopelessness of the subaltern, Lasswitz establishes an interior dialogue between the stance of his text and a perverted cultural theory harnessed to the imperial drive.

At first sight, the place of empire in each narrative seems clear. Both Wells and Lasswitz hypothesise an existing human empire suddenly under attack by an empire of an extraterrestrial genesis. Neither text is concerned with extraneous issues and both focus upon the single issue of invasion. There is little history in either narrative, except that intertextuality which the reader brings into the act of reading. The acknowledgement of empire begins with the first contact with the Other, when readers are expected, implicitly, to range themselves on the side of 'good'. With the Wellsian Martians this is a relatively easy matter – who does not instinctively oppose lawless slaughter? However, with the Lasswitzean model the image is blurred by uncertainties. Which is the 'good' side? Do we oppose the colonising invader on the grounds of principle? Does any culture have the right to deny its membership the benefits of freely offered medical and technological advancement? At what point must a culture concede that the Kantian good of the many outweighs the nebulous virtue of dogma? To resort to cliché, what price freedom?

And it is surely the question of freedom that links the two narratives, rather than the mundane and temporal maintenance of any political status quo. Lives may be lost, property destroyed and cultural traditions negated, but it is the most fundamental aspect of freedom, self-determination, which forms the essential issue in both texts. And here we reconnect with the path of the imperial project once more. Self-determination and the existential capacity for authentic behaviour are the cornerstones of individual and cultural rights: rights that the Martians now see fit to abrogate. The textual experiments of Lasswitz and Wells both uphold principles of autonomy, although in the one we are shown a deconstructed autonomy of self, and in the other a deconstruction of the ideal. Though one model of invasion is imposed by bloody violence and the other by insinuation, both are versions of the conventional imperial act. Which model may ultimately prove to be the more effective offers a serious debate, one questioning the relations between benevolence and domination. Does the formulation of empire and the imperial endeavour finally depend upon violence to the individual, or devastation of the ideal?

From this perspective, the monstrous ululating tripeds will likely effect the greatest physical damage. If sufficient individuals remain free, *ipso facto*, their ideals remain also, but nothing eliminates a culture's sense of self-determination more effectively than a blind offensive determined to eradicate all who stand in its way. As Gary K. Wolfe comments, 'Wells' Martians threaten us on a racial level: by subjecting us to the kind of examination and subjugation that we characteristically visit on lower forms of life'.[27] This 'racial threat' is something modern human society has become all too familiar with since the industrialised slaughter of World War I and the horrors of Auschwitz, although it was already prevalent in the 1890s in the Congo and south-west Africa. Stripped of the smallest ability to resist intact, of even the will to resist, Wells's human centre falls and is all but destroyed.

The Nume, however, wait until the final third of the novel before offering even a hint of their destructive capabilities. Their message is one of peace and goodwill, of cooperation and of unparalleled advance for the entire planet.

Because the Nume seek consultation and representation, their intrusion is much mitigated. They stroll gently into the world rather than blast their way across it. This manner of invasion does not accord with European historical precedent and may be seen more in the light of speculative idealism. How do we deny the undeniable reason in the Nume's wish to extend their 'goodness' towards the Earth? Is it wrong for the technologically 'rich' outsiders to wish to bring prosperity, comfort and plenty to their less fortunate neighbours? As Terry Eagleton notes, 'It is not in the end questions of language, skin colour or identity, but of commodity prices, raw materials, labour markets, military alliances and political forces, which shape the relations between rich and poor'.[28] The Nume seem to offer more than they wish to take and this, above all else, is Lasswitz's critically decisive moment of empire. Should humankind accept or reject the Nume's imperial overtures?

The stage is now prepared for either conflict or cohabitation. Wells's tripedal monstrosities rampage across the Home Counties of England, leaving death and destruction in their wake. The God of Man has abandoned even the faithful, as illustrated by the behaviour and ultimate death of the curate. Lasswitz promotes goodwill to humankind and ferries selected Earthlings up to Mars to see a potentially idyllic lifestyle for themselves. The conflict engendered by the Wellsian Martians is clear and unambiguous. They wish to destroy all human resistance, domesticate the remaining population as cattle and revitalise their dying race on a planet still in its youth. The Nume advocate non-violence, and even attempt to save those humans who do violence against them, while simultaneously engaged upon an ineluctable critique and deconstruction of the human ideology. Wells has England under physical attack; Lasswitz surrounds England with a *cordon sanitaire*. Interestingly, and in both cases, this country is singled out for the specific attention of the invaders. Why? Is it because England in the 1890s was seen as the most powerful imperial nation in the world, and to crush it was to crush civilisation? Did the fact of Britain's island geography alone support a fictional plausibility of both attack and blockade? Was the notorious British isolationism itself under attack? The likely explanation is that a combination of these circumstances had made Britain the most appropriate locale for the development of either narrative. In addition to the immeasurably ironic but legendary dislike of the British for any form of unwanted cultural encroachment, their equally vaunted fighting spirit would have made them the perfect quarry for an invasion force of any kind.

Thus England was singled out by both authors. Wells's Martians seek to consume the English and he has his invaders hound the population into the sea. Lasswitz, however, maintains the Nume's aloofness from physical destruction, and they are content to blockade and starve the entire nation into submission. Again, we see two distinctly differing approaches. Wells understands that only a massive and concerted effort that destroys the heart of Britain (London) would produce any immediate or lasting effect on such a culturally inverted people. A protracted but lesser conflict would see the British rise up against the Martians and eventually hunt them to destruction. But with the centre abandoned and the infrastructure of the whole cast into disarray, Wells illustrates the liquefaction of the social body. Lasswitz, on the other hand, has the Nume wanting to destroy not the people, as may be seen by their entirely pacifist principles, but the ideology of a people. In this, their intent is far more amoral, aimed as it is at the soul of a nation.

There is a plateau in both narratives that serves as foundation for the remainder of each text. Wells's narrator emerges from his hiding place in the chapter entitled 'The Work of Fifteen Days'. During this short time, the Martians have turned the centre of the country into a perversion of Mars. The bleak vista of destruction is everywhere. The red weed of Mars symbolically smothers the green of England. The narrator's barely endurable confinement and almost complete lack of sensory input has heightened his perceptions of defeat, as is plain from his first thoughts:

> I felt the first inkling of a thing that presently grew clear in my mind, that oppressed me for many days, a sense of dethronement, a persuasion that I was no longer a master, but an animal among the animals, under the Martian heel. With us it would be as with them, to lurk and watch, to run and hide; the fear and empire of man had passed away.[29]

There is a real mood of loss in this admission. The narrator indicates an idealisation of a passing ethos through his 'sense of dethronement', and his awareness that the 'empire of man had passed away' speaks to the core of Wells's narrative of conquest. Wider than politics, Wells has his narrator accept the complex Darwinistic notion that humans are animals, but with the unspoken conviction that they are also *more* than animals. The Martians pose a frightening blocking of the Darwinian view, in that they are both civilised and uncivilised in ways that the lower orders of animal species never are. The narrator discovers, in this one moment of clarity, that the maintenance of empire, its continuity, is, at heart, a philosophical supposition. Wells's England has reached the point of decline; its people are refugees; its notion of self is shattered; its future is terrifying. To have something so vast and invincible as England crumble as the broken rocks the narrator stands upon is to comprehend the ironic intangibility of physical power. As he gazes around the shattered landscape, the narrator finally understands the place of all humankind, as 'an animal among the animals'. His recognition of the displaced British hubris comments directly on the paradox of imperial thought: empire depends solely upon the perception of itself.

Lasswitz maintains the Nume in their saintly role of benevolent 'teachers', an engrossing and central theme of his text that saturates it with the Nume's innate chauvinism. Where does their aggression come from? If they are so 'saintly', why do they resort to overt domination? It would appear that the Nume are blind to their own failings, assuming their 'goodness' to be sufficient in itself to negate and hide their baser impulses. But those impulses remain, despite their containment, and rise to the surface as an imperial urge as soon as a 'suitable' political climate occurs. By this means, Lasswitz suggests the implausibility of the perfect being or a perfect desire. To be human, or remotely human, requires the having of these base impulses. The only thing which separates the 'good' from the 'not good' is the level at which these impulses are recognised and contained.

Lasswitz's insistence that these particular Martians are of potential value to humankind locates his narrative within a psychological dichotomy. As Angelika Bammer observes:

> When an other is perceived as threatening, it is precisely the degree to which this other seems not just 'different' but – uncannily – strangely familiar, even, one might say 'same'. The resulting dilemma is how to respond to this threat in a way that removes this other(ness) without undoing one's self in the process.[30]

This identification of the Other with the self both problematises and simplifies the issue of the Nume on Earth. Since they are so like 'us', their advanced technology and veneration of individual life appeal to the human sense of vanity. They represent a state of being which humankind *thinks* it would like to achieve. The Nume are positioned far in advance of contemporary human reality and appear to offer a shortcut to the cultural and social blessings supposedly sought by an enlightened people. However, the offer is Faustian and complex: the Nume's lifestyle is available only at a price. Before humankind can avail themselves of the Martian bargain they must willingly apprentice themselves under the Nume's tutelage. To gain much, all must be risked. Conversely, should humanity decide not to embrace the foreign entity now among them, neither the physical nor the ethical, then the Nume presence is reduced to the lesser problematised status of invader. As with Goethe's Faust, who, disillusioned with and despairing of the world, is tempted by the Mephistophelian desire to make his life worth the living, so too are the characters (Saltner, La) in Lasswitz's narrative torn: tempted by the Martians' wish to ease the burden of humanity, and equally fearful of the consequences of cultural subhumation and appropriation. The imperial package was never more enticingly presented.

Analysing the process of cultural appropriation, Jonathan Hart argues that:

Imperialism is about the expansionism of political property through the acquisition of colonies. That colonization involves setting up the cultural example of the imperial centre, while that centre also appropriates aspects of the colonized cultures officially and unofficially. In the wake of empire and the migration of peoples, especially in this century in the postcolonial period, the debate over what constitutes cultural appropriation by the dominant culture has become an important concern in multicultural societies.[31]

This is an interesting comment in the light of the Lasswitz assumption of Earth's cultural submission to the Martians. Given the Nume's stated values, any overt act of invasion by them that potentially involved the death of many would be anathema. Therefore they seek to conquer not by force of might but by force of reason and practical advantage, thereby distancing themselves from the archetypal form of imperialist. Moreover, without the threat of overt oppression, humanity would appear to have little to gain from a violent rejection of the imperialist project. But if the humans in Lasswitz's text freely give themselves up into a Numian overlordship, who is appropriating whom? The Nume are already sufficiently similar (in physical form) to humankind for Saltner to fall in love with a Martian female, and the suggestion of Lasswitz here is that there would be few obstacles to physical integration between the species. In fact, that the two peoples could easily merge into the postcolonial hybridity of cross-culturalism, with neither able to claim primary status, has already been proven by the birth of Ell, who is of mixed parentage, human and Nume, and the son of the first Martian to 'discover' the Earth.[32] Certainly the Nume possess significant technological advances, but if these are to be freely provided to the people of Earth, the gain appears to be strongly biased towards humanity. The Nume are even ready to educate humanity in matters scientific, their advances formidable but not incomprehensible to the younger race. Therefore the term 'cultural appropriation' does not seem immediately legitimate in Lasswitz's story.

It is only when the Nume, their hand forced by the outright antagonism of humanity, finally resort to totalitarianism that the will to any such domination is explicitly acknowledged. Lasswitz has, of course, provided earlier hints as to the assimilative desires of the Nume, before their otherwise inexplicable fascism becomes manifest. When Saltner and La's friend Isma are taken to Mars to see the Nume's lifestyle for themselves, they visit a series of 'museums', one of which exhibits things Earthly. It is obvious not only that the Nume clearly enjoy their ability to reconstruct the 'place' of Earth (complete with artificial gravity and heavy atmosphere) but also that their interest in presenting data in this format indicates an underlying belief in the moral correctness of such a display. The planet Earth and its indigenous 'animals' are in one sense contextualised by the Nume museum: humans are paraded as specimens. To the horror of the Earthlings and to those Martians who have come to respect the dignity of humankind, the museum also contains a theatre in which a weird play, a re-enactment of the scene of first conflict between the two races, is shown. The performance is nothing less than a presentation of human barbarism. That the Nume delight in such display of an inferior race says much about their self-perception. Other races are mere specimens and toys for them; they have no true regard or recognisable ethical standards in the human sense. They may not even perceive their chauvinism as oppression, but as a continuance of diplomacy by other means. The Nume smile upon the Earth, but the equivalent of their tabloid newspapers declare 'humans have hardly any inkling of justice, honesty, freedom.... Deprivation of liberty is an everyday affair. Thefts occur at every hour ... and this gang of semi-animals should be recognized by us as beings of reason?'[33]

If by 'appropriation' we project a reductive process, whereby a dominant society systematically assimilates some or all of the 'desirable' elements of a subordinate culture, then the issues of conventional cultural appropriation do not enter into the Wellsian narrative. Wells's interest and academic qualifications in zoology and comparative anatomy enabled him to render the Martians as monsters in the physical plane. These Martians bear no resemblance to humanity. They cannot survive outside their technological creations; nor can they live on the natural products of the Earth, unless a diet of human blood is considered 'natural', although this may be exactly what the narrator is beginning to consider. Lacking any measure of shared physical characteristic, it is understandable that nothing suited for human life would obviously benefit the invader. The Surrey Martians possess no desire for anything human other than to maintain humans as livestock. There is no value for these invaders in the cultural attributes of humanity; our arts and sciences meet no Martian attraction or aspiration. Even the planet that has drawn them across space offers limited service, other than a less severe climate and a potentially extended survival of their species. In the Wells narrative, the only form of cultural appropriation, if we may judge it that, is the annexation of the human race as a whole: the forced removal of *Homo sapiens* from its 'place in the Sun'.

The penultimate section of the Lasswitz narrative is concerned with the awakening of humankind to the true designs of the Nume. England has surrendered, enabling the Martians to establish a 'Protectorate' over Europe and thus defend the once belligerent nation from its earthly neighbours, which seek to divide the British empire to their own benefit. In the chapter entitled 'The Defeated', Torm, one of the original German explorers, reviews the changes that have taken place since the inauguration of the dependent territory. His summation of forced education, radical social change, the demobilisation of the military, the barrage of new civil laws and (a tongue-in-cheek gesture to Germany of the 1890s) the 'no duelling' law describes the first steps of imperial constraint emanating from the centre. The Nume have disabled Europe. Mechanical, industrial and agricultural revolutions have arisen almost overnight after imported Martian technology has dismantled the social structure of generations. Though physical force is prohibited by the Nume, their revenge upon a Balkan village whose inhabitants attacked one of the invaders' ships proves the Martians capable of unmerciful violence. From an initial superficial guise of benevolent teachers, Lasswitz's text has skilfully shown the evolution of the Martians into the most ardent of colonisers.

The Martians in Surrey seem invincible. They cannot be stopped or killed other than by a direct artillery strike, but no defensive position has been able to stand before them. As the narrator wanders through the chapter 'Dead London' what he sees suggests the end of human civilisation. The exact centre, indeed the 'dead centre', of a once mighty empire is now reduced to black powder and red weed. Everything that England and its empire stood for is gone. Structures of power, both of the physical and of the intangible kind, lie broken on the ground. There has been no appropriation and no assimilation, only destruction. Wells's Martians did not come to colonise a world: they came to cull the herd. The mass anthropogenic cleansing is not the goal and object of colonisation, but of ultimate competition. It is an unnatural Darwinistic obscenity. The narrator finally realises that the Martian Others are not colonists in the true sense but exterminators, and that their scourge will claim the Earth itself. The last words of the artilleryman, 'This isn't a war ... it was never a war, any more than there's a war between men and ants',[34] are erroneous. It *is* a war, but not a war to appropriate humanity in the accepted colonial sense. The Nume are equally prepared to destroy all life on Earth – in their case by stopping the planet's rotation because it is of little of value to them (except as a planet with a longer life expectancy than their own). Their logic argues that if the humans will not follow peace and reason, they do not deserve to live, and the easiest way to destroy the species from a Numian perspective is to kill off the entire planet. On a different level, the object of Wells's war is time itself, the goal of empire in its conventional sense being an unknown object to his Martians. These particular Others are not imperialists in the political motif: they are merely thieves and pirates intent upon general despoilation and the acquisition of a new food source.

Thus the two texts do not argue the force of the imperial drive from a shared frame of reference. In effect, the narratives share little except their synchronicity and coincidental choice of antagonists. Lasswitz has taken the once benign Nume through a distinct progression of devolution, every stage eradicating a further layer of their self-comprehension. From god-like benefactors they become fascist tyrants, imposing their will over the Earth simply because they believed it was in the better interests of humanity to do so. However, the narrative does not end with the Nume victorious. There are suggestions throughout Lasswitz's text that even Martian technology is finding the demands of life on Earth to be problematic. Furthermore, the atmosphere is too heavy and wet for the Nume, which causes recurrent outbreaks of 'Earth fever', a condition that may be remedied only by return of the sufferer to the colder, drier atmosphere of Mars. Nor can the Nume live easily beneath gravity three times too heavy for their physique. But they endure. Under adversely hot and sticky climactic conditions, and facing a constant low rumbling of native discord, the imperial Martians remove the power of human self-determination in favour of an extrinsic power of Other. It is hardly surprising that Lasswitz required England to take the role of primary adversary in this narrative, so closely does he equate the Nume with the British experience in India.

In a text entitled *Faces of the Future: The Lessons of Science Fiction*, Brian Ash perceives that:

> There is much in science fiction which can be regarded as criticism of 'progress'.... What makes this valuable, if harrowing, for students of the future human condition is that so many writers who have let their considerable imaginations play about the ultimate direction of present trends, have come to a similar conclusion: unless man himself progresses, his future – for all its technological wonders – will finally be little better than the primordial slime from which he so painfully climbed. That, of course, is hardly a view unique to the authors of science fiction.[35]

Precisely analogous to this observation, Lasswitz has taken the reader of nineteenth-century Germany on a journey into the possible future of humankind. 'Look!', he is saying, 'See what could happen to us!' From this stance, it appears that the author has produced an experimental postcolonial narrative, or, at least, a politically oriented anticolonial protest.

In London, Wells kills the Martians off with a fitting biological *deus ex machina*. It seems that the bounty of Earth, the one object of Martian desire, has become their ironic downfall: indigenous micro-organisms (vital on Earth but lacking on their barren home world) render them unable to survive in an atmosphere of plenty. This is a triumph of narrative and typical of Wells's fascination with the consequences of scientific knowledge. Deranged, the narrator wanders around deserted London, his movements accompanied by the mournful and eerie cries of the last dying Martian. The entire scene is surreal and echoes a general derangement and destabilisation, fascinatingly paralleled by Lasswitz's Nume as they endure the torments of 'Earth fever'. The power of Wells's writing in this moment of bleakness is compelling as his dramatic realisation and vivid narrative expression illuminate the potential of the SF text to create dramatic social imagery.

Meanwhile, the Nume finally understand the geographical issues of empire as their limited foothold on Earth begins to erode. There is a movement of rebellion among the dissatisfied humans, notably the people of North America, home of radical change and a lack of enshrined authority. The Nume begin to experience the first signs of disintegration, aptly echoed by W. B. Yeats in the poem 'The Second Coming' (1921), where 'Things fall apart; the centre cannot hold'.[36] The Martian home world is deeply divided by pro- and anti-Earth factions; there is overt rebellion on Earth itself; the colonisers cannot hold their ground and begin the retreat to Mars. If colonialism is the means of enforcing or fabricating the unity of an imperial power, then the defeat of an attempted colonialisation rebounds in shock waves to the centre. Once centrally based citizens become unsettled and at odds with the central authority, peripheral members of the home community are very likely to become fearful of their status. While it would be an exaggeration to suggest that imperialism at the periphery provokes disunity at the centre, this is clearly the scenario envisaged by Lasswitz. Though not entirely defeated, the Nume realise the combination of the anti-human movement on Mars and the growing powers of the Federation of Humans on Earth makes the peaceful appropriation of humanity impossible. After a brief frenzy of despotic behaviour by the remaining Nume on Earth, the Martian presence slips away.

Thus these two tests of the imperial project are reconciled once more into the single timeline of history. The Martians did not come. The British empire did not fall under the heel of the monstrous Other. And the secret of anti-gravity remains a secret. But the experimental acts of a postulated empire are not any the less legitimate when the concept and precepts of empire are so critically examined as in the narratives of Lasswitz and Wells. These authors provoke a sharp review of the ways in which colonisation affects both the coloniser and the colonised, and demand that we scrutinise the imperial project in all its guises. The experimental nature of SF appears to depend upon an endless expansion of the centre (either of the human centre or of the Others'), where scientific discovery and technological advance present us with the ability to postulate our maximum potential as a species. This is the function and paradox of the genre, as we are forced to recognise and digest the ugly and the unpalatable side by side with the more enlightened alternatives, as explorations of imperial power in SF create a bridge between language, accountability and history. To see how these early experiments of Lasswitz and Wells opened the way to a more contemporary view of colonialisation and a development of both the human culture and the culture of the Other, we now examine several more recent texts, written from an American perspective.

6. Exoticising the Future: American Greats

While the history of SF may arguably stretch back to the fables of the ancient Greeks, one of the first conventionally recognised speculative narratives was Sir Thomas More's *Utopia* (1516), which describes the travels of a Portuguese sailor, Raphael Hythloday, and the controversial but wondrous socio-political climate on the island of Utopia in the New World. Following this, but written for different reasons, came a work by the pantheist martyr Giordano Bruno, *De l'Infinito universo e mondi* (1584), which argued that the universe was infinite and that it contained an infinite number of worlds, all inhabited by intelligent beings. Bruno's text is credited by Frances Yates[1] as being the origin of Hermetic influence on science, since it involved magical interpretations of nature and of humanity's ability to conjure and understand the world, philosophical aspects that dovetail pleasingly with some perceptions of today's science and technologies.

More's and Bruno's works may be considered an excellent genesis of a genre unlike anything that had been experimented with before: not conventional literature, not scientific or parable, nor yet historical or plainly political, but a creative amalgam of all, a blend of the rational and the extrapolative, bound together with a touch of sixteenth-century optimism. Following the production of Galileo's telescope in 1609, and the then heretical notion that the Earth was not, in fact, the centre of the universe, many notable authors launched their writing into the genre space of speculative fiction, of which SF has become the leading and most popular element: Tommaso Campanella's *Civitas Solis* (1623); Cyrano de Bergerac's posthumously published *Histoire comique des états et empires de la lune* (1656) and *Histoire comique des états et empires du soleil* (1662); Voltaire's *Micromégas* (1752); and, of course, the magnificent opposing talents of Jules Verne and H. G. Wells in the latter part of the nineteenth century. But the idealistic vision of More has not been the only one forthcoming, with contemporary SF depicting not necessarily utopia ahead but also a variety of insane futures, prone to atavisms and socio-political structures which drive humanity outwards, to experience enmity without respite in the midst of abundance.

It is against such an extensive background of possibility and uncertainty, of utopia and dystopia, that modern SF authors have sought to illuminate plural social contingencies – different ways forward, where science and technology become the heralds of human progress. There may be room for More's *Utopia* but there is equally space for the dark and subverted machinations of William Gibson's 'cyberworlds',[2] where nihilistic cultural structures conflict endlessly with the desire for human spirituality. And while SF has no autochthonous nationality, springing up wherever writers look beyond their current circumstances into the unknown of a future time, the place where science and technology have most displayed themselves, and where SF writers, fuelled by the exotic excitement of the machine and of modern expansion, instigated the great wave of current SF popularity, is America. Many now accepted fundamentals of the genre were cemented by twentieth-century American authors, and this chapter examines works by two of the most influential, Isaac Asimov (1920–92) and Robert A. Heinlein (1907–88).

It is partly due to the significance of these modern American texts, whose prejudices seem coloured with even earlier cultural inculcations, that many subsequent narratives may be seen as tainted with echoes of a radical, if scientific, neo-imperialism. It is the relationship between the mind-expanding and imperial aspects of SF exemplified by the experiments of Asimov and Heinlein which this chapter specifically explores, since it is from their mid-twentieth-century narratives that many later SF writers have taken their cues. Full of an emergent American superpower, newly published SF authors preached the principles of human action, settlement and exploitation, though not necessarily in the traditional form of political empire. Yet even with their sight flitting between the past and the future, there emerged from the golden age of SF (1938–46[3]) a vista of diverse and inspiring texts, which produced a renaissance of science-based utopianist literature, where certain authors, mainly American, dominated the field with their remarkable visions.

Many of these visions were extraordinary. Not only did they provide the reader with wondrous imaginary vistas of alternative worlds, such as L. Sprague de Camp's 'Lest Darkness Fall' (1939), in which the Dark Ages are ameliorated, or C. M. Kornbluth's 'Two Dooms' (1958), which has Hitler succeed, but they were also places where the unfettered mind might once again discover the strengths of the human spirit. Beside the marvels of technology, they offered darker images of what might happen should humankind proceed blindly along the paths of Malthusian extravagance or misguided political Machiavellianism. Occasionally they also foreshadowed the course of real scientific achievement, although this is hardly a stunning revelation since a fair proportion of American SF writers were in themselves active scientists. Following the late-nineteenth-century innovations of Verne and Wells, ideas poured forth from America,[4] among which were:

Edwin Balmer's lie detector (*The Achievements of Luther Trant*, 1910); Hugo Gernsback's television ('Ralph 124C 41+', 1911–12); John W. Campbell Jr's description of the first hydrogen-powered rocket[5] (*The Mightiest Machine*, 1934); and E. C. Large's artificial photosynthesis (*Sugar in the Air*, 1937). Heinlein coined the term 'waldo' in 1942 in a piece of short fiction[6] that discussed the relative merits of various contemporary technologies, a term much in use in automated operations today. Even the much later *Star Trek* television series was partly responsible for the naming of the first US space shuttle, *Enterprise*. Yet these more obvious connections between science fiction and science fact frequently originated in the frustration of scientists as they sought to be heard outside of scientific realms.

In the wake of World War II, the late 1940s and early 1950s were a time of unusual literary activity among scientists and engineers, the aftermath of such technological conflict drawing the world of the real and the imagined much closer together. New writers such as Clifford D. Simak, L. Sprague de Camp and Lester Del Rey mingled personally and textually with such serious scientists as Fred Hoyle, Isaac Asimov and Arthur C. Clarke. The result was startling and frequently produced unstable results. Encouraged by the genius of John W. Campbell, editor of *Astounding Stories* and a physicist by education, American authors were inspired to reflect the dilemmas of their age in a new form of literature. With the broader implications of the Los Alamos project and the atomic bomb, the individualism of science was already giving way to the realities of a bureaucratically organised scientific community and a government that funded it. In an article in the *Johns Hopkins Magazine*,[7] Andrew Feenberg notes that changes were rapid and frequently traumatic as traditional value systems and models were subverted into 'progressive' scientific labour. Hostility grew towards the suffocating US government control over science, as the stereotype of the white-coated scientist boffin gave way to the almost commercialised laboratory entrepreneurship of Robert Oppenheimer. So keen were the politicised leaders of science to make their case known to the public that every forum was used, including fictional writing. Science, they demanded, should be returned to the scientists, to those who understood its nuances and idiosyncrasies. It was not the place for meddling politicians and accountants. SF became a voluble voice of dissent as its writers made their suit to the public, creating images of a fantastic future where all of humanity might share in an endless technological cornucopia.

It is understandable, given that the vast majority of golden age SF writers were educated, male and technologically enthusiastic, that their works were aimed at a predominantly educated, male and technologically enthusiastic readership.[8] Many patriarchal and male-oriented motifs were brought into the new mix of science and narrative, including the desirability of empire

and power over 'lesser' beings. It was not yet considered incorrect to have
gallant heroes (almost always male, of course) striding the galaxy in search
of wrongs to be righted and damsels to be rescued from various forms of
interstellar distress. The golden age of SF was a time when men were still
men and women were pleasantly ornamental, when the alien Other was
considered a threat[9] and when new planets were there to be conquered.
An entire genre was rapidly becoming popular, and basic but futuristic
threats were evolving into complete space opera and galactic fictions. The
enormous cult of pulp fiction turned to ideas of science, and deep space
became an endlessly thrilling objective for writers with a technological or
scientific bent. This mass enthusiasm ran parallel (and occasionally inter-
mingled) with serious attempts at future fiction, such as Aldous Huxley's
considerations of the large-scale social consequences of technology in *Brave
New World* (1932) and Jack Williamson's 'The Equalizer' (1947), a study in
the political implications of free power. But the great bulk of published work
relied upon the tropes of hero and villain in imperialist scenarios, where
only nightmarish monsters of the id denied the authors their expansionist
desires. Narratives of exoticised alien Others, themselves designed to be
eradicated or subsumed, multiplied in this great imperial scientific surge
from Earth. As Julia Witner observes:

> Science fiction has always been distinctive for its enemies. It departs
> from the tedious sameness of the Red, Yellow or Brown Menace one
> finds in 'realistic' adventure fiction, giving us green, atemporal, or
> amorphous menaces instead. It is rather refreshing to fight nightmares
> instead of people … to let oneself go, to externalise all that is hateful
> to one in some wildly original fashion and have at it with lasers.[10]

Scientific voices brought the apparatus and insight of their profession to
the new genre, but SF also provided the forum where older themes, attitudes
and biases, political and predominantly male sexual mores, were able to
continue and flourish. Just as it is impossible for the migrants to leave their
prejudices behind them on their voyage to Kim Stanley Robinson's Mars,
so it was difficult for many of the new-sprung authors to look far beyond
the cultural and social conditioning of the empirical scientist. Monsters and
galactic empires may have stepped from the intersection between the desires
of the writers and their audience, but the power to visualise a space-faring
humanity came from science itself, the latter opening up the wild frontier
of the former. And those who were able to understand that power were the
ones to wield it: the alien Other appeared doomed from the outset.

Guided by the knowledge of the past and attracted by the vision of the
future, it has frequently been the case that SF authors, driven by a scientific preference for fact and provable data, have sought to substantiate a

narrative's ideals and tropes through historical analogy. Though the concept of empire and all things imperial may currently be considered impolitic, the apparent convenience of locating empire in SF renders it dangerous on the modern cultural plane, regardless of the enlightened intent of the author. To preach the gospel of technology, many SF authors opted for the simple re-creation of a cultural dark age, against which advanced technology might be best contrasted; Frank Herbert's *Dune* (1965) and Michael Crichton's *Timeline* (1999) are good examples of this. SF may have opened the door to the stars, but it also offered *entrée* to a great deal of historical baggage in the form of prejudice, religious bigotry and political fundamentalisms. Yet the vast movement of SF began for the simplest, almost innocent of reasons: the compulsion by science-oriented writers to be heard.

While it may seem unfair to invest SF with attributes of negative social propaganda, some clearly believe this to be the case. Gary Wolfe's opinions are quite candid. 'Science fiction', he says, 'which begins with a child-like sense of wonder at the Universe and its possibilities, often ends in an almost cynical sophistication about social change'.[11] Similarly, Darko Suvin observes that 'it is understandable that its major breakthroughs to the cultural surface should come about in the periods of sudden cultural convulsion'.[12] Roger Luckhurst goes even further, suggesting some ironic synchronicity between SF and the advent of radical and often disastrous political events:

> The historical coincidence of decolonization and the production of science fiction catastrophe texts in the 1950s is marked. The period between 1945 and 1951 saw the reduction of imperial subjects from 475 million to 70 million, and the 1950s continued with a series of violent and unceremonious colonial withdrawals from Palestine in 1948 to the repression and systematic killing in Kenya.[13]

A fine satirical comment on the political machinations within the post-war scientific community may be gleaned from the short-story anthology *New Arrivals, Old Encounters*. A polemic masquerading as a piece of fiction gives us:

> 'We're made, you realise that, made! Grab a few of the higher life forms, take them back to Earth. Imagine the sensation.'
> 'Could be some nasty things out there.'
> 'We can handle anything that goes. From now on in, we're in charge, baby.
> And remember, we came in peace.'[14]

Thus, the scientist entered the political forum as did so many of his characters: walking softly but carrying a large authorial stick. One such writer was Dr Isaac Asimov, a long-time professor of biochemistry at the Boston University School of Medicine. During the war years he spent most of his time working in the US Naval Air Experiment Station in Philadelphia beside L. Sprague de Camp and Robert A. Heinlein, with whom he would become long-term friends, and who with him formed part of the great inner circle of influential SF writers destined to set the stage for much of the genre's development. Though born in Russia, Asimov was raised in the United States from the age of three, where he discovered the fantasy of the future in the comics sold by his father at the family shop. Asimov's *entrée* into SF began with short stories, his first published short fiction being 'Marooned Off Vesta' (1939). His later career produced nearly 500 books on a broad variety of subjects, ranging from scientific to literary criticism and religious studies, including a fascinating range of 'robotic' stories – narratives about the future of artificial intelligence and the forma- tion of 'positronic' brains. His development of the 'Three Laws of Robotics' provided not only a self-referential base for his later novels but also a main- stay for younger writers in the genre. In a speech to the State University of New Jersey in 1980, Asimov speaks of robots, saying 'The time will come when we will think back on a world without computers and shiver over the loneliness of humanity in those days'.[15]

Heinlein was a wartime colleague of Asimov. After serving in the US Navy for five years, Heinlein studied physics at the University of California, Los Angeles, before he began to write SF, both short fiction and novels; his work is credited with having some of the profoundest effects on the genre. By the time Heinlein met up with Asimov he had already published thirty stories, beginning with 'Lifeline' (1939), as well as three novels. In establishing a series of novels surrounding the saga of the Howard Families, Heinlein came close to producing a future history of humanity, linking his disparate narratives into a single continuous theme, only to find Asimov had achieved exactly such a placement before him with his *Foundation* and *Robot* series. Rising to pre-eminence between 1940 and 1960, Heinlein's texts are noted for their outspoken libertarian stances on sexuality, politics and socio- economics, and these render his narratives forever things of provocation and dispute. Like Rudyard Kipling, Heinlein antagonises and enlightens in equal measure. Salman Rushdie's feelings on reading Kipling apply equally to Heinlein: it is often difficult to appreciate such skill when annoyance and admiration are mixed in equal measure.

Asimov was a vastly prolific writer, his interests covering a broad and eclec- tic span. He also possessed the enviable ability to translate the most technical thought into generally digestible terms. His Three Laws of Robotics lay out precisely what a future humanity might expect and anticipate these positronic marvels to do. However, Asimov was also a social scientist, comprehending and extrapolating the moods and fears of ordinary people in concert with his insightful anticipations. This ambition to reflect and empathise with mainstream society differentiates SF from a great deal of *avant-garde* literature, although it also runs the risk of reflecting negative as well as positive prejudices. In his writings, both fictional and non-fictional, Asimov always appeals to the human element, the reader. He makes his science comprehensible to the layperson, injects a familiarity into the unfamiliar and deliberately removes much of the estrangement of 'hard' SF. Since Asimov wanted his readers to admire and embrace robotic technology his works never strayed far from an understanding of the human perspective; therefore while his robots are always Other, they are a friendly, non-combative Other. His narratives seek not to detach humanity from its technological future but to provide a form of authoritative yet comfortable solace, where technology and science may have a softened pathway into homes and lives. Unlike Philip K. Dick's androids, Asimov's robots are forever chasing the human ideal, elements of metaphor seeking a metaphoric whole.

On a quite different slant, Heinlein was acutely dismissive of contemporary society; his textual challenges to the socio-cultural status quo of twentieth-century Western ideologies were loud and unashamed. He chose to ridicule bureaucracy in all its myriad forms, to take the establishment to task at every opportunity and to poke the sacred cows of postwar America with a variety of deliciously pointed sticks. Something of a cultural rebel, Heinlein seemed at times both a Luddite and an Einstein, capable of suggesting a return to the fundamentals of the land and the vital need to expand science into different dimensions within the same narrative. It is partly this dichotomy of desires that makes his writing contradictory as well as vital and exciting, since his characters, often maddeningly perverse, encapsulate the widest spectrum of the human condition in the most unexpected manner. Like Asimov, Heinlein also paid homage to the future of the robot/computer mind, by granting his computer characters the ability to transcend their mechanical genesis and attain a more perfected humanity.[16] Given that Heinlein displayed a distinctly American ethos, the fact that his narratives embrace a personal abhorrence of the imposition of governmentalised social justice is hardly unexpected.

Although each of Heinlein's works gallery a portion of his mindset, there are a few which paint a larger canvas of his thinking. *Stranger in a Strange Land* (1961) tells us of Valentine Smith's transformation into a messiah figure who is guided by the patriarchal voice of the ultimate surrogate father and mouthpiece for Heinlein himself. This text speaks of a painless process of physical discorporation, where all needs of the body are removed to a higher plane, a process that might be easily imposed upon others. Likewise, his notion of the paterfamilias as central and iconic is discussed endlessly in such texts as *Time Enough for Love* (1973) and *The Number of the Beast* (1980). Before the publication of these works came a novel which dealt with many historical parallels, as well as clarifying his views as right-wing anarchism rather than those of fascism or social Darwinism. *The Moon Is a Harsh Mistress* (1966) is possibly one of Heinlein's greatest later works, embodying almost all of his essential paradigms, yet which still offers the reader faint echoes of a positive and hopeful utopian future.

The Moon Is a Harsh Mistress deals a revolution of the periphery against the centre, between Moon colonists and the overweening imperialism of the mother planet. The strongest parallel to events and thinking in the novel is with the American War of Independence (1775–83), where Heinlein's metaphorical colonist backwoodsmen take on the might of empire. Instead of fighting the British redcoats, Heinlein's unprepared 'Loonies' tackle the mighty injustices of Earth's remote but overwhelming central authority. The characters in this text, like Heinlein himself, are idiosyncratic and iconoclastic. Mike, the computer, through its growing complexity, awakens to the consciousness of a child and is representative of Heinlein's perception and desire for scientific achievement.[17] Wyoming Knott, an intelligent and beautiful woman, while never quite reduced to domesticity, is secretly filled with Heinleinic impulses for tradition, convention and babies. Professor Bernardo de la Paz is a logical political activist for rational anarchy and the voice of calculated obstructionism. Finally, there is Manuel Garcia O'Kelly, computer technician, partial cyborg, omniscient narrator and mouthpiece for Heinlein's humorous cynicism. These four main characters control the unfolding of the novel, first setting out the problem at hand and then devising the manner of its appropriate criticism and removal. As with many of Heinlein's characters, these four contribute to utopian ideals in the same manner as More's Hythloday and Albertino from Bruno's *De l'Infinito universo e mondi*. This powerful similarity reminds us that Heinlein, no matter his economic rationality or political satire, is writing in the tradition of speculative fiction that began with the renaissance utopianists. Like Hythloday and Albertino, Manny, Wyoh, Mike and the Prof are representatively rational, schematic and not given to casual fantasy, and yet all are able to construe a 'better' place. And just as the renaissance characters are seen to be expressing the cultural mores and ideals of their time, so too do Heinlein's actors, although in this novel the ideologies are emphatically American. Interestingly, an earlier novella, *The Man Who Sold the Moon* (1950), depicts the entrepreneurial activities of one D. D. Harriman, who, desperate to reach the Moon himself, does much to facilitate the space ambitions of the rest of the human race.

From the beginning of *The Moon Is a Harsh Mistress*, it is clear that Earth's authority, imposed upon the Moon and its inhabitants, is both unjust and unsupportable. The characters of the periphery are forced into the position of rebellion by the impossible demands of the centre. And just as history portrays the early American colonists as unwilling revolutionaries against the British, so too does Heinlein's novel initially depict the beguiling though unrealistic safety of dependence on the whims of empire. The lunar farmers are as much slaves to the mercantilism of the colony as ever were their North American predecessors; they are reluctant to endanger their current trading conditions, even though such conditions are unfair and will eventually become unendurable. Commerce and industry on the Moon cannot be self-supporting owing to heavy taxes and shipment quotas, yet the manufacturers and primary producers are fearful of retribution in an environment where life is cheap (some deaths, according to Heinlein's rationalistic and slightly callous view, are already inconsequential). Therefore, from the outset, the power struggle of rebellion is necessarily covert and discreet. Through Mike's technical endowment it is simple to redirect funds from the central Lunar Authority into the hands of the revolution. Subversive cell systems are set up; that these rely more upon friendship and familial loyalties than on any great political principles again illustrates Heinlein's fundamental belief in the centrality of family and blood ties. That these loyalties are expressed through entirely Westernised or Eurocentric family forms, even if subversive interpretations of these forms, is a matter of the author's own cultural influences. Even while preaching revolution against conventional power and social structures, Heinlein is unable to discard personal conditioning and clings to a mass of accepted historical precepts. He clearly sees 'family' as possessing certain limitations, of size and content, even within his 'line marriages'. Heinlein grants male superiority in terms of organisational skills, rationality and detachment over either female or even computer attributes; the illusions of personal freedom and the acceptability of violence in defence of the nuclear family are suggested, even while Heinlein simultaneously urges a disbandment of that nuclearity. Furthermore, though he interprets family as an essentially patriarchal structure, his women seem to be the most practical at enacting and enforcing that structure. It is almost as if there is a conflict in him between the intellectual desire for male leadership and the realistic comprehension that it is only through a woman's agreement and cooperation that such leadership may be instituted.

Heinlein's text is also interesting because he makes his argument for revolution using broad ideals and a big-brush technique, which once again reflects the wider form of speculative fiction working within the narrower SF tradition. Other than the four main protagonists, we are given few intimate details of the supporting characters, as if the power and momentum generated by these four are sufficient to carry the narrative, with need for little more than minor characters who collectively take the role of a Greek chorus. Heinlein's writing is so powerful that he sees no need for fine print and it allows his passion and convictions to propel the narrative through these four main characters. His essential protagonists represent not only aspects of Heinlein himself but also aspects of the scientific, social, political and cultural drives which so often illustrate the schism between periphery and centre. Mike, the computer, has the innocence of an uncorrupted child-hood, and looks at his existence with an untainted vision, but also has the power to create his future in the way it (according to Heinlein) should be. Mike is the stuff of Man before the Fall, who cleverly avoids falling by redesigning the nature of Eden through technology and new power. Manuel plays the social commentator, whose omniscient narration foregrounds the idiosyncrasies lurking within each of the main characters' attitudes. 'We were as non-political a people as history ever produced. I know, I was as numb to politics as any until circumstances pitched me into it,' he says.[18] It is Manuel who provides the most human of faces, the joker and clown, when he toys with technology, and mocks it mildly through satirical and ironic discussions of his replacement arm, of which he has a number of intriguing versions. Wyoming is problematic, in that, on the one hand, Heinlein creates her as the archetypal pioneering woman, strong of body and mind, fearless, intelligent and resourceful, but, on the other, her charac-ter, as with most of the other female characters in the novel, is also defined by her desire for the more conventional role of wife and mother. It is as if all of Wyoming's assets are there merely to prepare her for future motherhood, just as the post-revolutionary culture of the Moon colony depends upon its earlier political and survivalist grooming in order to meet its full potential as a new society. Wyoming represents Heinlein's image of a keystone within the fundamental family, the strength upon which great cultures are based. Professor de la Paz provides the narrative's historical and social context, as his quiet and restrained observance of protocols and due process become the political guide of Heinlein's neo-history. The Professor is the voice of the ultimate victor, who will be heard long after the revolution has ended and been forgotten, even, in fact, after he dies in the narrative. And just as his character reiterates an earlier declaration of independence, Heinlein's novel seems to reiterate the need for an end to externally imposed imperialism.

Unlike Ayn Rand's calculatedly objectivist stance, urging individuals to realise the super-human potential inside themselves, Heinlein's slightly more gentle existential libertarian approach argues that some are born to lead and some to follow, and that the difference in abilities is an important one to recognise. Intriguingly, while his text places enormous responsibility on the shoulders of individuals to take charge and be held accountable for their life and obligations, Heinlein is simultaneously critical of a 'ruling elite', which is a contradiction. Yet he maintains that there are specific placements for individuals that need to be observed, hence his clear but often debatable demarcations between the active roles of his main characters. Only the Professor, it seems, is able to plot and design the revolution, despite the fact that there is a quorum of four. Only Mike is able to carry out the technological magic that provides for the dissolution of the old central control[19] and only Manuel is able to offer the idiosyncratic musings of humanity. Yet, despite Heinlein's fascinating reprise of an earlier revolution, his novel does not actually object to centralisation, but in fact argues for a different version of the same form. Rather than be beholding and dependent upon the centrality of Earth, the Loonies are provided with an opportunity to recreate a new centre on-site, to renew the structure of imperialism under the guise of an independent authority.

Though Heinlein's words decry the power of control by one state over another, he does not renounce the concept of control altogether, but calls for an economic, libertarian stance, as opposed to a conventional imperialism. This illustrates a central issue of empire in SF: that no matter how revolutionary the thinking, and no matter how *avant-garde* or incredible the scenario, the desire for freedom and an ability to break away from the imposed control of others never really changes. Yet in order to embrace this freedom, SF writers have necessarily been required to maintain the atmosphere of imperialism in order to have something against which to revolt. Through the very act of rebellion against the old centre, the author has maintained the ideology of the centre, although there are two distinct reasons for doing this. Without a rationale for the lunar revolt, Heinlein would have no story; therefore the Authority's 'centre' provides something to fight – the resultant conflict presenting the author with all the narrative opportunities he could desire. But the secondary reason for a centre is that in any centralised society there is a need for some form of government, a fact recognised even by Heinlein. What we find in the novel is no real criticism of a central control but rather a consistent declaration of the need to be the one *in* control. SF does not criticise power *per se*, but continues to experiment with it in order that there will always be some justifiable or socially acceptable motivation for fictions of expansionism and colonialism. The shadow of power abuse in SF (of which imperialism is one form) is there to throw the act of cultural enlightenment into greater relief.

The abuse of the periphery by the imperial centre has become a crucial pivot, about which SF authors revolve an entire catalogue of experimentations: Heinlein and Robinson use it to justify conflict; Herbert uses it to illustrate economic politics; Clarke uses it as motivation for diaspora and colonisation; and Asimov uses it to highlight futuristic technology. In each instance, the centre of some form of empire is a vital component of the narrative. Following Asimov's and Heinlein's dealings with empire, countless other SF writers have used the premise of an imperium gone bad in order to investigate the human desire for exploration and settlement, even if that exploration takes them to an already occupied planet, an action epitomised by such works as Robert Silverberg's *Invaders from Earth* (1958) and Ray Bradbury's *The Martian Chronicles* (1950). Regardless of how much the fact of empire may be disparaged, it has been the linchpin of many great SF novels. Thus Heinlein is not arguing against the power of empire itself but rather (in this case) for the form – economic versus political – he prefers. Control through an imperial centre, he suggests, is not intrinsically bad unless it is someone else's centre with the power, the problem being in the manipulation, domination and abuse of the periphery by that centre. Heinlein, unwittingly inexact to his own libertarian premises, is not removing a controlling structure at all but replacing it with a different version: exchanging the old, remote, political centre for a new, local, economic one. While the new form of power may not display the outward trappings of imperialism, there is a sense that some basic precepts remain.[20]

Heinlein's use of historical reprise is characteristic of many modern SF narratives. Since the author of SF often deals with a limited number of events (typically war, peace, development, exploration, disaster, invasion and diaspora), as well as the variable to each of these induced by particularities of the human condition (such as love, hate, death, revenge), it is virtually impossible for any narrative to avoid some form of prior intertextual referencing. Heinlein's narrative is no different, as it follows in the footsteps of works such as 'The Birth of a New Republic' (1931), by Miles J. Breuer and Jack Williamson. Moreover, it is this constant recycling of empire and things imperial which provides and illustrates a problematic issue within contemporary SF. In order to create new worlds and new civilisations it is necessary for the writer of SF to invoke the political concept of imperialism (i.e. centre and periphery). New freedoms may not be contrived unless there is an older, less free environment against which to rebel, and yet, and most ironically, it is in this very act of neo-rebellion that SF writers refresh the concept of empire against which they have their characters struggle. Paradoxically, that which we most need (the freedom to explore and colonise: to create a new periphery) generates that which we most criticise (an expanding periphery creates an increasingly remote centre: the centre is necessary to support the periphery). For the utopianists of SF there is no end in sight of human expansion, of the exploration and settlement of new planets. Exploration and settlement must persist if writers are to continue their literary experiments in the human condition. Without the ability to embrace the inherent structure of empire, SF would be limited to the purely scientific, and a dull, non-applicable form of science it would be where great new technologies are unable to be tested. What use are fantastic spaceships if there is no place to go? Why develop the ability to harness new powers and transform inhospitable landscapes if such powers and landscapes are forbidden? The conquest of the unknown in SF is both an ideology and a positive instinct: we might not always agree with it, but we have a need to follow it.

Thus SF has become the grand narrative of the child eternally leaving home, its texts continuously railing against the control of the mother planet as the archetypal centre, the very thing that gives them life. Off-Earth settlement is the new metaphor for the human struggle to grow and for the compelling urge to develop new centres on the periphery as humanity moves further and further away from primeval waters. SF narratives of control and revolt are not simple political things but Oedipal offspring, eventually responsible for reproducing another generation of stories where the periphery confronts the centre.

Heinlein's narrative does not argue a truly anti-imperial stance, even though this is the initial interpretation of the text. What it does create is a revamped plan for the disengagement of the peripheral, dependent colony from the control of the centre, but only so that it might set up its own central authority, in effect setting up a new base from which to spread a newer periphery. The rebellion, so carefully documented by Heinlein through his main characters, is less a manifesto of anti-imperialism than it is an agreement to continue, with parochial adaptations, the historical structures of imposed control. His narrative does not renounce the wielding of power, only the form in which that power is applied. The fact that the lunar rebellion has the support of the majority of the Moon's inhabitants does not render such a rebellion less conducive to the centre–periphery model of empire. Wearily observing this endless repetition of repression and rebellion, Manuel notes that there 'must be a yearning deep in the human heart to stop other people from doing as they please'. He continues:

> Rules, laws – always for *other* fellow. A murky part of us, something we had before we came down out of trees, and failed to shuck when we stood up. Because *not one* of those people said: 'Please pass this so that I won't be able to do something I know I should stop.' Nyet, tovarisschee, was *always* something they hated to see neighbours doing.[21]

Heinlein is attempting to achieve a number of objectives with this text. On a personal level he uses it as a soapbox from which he can aim an oblique criticism not only at US postwar scientific policies (an indictment of political interference and poor economic strategies) but also at those of any similarly directed Western power. Further, he offers commentary on the social ineptitudes of contemporary cultures that are too self-limiting to concede the value of a more libertarian perspective. Through Mike's omnipotence, he illustrates not only some of the potentials of technology but also, more importantly, what happens when that technology lies in the hands of those who do not properly understand its significance. Heinlein chose to re-enact a historical scenario simply because it was the most convenient vehicle from which to convey his ultimate distrust of powerful bureaucracies and remote government centralities. As well as recreating the struggle for independence between America and Britain, Heinlein touches upon but does not dismiss the human desire for control itself. Though the narrative may be read as a strong declaration for the removal of imperialism, it can be more properly examined as a testament to the author's own desire for freedom from the limitations of contemporary governmental encroachment into the realm of the individual. Because of this, the novel is not an authentic experiment in the unmaking of imperialism but more of a cleverly couched personal quest for an unfettered existence. But where Heinlein's lunar revolt is an experimental version of historical empire exoticised by the mysteries of science, Asimov achieves an entirely different effect, by exoticising both his characters and the future they inhabit.

Of the extensive archive of Asimov's published works, two early texts stand out as being both seminal, that is, providing the basis for future development, and unique for their time, *The Caves of Steel* (1954) and *The Naked Sun* (1957). Forming the 1950s link in his extended *Robot* series (1940–85), these two narratives present the reader with a future Earth where the overcrowded inhabitants of the planet have descended underground, living in vast, steel-encased cities in a permanently artificial environment. Earlier migrants, who escaped from the hyper-Malthusian Earth, have developed into a hubristic race known as 'Spacers', who live amazingly extended technological lives beneath their own 'naked suns'. The conflict between these two radically opposing lifestyles provided Asimov with an enormously productive setting, enabling him to explore and experiment with variations of imperialism in two quite separate human states.

In the earlier novel we are introduced to the characters central to both narratives, Elijah Baley and R. Daneel Olivaw. 'Lije' Baley is a straightforward Earth detective, living in the massive subterranean enclave of Greater New York. He is partnered, initially as an act of political sabotage, with the Spacer Daneel Olivaw. Olivaw is a robot, hence the 'R' prefixing his name. However, neither of these characters is quite what we expect them to be from a superficial evaluation. Baley is not a prosaic police officer, in that his detection talents are real and effective, and Olivaw never falls conveniently into any of the comfortable or predictable robotic stereotypes. Baley is less bound by stifling convention than many humans of his generation, while Olivaw appears at times more compassionate than the humans he was designed to protect and serve. That Asimov keeps the setting for both novels inside a comprehensible although significantly future landscape is deliberate, just as are the choice and placement of the two main characters. It was not the author's intent to shock the reader with either maddeningly bizarre locations or characters with whom it might be problematic to identify. Instead, Asimov carefully selected an advanced Earth that might be sufficiently unusual to form part of the unknown, just as Olivaw is partnered with a normal human in order to make his robotic genesis and behaviour less startling, or, at least, more easily observed in contrast to Baley's.

Thus the infrastructure set up by Asimov in the first narrative not only informs the subsequent text but also acts as a link between the society of the reader and the society of the characters. It was important for these novels to be exotic but less than alien in their predominant aspects because Asimov was more intent upon dissecting and analysing relationships of far greater subtlety. To place the narrative in too profoundly different a future or with characters too far removed from the accepted human norms of the time would have been to focus too much interest on place and individual. Asimov wanted the reader to identify easily with both place and characters so that he might better locate the main drive of the narratives as being of social historical importance. Earth is still recognisably Earth, but the use and abuse of the planet have followed Malthus's predictions of a precarious, barely operable stability. The slightest imbalance would mean catastrophe and ruination for millions. Although he is far from conventional, Lije Baley is the epitome of stability, until he, too, is unbalanced by the introduction of an unknown quantity in his life – the constant presence of a Spacer robot. In turn, Asimov removes almost all things from Olivaw that render him conventionally robotic. The embodiment of a handsome human male, Olivaw acts at all times in a socially acceptable fashion; he is articulate, well mannered and is capable of reasoning as complex as a human's. Only a highly qualified and experienced roboticist might identify Olivaw as other than human, and even this identification is not immediate or instinctive. The reader readily accepts Olivaw as both familiar *and* part of the unknown, integrating this knowledge throughout both narratives. With this technique, Asimov has achieved the orientalist's desire for mystery and familiarity simply by changing the status of a major character. He also raises questions that make us reflect on the endowment of character upon the not-human. If Olivaw is heroic, does this mean that all robots might be heroic? If he suffers upon witnessing a human's pain, are robots really the unfeeling machines of conventional stereotype? There are just enough questions about the text's depiction of Olivaw to make him appropriately exotic and 'different'.

Significantly, Asimov invokes a form of doubly inverted alienation with the robot, in that, on the one hand, Olivaw is capable of great strength and purpose but, on the other, is capable of being instantly diverted from that purpose at a single command from his 'masters'. That he is vastly intelligent and able to reason for himself is not questioned, and yet he must submit to the less articulated desires of his flawed, human programmers. Asimov's involvement with robots speaks to the reader of a form of *acceptable* enslavement, this time not of people but of a *thing*. Interestingly, this is the diametric opposite of a shockingly revealing work of short fiction by Harry Bates, 'Farewell to the Master' (1940, filmed as *The Day the Earth Stood Still*, 1951), where the central role of the robot is not in the least subservient. Commenting upon the reversal of the roles in the Bates text, Andrew Feenberg observes a distinct social estrangement:

> As the robot prepares to leave, Cliff asks him to 'tell your master' that humanity regrets his rude reception. 'You misunderstand', the mighty robot said. 'I am the master.' And with these words, the space-time traveller departs, leaving Cliff in awe and bewilderment at what is evidently the future fate of humanity in a world ruled by robots.[22]

Though Asimov's robots are friendly and apparently well adjusted creations, the insidious principle of subservience is invoked by the way in which the submission of a machine, of the technological Other, is deemed perfectly normal. As the Spacers behave towards Earthers, humanity behaves towards the robots: far too superior to consider that any form of thinking, reasoning and feeling being is in any way their equal. And once that concept is accepted, the future subservience of Others becomes simply a matter of degree. Asimov might like to think his robots are the equal of humankind, but his consistent placement of Olivaw in situations where control is removed far from the robot's grasp suggests either that the author was unaware of the depth of his own inculcated desire for cultural superiority[23] or that he was simply unable to find narrative means of accommodating such an equality.

In *The Caves of Steel*, a murder has been committed. Asimov was exceptionally fond of the detective story format, often analogising it to the pursuit of science. By invoking this genre within a genre, the author was able to ask the most direct of questions, by placing readers in a situation where they must not only assess all the clues but also reassess the paradigm through which the evaluation was drawn. Like Heinlein, Asimov sets the narrative against a general backdrop of social unrest and a fear of worse things to come. Though he has no overt revolution taking place, Asimov draws attention to his main topic – the cultural fear of science and progress – by gently hinting at the underlying trend towards poorer living conditions and the collective anxieties of a race of people doomed – just as are the robots – through their own lack of exploratory initiative. The novel reveals, through various mechanisms of police interviews and dialogue, that each

protagonist harbours some fear of scientific development, even displacement, enabling the reader to see that Asimov's true goal is pluralistic. In a
design both to ennoble the potentials of technology (through the settlement
of new planets) and to criticise his own culture for its short-sightedness
and timidity, the author creates an allegorical 'straw man'. Yet in doing this,
Asimov also fosters a tacit neo-imperialism, the subtleties of which are so
embedded in the plot that it is not until the end of the narrative, when
Baley, the staunchest and most upright of humans, throws his ideological
weight behind an exodus to the stars, that it becomes visible.

Olivaw plays an intriguing role in both novels. Asimov cleverly places
him in an indefinable limbo, where the robot refuses to be designated as
any one particular archetype: he is heroic but lacks heroism; he is gentle
and nurturing, but only because not to be so might damage his delicate
positronic circuits; the robot is a fine picture of a healthy male, yet he
does not need to eat or sleep, or require any of the basic amenities we currently associate with civilised living. Asimov has rendered Olivaw effectively
bodiless, removing from him all those aspects of humanity that make us
the susceptible creatures we are. The robot is honest, but only as far as
he has been programmed to be honest by his designer, the Spacer Dr Roj
Sarton, who is also – and not incidentally – the murder victim. Asimov
uses the flow of crime detection to reveal not only the hidden fears and
dissimilarities between Baley and his fellow Earthers but also the equally
hidden motives and similarities between Baley and the Spacers. Baley is the
true hero. Deeply concerned over the welfare of his wife and young son,
still saddened by the tragic demise of his disgraced father, he nevertheless
continues the heroic tradition of placing the needs of others above his own.
It is precisely because Baley is himself flawed by ambition and materialistic
desires that his heroism resounds all the more convincingly in the narrative. To be created perfect – like Olivaw – is to have nothing to overcome,
no demons to fight, and thus Baley rises to his appropriate heroic stature
simply because he is imperfect. This gradual revelation of genuine heroism
also forms part of Asimov's design in the text. If we align ourselves with the
petty weaknesses and desirable strengths of the hero, how are we then able
to pull back from acknowledging the logic and sense of Baley's new-found
ambition? Lije Baley is a born-again colonialist and the reader cannot help
but admire that aspect of the character, since it is so essentially ingrained
in every move he makes.

It is also worth noting that Baley's advocacy of colonialism is partly
offered as an achievement for the Earther. For so long have the inhabitants
of Earth been conditioned into a belief not only that the Spacers are vastly
superior to them in every measurable way (intelligence, health, wealth, etc.)
but also that it is only the Spacers who are capable or even fit to explore the

reaches of space. Baley's movement towards a new programme of settlement and general expansionism overcomes his prejudice about the superior
Spacer and robots as well as his fear of exploring the 'outside'. By linking
Baley's triumph to the achievement of these lesser objectives, Asimov is also
urging the reader to become more open to the idea that other, unmentioned
prejudices (such as racism and aversion to social change) may also be overcome. However, since an encouragement to grasp the colonialist perspective
also carries with it the darker shadows of neo-imperialism, Asimov is caught
in an interesting ideological complexity.

The Caves of Steel is powerful because of its very lack of overt seductive-
ness. It does not tempt the reader with Heinlein's exoticised Moon, or with
the carefully sculpted mysteries of foreign landscapes. Nor does it seek to
fascinate with spectacular, gaudy technology or the repellently monstrous
and invading Other. It is more a narrative about how and why people
change, and about why the fear of containment may be resolved only
through embracing the inherent exploratory drive in all of us. Moreover,
because the novel is so quietly persuasive, it is doubly dangerous from a
postcolonial perspective, in that it does not present the desire for cultural
increase and new settlement as anything but right and proper. It does not
urge the reader to examine more closely the ramifications and consequences
of colonialism, nor does it suggest anything less than worthy in its motivations. While the Earth struggles to sustain its countless millions of relatively
low-tech humanity, the Spacers are held up as examples of the purity of
scientific advancement and of what humanity might achieve. Gaining by
their willingness to embrace technology and space exploration, the Spacers
have completed a rite of passage, something the planet-bound Earthers
have not yet attempted. The implication here is those with a healthy desire
to expand and take what is theirs by right of discovery do not necessarily
have to share their good fortune with those who do not take up the same
challenge. The elitism of the Spacers strikes directly against the proclaimed
maxim of America, best encapsulated by the inscription on the Statue of
Liberty: 'Give me your tired, your poor/Your huddled masses yearning to
breathe free/The wretched refuse of your teeming shore'. Asimov makes an
authoritative point by making no overtly authoritative statement.

If Baley is the unassuming hero who sees the delinquencies of his own
culture through the alienated eyes of a new companion, then Olivaw is the
intentionally silenced voice of the colonised Other in an expansionist human
future. Asimov has taken the paradigm of the subordinate Other and built
an immoral subservience into a helpless creature of the future, to produce
this insidiously admirable form of a moral robot. Additionally, Olivaw's very
subservience poses a threat, in that he represents not only the repressed
Other but also a *machine*. His lack of faults makes him the perfect worker,

tireless, strong, very moral, but also quite capable of replacing a human. Thus Olivaw is as much a contradiction as is his creator's thinking: free but not free; moral and immoral; both an aid and a threat to the humans he is designed to serve. With an authorially unseen yet exquisite irony, the novel ends on a comment from the police officer. 'The colonization of space is the only possible salvation of Earth', Baley announces calmly to his commander. 'You'll realise that if you can think about it without prejudice.'[24]

It is partly because of Asimov's subtlety of expression, of scientific authority and *gravitas* that he is one of the American leaders of early modern SF. His robotic laws and positronic marvels have taken their place in the foundations of the genre. And it is his gentle introduction to science and SF that makes it so attractive. There is no immediate affront to the senses, nothing too hideous to willingly consider. As Wolfe notes:

> In science fiction, it is less important to conquer the villain than to conquer the unknown, and the importance of this conquest is what the ideological structure of many science fiction narratives teaches. The unknown is an overwhelming presence in science fiction, and it is the transformation of the unknown into the known that accounts for its conventions and formulae.[25]

Much of early modern SF borrowed greatly from the techniques of nineteenth-century realism, in that it required believable characters whose lives reflected real historical states and who represented a human involvement in events of history. Yet SF has a distinct problem, in that it also endeavours to portray events that have not yet occurred and therefore seeks to present its various scenarios against a human base that is, at best, projective. Asimov's solution to this problem is to adopt a certain form of exoticised foregrounding of technology. In *The Caves of Steel* he posits a mundane Earth, with the average and the commonplace taking a greater role than the rare and the unusual. His characters are usually of middle or working class and endure the normal experiences of childhood, marriage, parenthood and death. The predictable ordinariness of their lives is interwoven with staggeringly extraordinary details, such as the pedestrianised 'strips' that everyone takes as a matter of course, or the fact that nobody on Earth willingly visits the planet surface. It is this oscillation between the expected and the unexpected that prepares the reader for the opening of doors such as Baley's new-found desire to migrate. The reader not only begins to expect innovations but waits for them, anticipating the next revelation on the next page. Then R. Daneel Olivaw, an entrancing *object* of science and technology, is dramatically foregrounded, producing what Feenberg describes as 'an example of what might be called the "technological exoticism" of science fiction by which it focuses the attention of the reader on objects instead of character'.[26] This reversal of conventional foregrounding–backgrounding is another way in which Asimov shifts what might otherwise be considered mundane into stark prominence and vice versa, an even more intriguing situation when we consider that Olivaw is in many ways the most 'human' character in the narrative. Such a technique also pushes the underlying theme of the narrative, that of a neo-colonialism, into a supporting rather than a confrontational role, making it less threatening, less of a flag to the alarmists. Thus the desire for expansion mingles with the continuous juxtaposition of ordinary and extraordinary, eventually forming the thrust of the primary objective while remaining seductively in the shadows of the text.

In the second of Asimov's Baley/Olivaw novels, *The Naked Sun* (1957), the two protagonists are once more paired in a murder investigation. However, where the first narrative was set in the dark and crowded spaces of an overpopulated Earth, the second one is located on the planet Solaria, where the level of population is rigorously maintained at 20,000 humans. There is a deliberate and massive difference between the two novels in almost every respect. In the first there are literally millions of human spectators, while in the second there are, equally literally, none. In the former there is a dislike and deep mistrust of robots, while the latter contrasts by describing a society that could not possibly survive without vast numbers of them. In the one narrative there is the sense that only Earth offers humanity an authentic model, yet in the other we are shown its binary opposite, where Earth's isolationism is seen as misguided and providing little more than a deformed and regressive mutation of what humanity might be. The second novel, set in the empty landscapes of the garden planet of Solaria, is actually the forum for a continuation of Baley's earlier thoughts on expansion.

This second narrative provides the reader with a realistic representation of what might happen should the masses of Earth take it upon themselves to continue a human diaspora to the stars. It is a pleasantly non-confrontational scenario where, again, through the devices of a typical detective theme, various aspects of the Spacer planet are gradually revealed. In Baley's alienated vision, the distant world of Solaria compares favourably in almost every way to his seething Earth and his initial inability to tolerate the open spaces indicates Asimov's own concern that the humanity he knows is already coming to accept a lesser life than they should. That Baley eventually conquers his agoraphobia is Asimov's way of advising the reader that we are capable of overcoming anything when we follow our natural desires. In this instance, the natural desire is to leave the mother planet and to strike out for new and untouched habitats.

Just as in his earlier work, Asimov's message is subtle and more persuasive through imagery than through direct political exhortation. If he chose simply to tell his readers that colonisation was a 'good thing', the result would not be a rally-call to the wonders of the technology that might assist such an endeavour. But by incorporating a certain degree of subliminal temptation, and by adding the very specific overlay of glamorous exoticism, the author seems to be urging a consideration of these things by his anticipated readership: the educated, technologically oriented male. Thus Asimov achieves a twofold objective: to critique the contemporary political status quo through an illustration of what might be in a less conservative social and scientific environment; and to laud the potential results of returning to that most natural of human states, exploration. As Baley returns to Earth having successfully solved this latest puzzle, he considers his life now:

> He had told Minnim the Cities were wombs, and so they were. What was the first thing a man must do before he can be a man? He must be born. He must leave the womb; and once left, it could not be re-entered.
>
> Baley had left the City and could not re-enter. The City was no longer his; the Caves of Steel were alien. This *had* to be; and it would be so for others and Earth would be born again and reach outwards.
>
> He remembered his dream on Solaria and he understood it at last. He lifted his head and he could see through all the steel and concrete and humanity above him. He could see the beacon set in space to lure men outwards.[27]

That both Asimov and Heinlein were such powerful writers in their own unique fashions set the scene for many SF texts that followed. The idea of colonising other star systems, though often confounded by later astronomical acknowledgement of the sheer distance of the further stars, nevertheless remains an enticing and compelling one. The narratives subsequent to the works of these two American greats echo and reinvigorate the inherent desire for outward movement, which appears to be a deep impetus within humanity. Not even the cautionary tales of such writers as Robert Silverberg or Ursula Le Guin, containing some of the harshest criticism of expansionary human behaviours, would quench the drive initiated by the creators of the robotic Olivaw or the exoticised Moon. Likewise, the recurrent themes of colonisation and of eventual rebellion against the mother planet seem destined to perpetual repetition, since the mythology of the pioneering spirit is still so much celebrated at so many levels. Such celebration is indeed the beacon set in space to lure humankind outwards.

It is at this point we turn to the examination of a classic work of SF by Walter M. Miller which provides both a movement away from the imperialist golden age behind us and an anticipation of perhaps more genuinely postcolonial texts which lie ahead. Miller's narrative experiment engages not only with the issues of cultural determinism but also with a peculiar circularity of events which incorporate the increasingly dystopian mood of SF in the latter half of the twentieth century. This politically critical text also opens the door to a further extrapolation of science and heralds the way for the often bitterly realistic works of such authors as Joe Haldeman and Kim Stanley Robinson.

7. The Shape of Things to Come: *Homo futuris* and the Imperial Project

Where is empire in SF going? Is it, as Neil Easterbrook suggests, likely to continue its 'dedication to the serious exploration of political models'[1] or is it content to iterate the imperial cycle? Is SF taking inspiration from real scientific development or will it evolve more into the realm of fantasy and fable, further softening hard realities into mythical heroisms and broadening the territory of the genre? Will it continue to reflect and articulate contemporary social concerns in an estranged landscape or is SF to become a popularist parody of itself, as has its cinematic sibling? Since the term 'science fiction' came into general use in the 1930s, the tropes of the alien Other, of exploration, contact and settlement, of conflict and of human supremacy over marginalised indigenous species have fuelled the genre, but is the fire burning low? Will the transmutation of cyclical history into fictional scenarios maintain its fascination, or is SF already becoming blasé and predictable?

In fact, recent SF texts suggest that the genre is indeed able to maintain its fascination. Examples would include Alastair Reynolds' *Redemption Ark* (2002),[2] Richard Morgan's *Altered Carbon* (2002),[3] M. John Harrison's *Light* (2002),[4] Ken MacLeod's *Engine City* (2002),[5] Elizabeth Moon's *Speed of Dark* (2002),[6] Allen Steele's *Coyote: A Novel of Interstellar Exploration* (2002),[7] David Weber's *War of Honor* (2003)[8] and Charles Ingrid's *The Marked Man Omnibus* (2002).[9] These novels share themes of humankind's continued expansion, in both an external form (conquering new planets or rebelling against an existing hegemony) and an internal one (examining those things which make us human). Though they may share ground with many earlier works, the advent of modern scientific discoveries – the mapping of the human genome, for instance – allows the authors to speculate on a number of fascinating complexities unimaginable even ten years ago. It appears that many contemporary authors, such as Ken MacLeod and even Neil Gaiman, are already aware of and writing about those issues directly or indirectly bordering postcolonial criticism, possibly even to the point where fiction and academic writings begin to converge.

After Mary Shelley's monstrous Other, Isaac Asimov's galactic power blocs and Ursula Le Guin's dystopias, what is there left to ignite the heat and passion of this most original genre? The answer lies in SF's unseverable association with the production of science, and the certainty that there is always another conjunction between the past and the future waiting just around the corner. Just as new scientific discovery is based upon existing knowledge, so too will SF continue to explore the social aspects of developing human history as it is affected by each step the scientists take. And it is this sense of historical, social and political connectivity that will propel SF into its own future and, eventually, a postcolonial one. Because much of human history is implicitly linked with the machinations of political power brokers, it is certain that where go science and SF, there must also go the exploration of the use of power and the organisms which display that use. What does seem to be happening in many of the most recent publications is a change in the form of power control, as the narrative moves away from the traditional shape of empire into something much more flexible. The empire of the future is metamorphosing from a concrete, geographical and tangible entity into that of an adaptive organic body, where *knowledge* becomes the power behind the control. We cannot halt the advance of science as it enhances the power of humankind to control both existing and new environments, nor can we stop the translation of this advance into the fictional field. All that remains to be seen is precisely how the acquisition and display of such power will be extrapolated in our fictions. The maturation of SF may indeed be likened to a *Bildungsroman* of human evolution, where it shows us not simply the development of a single character but also the potential social maturation on a grand scale of an entire species.

If we consider how the genre of SF has, in the short period of its modern existence, incorporated much of the known or semi-known history of humanity, it becomes fascinating to speculate on which portion of our background it might next focus. Will the myths of early America's 'Wild West' ever cease to be an animating force behind stories recounting the exploration of the universe and the rigours of colonisation? Will we discover other philosophers like Arnold J. Toynbee or Oswald Spengler, whose thoughts of the deterministic nature of existence sparked such great mid-twentieth-century sagas as James Blish's *Cities in Flight* series or A. E. Van Vogt's *The Voyage of the Space Beagle* (1950) or even Frank Herbert's *Dune* series? Asimov plundered and transmuted Edward Gibbon's *The History of the Decline and Fall of the Roman Empire* (1776–88) into one that is more galactic and recent authors such as Kim Stanley Robinson and Walter Jon Williams have exploited the advent of the atomic era in texts that 'replay' a specific period of known human history. Though this is a complex issue – most SF writers have to draw on some past pattern of events in order to project a future history – it probably does not matter hugely to the reader where the SF writer finds inspiration. What seems clear is that no matter how fabulous the imagination, and regardless of readers' skill at suspending their disbelief, there remains a mutual desire for a recognisable point of departure, some moment, some threshold of connection upon which the new narrative is built. Darko Suvin argues that neither readers nor writers can be divorced from their own time and that some overriding historical sensibility will always make the text bear critical reference to *its* own time. According to his theory, SF cannot escape the past or the present; Suvin borrows the term 'novum' from Bertolt Brecht but reframes it as 'a totalizing phenomenon or relationship deviating from the author's and implied reader's norm of reality … a novelty entailing a change of the whole universe of the tale or at least the crucially important aspects thereof'.[10]

Many critics agree that intertextuality, the literary link between the reader's existing knowledge and a narrative's hypothesis, is as crucial to the development of SF as earlier scientific experimentation is to technological development. Moreover, no matter how futuristic, metaphysical or culturally unconventional today's SF may be, it is still written for today's readers, and not for some future, metaphysical *avant-garde*. Even at the opening of the twenty-first century there remains an unspoken requirement in narratives for an intertextual linkage between the nebulous 'what ifs' of the time ahead and the more pedestrian knowledge of times past. Reading such works as Brian Aldiss's *Helliconia* trilogy (1982–85) against Robert A. Heinlein's *Stranger in a Strange Land* (1961) may benefit the reader, in that while the comparison of those contemporary 'realities' may not suggest either text is 'real', the *act* of intertextual comparison may lay the foundation for a better understanding of more abstract works, for example by an author like Iain M. Banks.

And so the contemporary reader of SF is well prepared to travel inexpressible textual distances, but even these journeys must have a contextual departure point – just as the great voyages of British exploration usually began at Southampton or Plymouth docks. There is a need for a recognisable beginning, some form of signpost that indicates what may lie ahead. Therefore our voyages into the far future must begin at some point of commonality, if not scientific then social or cultural or historical. It is as if the story needs to enter the realm of the speculative by some identifiable door if a full appreciation of the narrative's scope and dimension is to be realised. And to create a startlingly effective new story, the doorway is often paradoxically of a singularly ordinary nature;[11] the contrasts offered between the mundane of today and the extraordinary of tomorrow are yet another of those important cyclical archetypes, although an archetype of custom rather than of persona or mood. The important point is for the writer to provide the reader with some departure point that is linked to *contemporary* knowledge, since it is difficult to appreciate how far we have travelled if we cannot accurately gauge where we started. In *Metamorphoses of Science Fiction*, Suvin defines SF as the literature of cognitive estrangement, whereby SF uses the trope of novum to transform the tangible world we know into something Other, yet still offers us worlds which are recognisably Earthly: 'SF is a developed oxymoron, a realistic irreality, with humanized nonhumans, this-worldly Other worlds'.[12] Suvin's doorways and departure points are an alienised version of a thing we think we know well. Gary Wolfe makes a similar argument in suggesting that SF 'tries to achieve a "sense of wonder" through a juxtaposition of the known and the unknown, that it is often structured around symbolic barriers to knowledge'.[13] Therefore 'portals' into other worlds depend upon their efficacy not because they are alien and Other, but because they are recognisable and partially familiar. At the same time it should be noted that various postmodernist theorists, such as Hayden White and Richard Rorty, appealing to Friedrich Nietzsche,[14] are also in the process of undermining the notion that the past is a set of facts we can know; they question the concept of 'history' as a given, with the suggestion that history itself is a malleable construction. Therefore it is useful to find a departure point not only that is recognisably historical or suggestive of the past/present but also for which different readings are unlikely to significantly alter the perception of its meaning.

There are many other examples of these departure points: an awareness of the steam engine is needed if we are properly to appreciate the innovativeness of the hydrogen ram-scoop drive; a fascination with geometry begins a narrative of time travel in a suburban Victorian cellar;[15] and knowledge of the general mythos and conflict of Earth religions is helpful in order to begin to understand the possibilities of difference between humans and Others.[16] Likewise, it is necessary to recognise the old paths of empire if we are to grasp the power of contemporary literary experiments which engage with new, fictional imperialisms: how extraordinary and powerful is the Lansraad in Herbert's *Dune* series, for example, or *Star Trek*'s 'neutral zones' if they are without some form of historical context? Isaac Asimov took us to the isolationist Spacer planet of Solaria (see Chapter 6) but only after he was sure we were ready to depart an Earth cased in steel and crowded beyond capacity in cities that never saw the light of day. Yet before we are asked to consider the moment of departure from the known into the unknown and to examine the places where humanity's explorations might take us, many texts also offer some intimation of limit or control, a mechanism of antecedent which indicates and defines the human ability to survive its own imperial predations. To 'scale' the event ahead, a text will often refer to an older event or some assumed historical knowledge, as in Joe Haldeman's *The Forever War* (1974), where he uses a link to an Einsteinean past in order both to frame the scope of the novel as well as to legitimise his hero's longevity:

Twelve years before, when I was just ten years old, they had discovered the collapsar jump. Just fling an object at a collapsar with sufficient speed, and out it pops in some other part of the galaxy. It didn't take long to figure out the formula that predicted where it would come out: it travels along the same 'line' (actually an Einsteinean geodesic) it would have followed if the collapsar hadn't been in the way.... It made a lot of work for mathematical physicists, who had to redefine simultaneity, then tear down general relativity and build it back up again.[17]

Haldeman invokes Albert Einstein's theories of relativity as his starting point[18] and assumes that readers of his novel will possess at least a basic knowledge of space–time travel discussions and the theoretical effects of relativity on the human condition. In this book Einstein's well known theory provides the doorway by which the reader enters the narrative, which is an experiment in an imperial setting where humanity is embroiled in a seemingly eternal war with the Taurans.

Haldeman's novel is also an excellent example of a future narrative's placement against a general contemporary reality,[19] where it is useful for the author to illustrate (through hints of precedent) that any new empire will not take us too far beyond our capacity to control. A different illustration of this can be seen in the current fascination with George Lucas's *Star Wars* film saga. The Jedi knights are, as were their Arthurian predecessors, keepers of imperial virtue in a land of supposed fairness and parity, where justice and civility prevail. However, both Lucas and the various writers of the Arthurian mythos understood their audience well and glossed over much sordid individual suffering in favour of the stoicism of the sufferers. We are shown the villainy of Darth Vader's empire on a grand scale but not the intimate humiliations of his oppressed and marginalised subjects. On this intertextual point, the narrative of the film balances between the connective need for literary reality (the ability to link the narrative to something the audience or reader will understand as historically 'real') and fictional interest (the ability to create something which links the 'real' to an engaging speculative future). Too much reality (based on the documented horrors of imperial power abuse) and the narrative risks confronting audiences or readers with something they might prefer not to face. Too much fictional optimism and the SF text becomes trite and unconvincing. Haldeman's narrative, though grim, is equipoised between the two.

While there is nothing at all wrong with a text which focuses the optimism of SF on the more politically critical and dystopian realities of empire,[20] most narratives of this type centre on the anti-hero's progress into absolution, or the eventual overthrow of the narrative's argued status quo (as in *Star Wars*). While imperialism in SF may be a glorious thing (as long as we are 'of' the empire and not subjugated by it), the power behind empire is fascinating only so long as we are not required to examine too closely the costs of such power. The power of empire comes, after all, from the suppression of one culture by another and in today's more politically enlightened times the dark realities of this suppression rarely make for inspiring reading, unless we are reading of the overthrow of oppression. Therefore the most common attraction of empire is not through dystopia (George Orwell's *Nineteen Eighty-Four*, Margaret Atwood's *The Handmaid's Tale*) but through utopia (or a purposely unconvincing utopia), where everyone is apparently free to explore and colonise at will, and where even the colonised subjects appear happy about their condition, as exampled by the popular nostalgia of the *Star Trek* space opera, and especially seen in E. E. 'Doc' Smith's exuberant *Lensmen* series of the 1940s. In the 'best' empires, most outward aspects of real power and control are carefully hidden, as in L. Frank Baum's *The Wonderful Wizard of Oz* (1900) or Clifford D. Simak's *Cosmic Engineers* (1939), where subjugation has become almost a democratic process, or, at least, a benevolent dictatorship.

Thus we can accept almost any future empire as long as we have an appropriate context, an understanding of *where* we come in and at least some faint notion of the empire's boundaries and powers. That readers like to know 'where they stand' is one of the intriguing arguments for why the empire of Asimov is less problematic to some readers than is 'the Culture' of Banks. The Asimovean model is comfortably conventional – an amalgam of nineteenth-century adventure novels and a twentieth-century confidence in science – and fits neatly within well defined limits and parameters of a 'standard' empire. It is an empire of human proportions in a familiar galaxy. The characters are barely different from the people of our own families or from characters of nineteenth- or even eighteenth-century adventure novels. The essence of Asimov is an application of new technology and scientific theory focused through the lens of convention and tradition and, almost, a predictability of form, whereas the essence of the Banks form is the reverse of this: opposing and iconoclastic, with wildly incredible scales and frequently gruesome imagery. And here we see the development and maturation of the SF genre as it grows from its earlier, simple ideologies into something far more sophisticated and complex, its experiments mirroring – as SF must to remain a relevant social commentary – a heightened awareness of the changes in the cultures from which it springs. Asimov was 'right' during the 1950s and Banks is 'right' for the beginning of a new millennium. Often demanding uncomfortable new definitions from the reader, Banks's texts are written on a level which insists the reader leaves the old assumptions of Asimovean imperial reality behind, and this is one of the reasons why his novels may be considered authentically postcolonial, since, as Dawn Duncan argues, 'For the postcolonial to achieve identity that is genuinely new, old tools must not be used for the shaping'.[21]

Yet regardless of the individuality of imperial models produced by an author, the tacit collusion between all fictional patterns of empire transcends any specific mould, a facility which enables the reader instantly to position the narrative into a more or less comprehensible context. No matter where the authors of empire take us, they usually begin with some imperialised definition, often marked by a recognisable doorway or entrance. Consider three examples, from Robert A. Heinlein, Walter M. Miller and Iain M. Banks. First, Heinlein:

> Sure, we had trouble building Space Station One – but the trouble was people. Not that building a station twenty-two thousand three hundred miles out in space is a breeze. It was an engineering feat bigger than the Panama Canal or the Pyramids – or even the Susquehanna Power Pile.[22]

Heinlein's text speaks of a time when major works of near-Earth engineering are still considered significant and remain comparable to extant (though ancient) monuments of human endeavour. Thus we can locate Heinlein's narrative in the period after the Moon landings of the late twentieth century but likely before any interstellar engineering marvels of the twenty-second or twenty-third centuries. Therefore the positioning of this text is 'near future', and contemporary ideologies, politics and technologies may be applied with little dislocation of understanding by the reader. This is one of the attractions of Heinlein's novels. His reference to massive and breathtaking engineering was perfectly acceptable and exciting in the 1950s, whereas in the early 2000s such references are more likely to be perceived as ironic, since the reader is well aware that such things are not so simply achieved. Heinlein's narrative is sufficiently futuristic to permit him a few of his favoured libertarian urges but close enough to the present day for the reader confidently to apply current political 'standards' of empire, unlike the following example, from Miller:

> On one wall of the stairwell a half-buried sign remained legible. Mustering his modest command of Pre-Deluge English, he whispered the words haltingly:
>
> FALLOUT SURVIVAL SHELTER
> Maximum Occupancy: 15
>
> The rest was buried, but the first word was enough for Francis. He had never seen a 'Fallout', and he hoped he'd never see one. A consistent description of the monster had not survived, but Francis had heard the legends.[23]

Miller's reference to a nuclear war so ancient that the term 'fallout' has become legend places this text in the far future of humankind. The reader comprehends the author's intention that the nuclear threat contemporary to the writing of this novel has long since vanished and degenerated into the distant memory that is myth. Thus by this signpost readers understand they are entering a time of 'future myth', when the distance between what is fact (today, contemporary) and what is fiction (tomorrow, futuristic) is so significant as to stretch their grasp of reality. With Heinlein, both reader and narrator share some levels of knowledge, some common ground on which engineering references appear solid and 'real'. Miller's text contrasts this by taking the reader into a future so distant that virtually nothing can be assumed sharable. Miller's reader knows about fallout shelters and toolboxes but the monks of Leibowitz in his novel do not – everything is strange and foreign to them. They cannot perceive even the mundaneness of an ancient shopping list, for there are no longer such things as shops. Other than through historical references and certain analogies with other cultures of belief, Miller offers very few connections with known ideologies, and the reader is required to take a great deal on faith, supported only by the knowledge that the narrative is as much a myth to the monk's situation as their situation is to the reader's reality.

A symbiotic relationship exists between reader and text based on this dual and incredibly sophisticated use of deliberate myth and historical reality. As with Haldeman's use of Einstein's theory as an entry for the reader, Miller's text balances its historical references and futuristic extrapolations along the only thing any reader of SF might be expected to understand – the advent of a nuclear holocaust – although it presumes no superiority of 'our' time over that of the monks, for, according to Miller's novel, 'we' are the ones who loosed the holocaust in the first place. However, since humankind has not actually flung itself into that particular pit, Miller bases his extrapolations on the shared iconography of existing nuclear holocaust texts, an exercise in intertextuality which not only relies upon the commonality of nuclear holocaust images but also upon the reader's knowledge of the political mindset which might engender a nuclear conflict. Thus readers are able to locate themselves in a future environment not only where nuclear war is a dreadful memory but also where the human survivors of that war may properly be expected to have progressed beyond the deadly desire for the power and political control which once led to such a war. It is by this means that the full irony and rationale of Miller's narrative is revealed.

Contrasted against Miller's far future are Banks's extraordinary narratives, where even the passage of time itself has become an insignificant reckoning of the distance between today's reader and tomorrow's possibilities, as is illustrated by the following excerpt:

> We are a long-lived species, Ziller, and have been part of the galactic community for many millennia. Three thousand years are far from insignificant by our reckoning, but in the lifetime of an intelligent, space-faring species, it does indeed count as recent history.[24]

Banks's narrative offers the reader very few bridges to either a contemporary existence or to the political environments with which the reader may be assumed to have at least some knowledge or familiarity. The reader is offered only minimal doorways through which to step, in terms of science or social precedent (a decadent party; two drunken men about to join a battle; soldiers cowering in a dark foxhole[25]), and is expected to establish additional frames of reference as the narrative is digested. Everything is different. Nothing can be assumed familiar, not even the human-like beings around which much of Banks's stories revolve. The deliberate magnitude of time and history between today's reader and Banks's texts is so vast as to be unbridgeable, which is precisely the author's aim. In a setting where even the concept of history is archaic, everything becomes open to new translations and interpretations, including the notion of empire. Through the mechanism of a character's party conversation, entire millennia are dismissed. The measure of events affecting the human race (or human-type races) is massive and impossible to scale. There is virtually nothing of solidity here for a contemporary reader to fix upon as a suitable *entrée* into the Banksian future – the text has an almost postmodern intangibility – and therefore new demands are placed upon the act of reading. A Banksian empire extends beyond anything remotely resembling Earth history, and so the reader is asked to reconsider the very concept of such an imperial political mindset. We are thrown into a vacuum of comprehension, since nothing contemporaneous, not even a myth of self, exists inside this form of narrative, leaving us to walk into an unlit and unexplained future, without even a basic guide. Banks's novels ask readers to reassess their present as much as their future. The familiar political and social stances of Asimov and Heinlein are gone, supplanted by an intangible postmodern mood of fluidity and adaptation, where readers stand not on a recognisable street of hard fact but on a moving strip of elastic. Though occasionally uneasy to read, Banks's narratives, his breathtaking and iconoclastic form of SF writing, are fully justified, as the popularity of his novels has demonstrated.

Yet despite these differences in the potential dislocation of a reader's ability to digest massive ideas, there remains a legitimate connection between the Heinlein, Miller, and Banks texts. James Romm considers the basic attraction of the essential galactic empire:

> The most remote spaces of the earth shared with the most distant times in history an affinity for the fantastic, because things more exotic or

terrifying than anything in the familiar world could exist there without provoking disbelief.[26]

William B. Fischer refines this perception:

> The inhabitants of the imaginary world themselves may refer to the reader's own world as a spatially and temporally distant place peopled – or at least once inhabited – by strange beings with equally strange ideas and behaviour. After the reader ceases reading, his sense of the alien nature of his own world subsides. But he may well retain a sense of relativity and mutability, a new appreciation of the position of his world and himself in the immense expanse of time, space, and the possible forms of individual existence and social organization.[27]

The vital connection between all fictional empires of the future is that, at some point, they make contact with a known historical model. Many SF writers do this through an examination of empire in its most classical form, as in the case of Asimov's *Foundation and Empire* (1952), which built directly upon the foundations of Gibbon's Roman imperium. Blish's *Cities in Flight* (1970) owes much to Spengler's philosophy of cyclical history, and Van Vogt based such works as 'Recruiting Station' (1942) on Robert Graves's *I, Claudius* (1934), while A. Bertram Chandler's *Rim Worlds* series (1961–76), bears an uncanny similarity to the paternalistic hierarchies of America's old Wild West. Even the non-conformist 'Culture' of Banks may be considered connected to this theme, although his construct may be more properly seen as overtly anti-empire, as his texts oppose all those aspects of imperialism so often embraced by the majority of other SF writers. It is this basic connection, linking some form of recorded history to the posited future, which is shared by SF's prospective empires: by shape or form or political makeup, there is invariably something in the new narrative which links it directly to an earlier model of empire. In this respect SF texts may be considered a practical response to humanity's development; the genre reframes historical models and adds to the rise of humanity's comprehension of itself through the medium of literary thought experiments. It is also through this experimentation that the reader gains exposure to many forms and sub-forms of imperial thought (if only by implication), the result of which must be an increased understanding of why empire will not accord with human development and is most unlikely to exist in the future. Each imperial example, each model is examined and tested by its respective author in order that aspects of their particular version of empire may be tested for efficacy.

If the model is hopelessly flawed, the forces of good prevail and the empire is eventually forfeited (*à la* Lucas's *Star Wars*). If the model is even partially sound, it may triumph, but only at the cost of comprehending the model's imperfections and learning to live with those negative aspects in the scenario, as illustrated by Heinlein's *Red Planet: A Colonial Boy on Mars* (1949) and Alexei Panshin's *Rite of Passage* (1968). Examples of SF texts illustrating the 'perfect' empire, where both the dominant and the subordinate cultures are in utter harmony, do not exist, other than as narratives detailing symbiotic relationships, and which are not properly narratives of political imperialism. If we examine sufficient numbers of SF texts revolving around future empire, it is relatively easy to discern hundreds of minor mutations of a basic plot, as if each author is attempting to bake a slightly different cake though their ingredients are essentially identical. In hundreds of novels, humanity is at the centre of a neo-imperial surge, and while a significant portion of these end in the dystopic (or 'failed' utopic) collapse of the project, a great many more, like *Red Planet*, are seen to adapt their framework to suit a more liberal and ethical philosophy. What these adaptations are doing is to experiment with versions of an imperial mindset until a more mutually acceptable accord is achieved. No longer will humankind's literary heroes 'boldly go' as did Hernándo Cortés, but they will rather go with a greater moral caution.[28] In addition, the more SF examines not only our ability to expand, exploit and control but also the motivations behind our desire to do so, the less likely we are to find such exploitive controls satisfying or even all that attractive. Once this comprehension begins, the greater irony of imperialism in SF starts to become clear: despite the attractions of a utopian empire, one of the genre's most pivotal tropes is slowly working to negate the possibility of itself.

Yet if most SF texts involving empire are based in some manner or part upon the empires of history, what does this suggest for the continuance of fictional imperialism into the future? Is there likely to be more or less experimentation with empire in SF? As science itself provides a greater ability to explore and eventually move us around the solar system and nearest stars, fictions of science will continue in their extrapolation and expansion of the fringe technologies inspired by this greater research and progress. But regardless of authentic scientific gains or the growing awareness of imperial failings, the fictional *essence* or principle of human exploration and exploitation of the planets and stars shows little sign of altering, although the mode of exploration is subtly altering, as is the motivation for it. In all probability, humanity will learn from its old imperial mistakes only at a leisurely pace and will, through the genre of SF, continue for some time to discover, digest and discard the same cultural paradigms, a likelihood which Françoise Verges considers:

> What interests me here is to ask if the colonial impulse has entirely disappeared with the collapse of the European empires … I wonder if

the *model* of colonialization, i.e., occupying a territory, controlling its resources and justifying it, is not alive and well. The colonial impulse is still legitimized.[29]

And it appears the model (or at least an interest in experimenting with the model) is very much alive and well, judging by a recent crop of SF texts to reach the best-sellers list. The winners of the annual Hugo Award for science fiction and fantasy writing in 2000 included Vernor Vinge, for *A Deepness in the Sky* (1999), which deals with an ideological scheme of progressive capitalism and the building of new empires, and David Howard, for his satirical *Galaxy Quest*, which shows how even the most incompetent humans (brutally characterised as hapless Hollywood actors) may overcome the alien Other and once more raise the banner of human superiority. For the moment, at least, future empire is alive and well, with a dynamism all of its own, regardless of any connection to a previously extant historical form. Whether SF imperialism takes a social form, as in Asimov's texts, an economic form, as in Frederik Pohl and C. M. Kornbluth's *The Space Merchants* (1953) or the more ubiquitous political form invoked by Frank Herbert's *Dune* (1965), the construct appears irrepressible. One novel which well illustrates a melange of imperial aspects is Miller's cautionary tale of the power of imperialism and the cycles of history, *A Canticle for Leibowitz* (1959).

Walter M. Miller, Jr (1923–96) was an American combat pilot in World War II who converted to Catholicism in 1947. His preoccupation with matters religious lent an uncommon and complex morality to his novels and short fiction. He received a Hugo Award in 1955 for his story 'The Darfsteller'. Miller seemed focused upon the conflict between the scientific and religious mindsets of the postwar United States. He had a relatively short writing career, becoming reclusive and publishing nothing after *Canticle*, his best-known novel. Written in three parts – *Fiat Homo*, *Fiat Lux* and *Fiat Voluntas Tua*[30] – the narrative speaks of a humanity crushed by a nuclear holocaust but which then, after many hundreds of years, and after surviving an extended 'Dark Age', is 'reborn' into a time of supposed neo-technological wonder and science. While the first holocaust was caused by the now traditional horrors of territorial and political misunderstandings, which in themselves would have made an intriguing novel, the text is more concerned with the continuation of the Catholic Order of Leibowitz as it attempts to connect a portion of one pre-holocaust society to another. Miller's subtle work presents the awful nature of determinism, to which his version of humanity seems doomed, and his characters are racked by an uncontrollable circularity of politics, power abuse and fear. Though the narrative appears to act as a link between moments of human enlightenment, the text permits no real development of societal understanding, merely an extended period of physical healing and forgetfulness, during which time even the memory of hard-learned wisdoms is allowed to expire under the circular and ever-rising expediency of power.

Miller's text was published in 1959, a year after the US launched its first space rocket and two years after the USSR launched *Sputnik I* and *II*, and Britain undertook thermonuclear bomb tests in the central Pacific. As such, it is an ideal text to act as a bridge between past and future SF, as it stands between the decline of Western European imperialism and the rise of the Cold War power games. It shows a cyclicity of thought which (sharpened by Miller's own religious values) not only encapsulates the physical act of imperial oppression but also attempts to show the cultural circumstances which might unconsciously support such oppression. That the author's profound beliefs were aroused at events[31] which might appear potential transgressions of religious doctrine is not surprising, and his narrative features a doom-laden imperial cycle through which the reader is introduced to the present day through a series of flashbacks (Miller's 'doorways'). Highlighting the physical symbols of nuclear disaster with which contemporary readers have become so familiar, Miller weaves a story where the cycles of human political empire end in a contemporary version of apocalypse: a fiery destructive madness.

In the first part of the narrative, *Fiat Homo* ('Let There Be Man'), we are taken forward to the dreaded 'curse of the Fallout' and the 'rain of Strontium', as well as the 'misborn'. We are shown a land burned by fire, poisoned by radioactivity and now illuminated only by scraps of disparate memorabilia. Even the story of the travails of Saint Leibowitz (a minor twentieth-century physicist) is interpreted through a precious, though distorted and broken, memory of history, a nicely ironic touch since Miller's basic premise for the rise and fall of empire rests in the fallibility of human memory. The Leibowitzean canticle is a perfect catalogue of the cyclicity of empire, both political and religious: rise and fall, rise and fall. Charting human 'progress' from the threats of the atomic 1950s, Miller brings the reader out of a first nuclear devastation, then through a long interregnum of ignorance, fear and mistrust of science (the 'Simplification') and into a period of increasingly galvanised social and scientific activity, before finally returning to a resurgence of nuclear hostilities and deep social pessimism. What is most interesting about Miller's text is both how and, more importantly, *why* he illustrates the inevitability of each stage of the cycle, depicting his belief in the fatality of the human urge to empire. Whereas both Asimov and Heinlein see the future as a series of successful developments, each building on the previous one, Miller is suggesting that beyond each development lies an inevitable fall, and that humankind is unlikely to reach the stars except as a last act of desperation.

In this first portion of the novel we are introduced to the Catholic Order of Leibowitz, which has taken upon itself the guardianship of knowledge during the times of post-holocaust destruction and ignorance.[32] As civilisation retreats into semi-barbarity, the monks live almost as hermits in the desert wilds, but are sent into the remains of the wider community to collect memorabilia and disseminate information, in oral form.[33] Miller carefully documents the process of social decay from the 'pre-deluge' times into the years of the Simpletons (holocaust survivors who renounced all aspects of learning) and we see the great value placed on things historical because of their age. Blueprints of useless circuit boards and fragments of shopping lists are as treasured as tomes of history and mathematics. In some ways the characters we meet at this point in the novel are paradoxically the most innocent and virtuous. They believe because they find their belief fitting and righteous, because they are innocents born of the storm, whereas the characters in the latter part of the narrative have been developed by Miller to illustrate predetermined positions, where their innocence has become less authentic and more of an applied contrivance. Yet 'the monks waited. It mattered not at all that to them the knowledge they saved was useless, that much of it was not really knowledge now.'[34] Miller goes into some detail regarding the sheer devolution of post-holocaust humanity since this provides a suitable backdrop upon which to paint the picture of ever-renewing empire based on nothing other than the hubris of humanity. In the narrative's effort to remove all possible prior knowledge of empire, Miller has done his best to give his human characters a *tabula rasa*, an opportunity to rewrite their future away from the path of imperialism. The first devastation effectively wipes the cultural slate clean and brings the remnants of humanity down Abraham Maslow's 'hierarchy of need' to the point where only tribal authority, shelter and physical continuance matter. Stopping short of destroying everything, Miller leaves just enough clues for the newly emergent survivors to understand that their scientific ancestors have made a terrible mess of things. Intriguingly, he does not make it clear precisely *how* or *why* things went wrong, leaving an irresistible and unfairly enticing puzzle for those who follow.

Half a millennium later, Miller moves us into the second part of the text, *Fiat Lux* ('Let There Be Light'), where the Order of Leibowitz is confronted with a form of nascent science, many items springing from a limited understanding of some of the salvaged texts. The survivors of the first holocaust have taken up Miller's challenge and are busily deciphering scraps of their cultural heritage, discovering through them the printing press and the power of the electric dynamo. Localised power blocs have evolved, headed by baron chiefs whose power is of life and death. Parallels between Miller's narrative and our own history are at their weakest here, since in our reality, while science has frequently been channelled by both government and commercial powers (the development of the atomic bomb, the invention of Teflon), scientists have never abdicated the right to explore pure (non-applied) science or behaved 'immorally' without loud dispute.[35] However, Miller's barons covet the knowledge of the preserved memorabilia since it is now understood to hold much useful scientific information (i.e. is able to offer the holder an advantage of illicit power in some way). Trusted lieutenants are sent as pilgrims to the Leibowitzean abbey in order to examine and assess how much of this preserved knowledge could be used to reinforce baronial power and authority. Miller indicates the move to an immoral use of knowledge for power when he has one of these lieutenants address an assembly of the monks with the following words:

> Ignorance has been our king. Since the death of empire, he sits un-challenged on the throne of Man. His dynasty is age-old. His right to rule is now considered legitimate. Past sages have affirmed it. They did nothing to unseat him.
>
> Tomorrow, a new prince shall rule. Men of understanding, men of science shall stand behind his throne, and the universe will come to know his might. His name is Truth. His empire shall encompass the Earth. And the mastery of Man over the Earth shall be renewed.... It will come to pass by violence and upheaval, by flame and by fury, for no change comes calmly over the world.[36]

Miller's narrator, Thon Taddeo, suggests that humankind's tolerance of ignorance (lack of knowledge, an inability to change their condition) is an artificially passive state that has come about during (and due to) the absence of science. But once scientific discovery resumes its proper place in human society, humanity would fling off this unnatural lassitude and begin the slow process of culture building (and, *ergo*, empire building) all over again. Miller's deliberate lack of ambiguity in dealing with the character Taddeo is intended to clearly equate a scientist's knowledge and scientific progress with power and the political uses of that power, a philosophy that fits neatly into the author's deterministic narrative. The new scientific mindset is shown to be completely unfair since, although it carries both advantages and liabilities, the only people equipped to understand the new science are those individuals already favoured by the patronage of the local barons. Echoing themes in Asimov's *Foundation* books, the powerful accumulate more and more power, scientific knowledge adding to existing whirlpools of information, sucking yet further power into the hub. Each baron establishes a small centre with its own inevitable peripheries – an empire in miniature. Miller also takes great pains to demonstrate how the desire for personal gain and power corrupts leaders, as his characters walk a morally dubious path in order to wrench an advantage over competing interests. It is as if Miller is showing the reader that humanity is hopelessly flawed since, even with our imperial history utterly eradicated, we are doomed to covet power and control over each other. As the second section of the novel brings the resurgent and factionalised population of the northern Americas once more into potential conflict, the barons achieve a last-minute *entente* among themselves and continental war is just avoided.

The final section of the text, *Fiat Voluntas Tua* ('May Thy Will Be Done'), is set in 3781 AD, when:

> It was inevitable, it was manifest destiny, they felt (and not for the first time), that such a race go forth to conquer stars. To conquer them several times, if need be, and certainly to make speeches about the conquest. But, too, it was inevitable that the race succumb again to the old maladies on new worlds, even as on Earth before, in the litany of life and in the special liturgy of Man: Versicles by Adam, Rejoinders by the Crucified.[37]

In this last segment of his novel, Miller is done hinting at the corruption of temporal power brokers and now offers the reader a gruesome and unvarnished account of what happens when conflicting imperial desires escalate and eventually clash. Though the conquest of the stars is not presented as evil, and the departing Catholic ship bears clear parallels with Noah's ark, it is the force that motivates such activity which Miller considers transgressive and untenable. Were it not for the machinations of the little empires, the spectre of nuclear destruction would not have originated nor been reanimated. Therefore, once again, Miller's experiment has humankind embarked upon the road to self-destruction and, as his pessimistic narrative ascends into a new scientific enlightenment, so his characters descend into the bleakness of cultural antagonism. Read as an allegory, Miller's story is a hostile and cautionary tale about original sin and the fall of humanity; the framework of empire becomes the vehicle by which the allegory may be illustrated. But why did Miller select 'empire' as the vehicle? Writing, as he did, with a decidedly religious bent, why not choose any of the other human weaknesses, such as impaired morality, or the lust for wealth and status? Was it because the notion of empire conveniently encapsulates all of humanity's weaknesses, or was it because the historical notion of empire and the desire for imperialism are so entrenched as a trope within the human psyche that the reader becomes instantly aware of its iniquities? While Miller's textual experiment is not about the evolution of an empire *per se*, he attempts to illustrate the mode of thought that contributes to the imperial project. The rise and fall of empires are themselves part of the religious background Miller chooses to create for his future world and are very much part of the history of the Catholic Church extrapolated into the future. Reflected in the novel are the ample illustrations of the actual and recurrent oppositions of alternative faiths and the schisms within Catholicism, events such as the establishment of the Church of England and the religious vagaries of Mary and Elizabeth.

In contrast to Banks's novels, which share a postmodern mood of constant change and fluidity, and which depict the aftermath of imperial thought as a kind of loose curtain, Miller pins his characters down like insects into the rigid and fatalistic frames engendered by the human lust for power and control. Does *Canticle* evoke neo-imperialism to explore the potential of such control, or simply to provide the reader with a massive 'doorway' through which all things dystopian may be inspected? Either argument is possible, yet by using 'empire' as his leitmotif Miller is not only holding up the classical model of dystopia for his readers but also reiterating the power of the imperial model in SF thought experiments. *Canticle* relies significantly upon the reader's comprehension of the place of empire in human history and society if the allegory is to have the desired impact. The superimposition of a complex narrative upon an immediately obvious frame (the notion of the cyclicity of empire and, specifically, religious empire) gives Miller's story much of its hidden depth.

If we consider SF as a genre of social education and development (therefore not so much *Bildungsroman* as *Erziehungsroman*[38]) we are able to see in Miller's narrative a grand gesture which sweeps up all human history and condenses it into an allegorical warning. The secular desires of humankind sentence our race to return repeatedly to the point of beginning until we eventually outgrow the need to live as disparate tribes and coalesce into a true single organism without cultural differentiation (in this case, the ideal for universal unity being the Church). He argues for utopia by illustrating its darker sibling; he pleads the case of postcoloniality by demonstrating the failures of the imperial cycle. This form of social illustration is integral to both the purpose and the appeal of SF. Readers of SF *enjoy* their participation in the author's thought experiments, though it may seem an unusual experiment which simultaneously teaches theology, history, political science, sociology and philosophy. Once more, SF demonstrates that its place in the literary field is far more profound than some might consider. Not only does it provide humans with a forum in which to stretch their imaginations as to what may be but it likewise permits us to look back along linear histories to discover where 'new' ideas may have had their genesis. And just as the nexus of history and future speculation stands in the moveable light of the *now*, so too must this amalgam of yesterday and tomorrow mean something for today. In *Storm Warnings: Science Fiction Confronts the Future*, George Slusser and his co-editors spotlight the precise rationale of SF's function in this area: 'If SF lets us see the future, it is to enable us to experience dread, thus be warned away from an activity which, if pursued, leads us inexorably from bad to worse'.[39]

Yet the present and the future of SF cannot help but connect the past of our species to myriad potentialities and, in doing so, must increase a reader's postcolonial awareness of the imperialist taint in our past. The stain of empire indelibly affects contemporary perspectives and in turn is responsible for a continuing imperial element in some SF. Authors connecting our past with our future, providing 'doorways' for the reader, must latch onto some 'known' reality, and examples of imperialism are rife in our histories. As Jean Pfaelzer states, 'Both utopias and dystopias are extended literary metaphors embodying theories about social change. As narrated histories of the future, they extrapolate events, characters and attitudes from tendencies observed in contemporary life.'[40] While the human race is compelled to stare into the future, it cannot afford to neglect the images of the past if it is, as Miller suggests, to avoid recreating the imperial project and falling prey to its insidious beckoning. Yet if we are currently engaged in the production of tomorrow in our activities of today, what does this say about the contemporary mood of postcoloniality? Are today's societies genuinely postcolonial? Beyond empire? There are many reasons for reading fictions which indulge imperialist fantasies, or which offer a subtle critique on the contemporary nature of postmodern empire; however, if we consider the volume of newly published imperial fictions in SF it seems that *Homo futuris* is just as enthusiastic about empire, at least as a literary tool, as were earlier generations.

'Empire' in SF is not only a doorway to the future: by anticipating its existence, contemporary authors are casting a less than oblique glance at the present. Are they seeing the re-emergence of empires in our own societies? Is the division of the world's economic power into vast geopolitical blocs merely globalism in practice, or are we already witnessing, like the Leibowitzean brothers, the reformation of economic imperialism? In Ken MacLeod's *The Stone Canal* (1996), a character called Wilde poses the question in rhetorical form:

> When we want to know whether something was worth making, we look for the answer in a discovery machine called the market. When we want to know how something works, we have another machine, called science. When we want to know if somebody was right to kill somebody else, we have a discovery machine called the law.[41]

Is part of Wilde's narrative function to ask whether we also have a discovery machine called SF? Might it not be the case that SF plays with models of power or potential empire in order to find the answers to the questions societies are asking right now? Ursula Le Guin gives us this definition:

Physicists often do thought-experiments: Einstein shoots a light-ray through a moving elevator; Schrödinger puts a cat in a box. There is no elevator, no cat, no box. The experiment is performed, the question is asked in the mind.... They are questions, not answers; process, not stasis. One of the essential functions of science fiction, I think, is precisely this kind of question-asking: reversals of an habitual way of thinking, metaphors for what our language has no words for as yet, experiments in imagination.[42]

Thus in Miller's 1950s novel we see an author experimenting with his ideas of humanity's weaknesses. *Canticle* postulates the premise that we crave the powers of science but that we also are quite capable of misusing those very powers. Where Asimov has considered those issues as being surmountable, leading us into a utopian existence, Miller has perceived them as being our ultimate downfall. Where Heinlein looks at the struggle of a people powerful enough to break from the imperial past, Miller sees only the failure of that struggle. Was it Miller's deep religious beliefs that caused him to see the human lack of restraint when faced with the possibilities of scientific-based knowledge, or was he suggesting a certain determinism linking science and cultural decline? Was he implying that he found the lust for power and control hard to relate to his Christian beliefs in moral responsibility, or was it more that he saw future humanity adopting the pattern of all empires, rising and falling? An insightful novel, *Canticle* experiments with possibilities of human survival in the face of a potential scientific disaster. To see how a contemporary author experiments with similar difficulties but from a more strictly scientific rather than moral perspective, we turn now to the meticulous scientific realism of Kim Stanley Robinson's *Mars*.

8. A Postcolonial Imagination: Kim Stanley Robinson's *Mars*

With the publication of his book *Red Mars* (1993), Kim Stanley Robinson (1952–) began a fictional debate on the phenomenon of the imperial project in a supposedly postcolonial era. His next two novels, *Green Mars* (1994) and *Blue Mars* (1996), completed the 1,700 pages of a trilogy that skilfully reflected the Western process of discovery, first landing, colonisation, exploitation and eventual colonial revolt, encompassing the macro of the imperial act in the micro of fiction. Though an ongoing recital of the imperial project is a fundamental theme of the SF genre, Robinson's meticulous realism reprises the process of empire to such a degree that his works may be considered important pieces of mainstream fiction as well as seminal works of SF, the *New York Times* calling the trilogy 'a landmark in the history of the genre'.[1]

Based on the colonisation and gradual terraforming of Mars,[2] the trilogy charts the progress of the 'First Hundred', the original 100 scientists, engineers and explorers who begin the colonisation project. Though latterly joined by other pioneers and migrants, the actions of this initial group act as an anchoring thread throughout the timeline covered by Robinson's narrative. Opening in the year 2026, with the selection of the privileged few who will be the first to undertake interplanetary migration, this massive thought experiment of Robinson describes an immense circle, ending in 2206, at which point humanity is beginning a tentative flirtation with interstellar travel. However, the circular nature of the narrative is not limited to the major events in Robinson's timeframe, as the novel also offers an intuitive commentary on the unremitting nature of the imperial project. The text sets up a debate between the rationale of a geographical expansion and the reluctance of a more aware humanity to re-enact the ruinous behaviours of power-seeking associations.

As the text develops, we are shown how images of the contemporary are inextricably linked to the next rotation of imperial thought, how the production of empire maintains its grip even within postcolonial imaginations. With discussions not only of the social, cultural and political structure of the First Hundred but also of the emergent colony and of the practicalities of daily life on an 'alien' world, Robinson's dual project touches upon the history of colonial designs as well as their implicit continuity. Though set in the future, the text is solidly based on known history and experience, which makes it possible to read the trilogy as both a commentary on and a rendition of that history, as well as a meditation on things to come.

The first novel in the trilogy focuses on a number of issues likely to be significant during the immediate time ahead: hyper-Malthusian economics; global disaster through poor environmental management; critical depletion of the Earth's natural resources; inexorable transnational capitalism; and accelerated scientific discovery. Robinson's text interrogates the rationale of a technological drive as it interacts with these stimuli by repeatedly asking the question 'Why?' Why do we do a thing simply because we have the knowledge and ability to do so? Why, given our acclaim of science, are its imperfections inevitably perpetuated into fictions of the future? Can we look to the dictatorial drive of modernity for an answer, or is technological advancement necessarily subjacent to the larger movement we call human evolution? Is humanity already caught in the snare of a technological determinism? In keeping with his intellectual seriousness and interest in contemporary science, Robinson's massive work also presents the reader with apparently determined and sometimes stereotypical characters, since the *Mars* trilogy is not so much a series of novels as an extended treatise in which these characters can usefully be mouthpieces for fixed positions. As with the Lasswitz text considered in Chapter 5, Robinson is not content to give us a superb and realistic vision of one possible future but also intends us to see, through the eyes of his characters, the political and cultural developments within the narrative as it moves into the postcolonial. Is it the narrative which modifies the stance of his characters, or the placement of the characters which ultimately informs the narrative?

While a discussion of these issues is certainly not restricted to SF, the genre does provide a fertile forum for their consideration, even though, as Gary Wolfe unhelpfully remarks, 'In all probability, science fiction will ultimately have to be characterized by the questions it raises rather than by the answers it offers'.[3] As well as questioning contemporary society's role in its own future, Robinson's narrative devotes substantial effort to exploring the assumptions that technological evolution is unstoppable and that, once invoked, its effects are irreversible and inevitable. His reflections on the doctrine of technological endeavour offer a cautionary insight into the behaviour of an inherently curious species driven by an endless and unremitting covetousness. The vista of Robinson's *Mars* is changed and developed as he poses his questions to the characters, stirring the ingredients of his future realities together in a pressured environment of economic necessity and political intrigue.

Beginning with the stringent selection process, we see what makes a 'good' pioneer and learn that, even at this stage, the First Hundred have begun to modify their emotional behaviour in order to better meet a pre-formed 'colonialist' selection criterion: 'they were crazy enough to want to leave Earth forever, but sane enough to disguise this fundamental madness, in fact to defend it as pure rationality, scientific curiosity'.[4] Michel Duval, the group's psychologist, hints at the problems that lie ahead: 'Since they're going to go crazy anyway, why not just send insane people in the first place, and save them the trouble?',[5] a psychological allusion to the problems awaiting the colony. This criticism of colonist selection by Michel opens Robinson's ironic observation of a supposedly scientific process that is as flawed as the individuals who participate in it. But we soon realise that it is the emotional imperfections of each individual that enable them to survive the maelstrom ahead, implying that we might be wiser to rely more on our instincts and less on 'scientific' psychological assessments. The text also intimates that the human ability to camouflage basic emotional needs is an essential part in the formation of our society. This is the beginning of Robinson's postulation that the First Hundred are simultaneously their own worst enemy and their own best hope, or, as Wolfe affirms:

> [man] is the beast and the symbol of the limitless human spirit. He is imperfect, arrogant and brutal, and yet he perhaps most clearly symbolizes what the icon of the monster means in the myth of science fiction: the potent and threatening unknown that in the end is humanity itself.[6]

If we are necessarily flawed and emotionally mute, are we fated to act accordingly, even to repeating past practices that have made us this way? But if humanity depends upon these very characteristics to survive, can we condemn ourselves by denying them? Robinson's First Hundred are insightful enough to identify the only acceptable imperfection: an obsessive passion for Mars. The stage is set for a confrontation between the human will to fabricated behaviour and a deterministic society that cares only for the maintenance of a rampant capitalism.

As might be anticipated when discussing an imposition of remote authority, the issue of determinism is a significant theme within the text. Events such as Sax's kidnapping or Phyllis's wholesale conversion to capital-ism occur because there appears to be no alternative to the pressure applied by external causes. From the beginning, Michel seems destined to prolong psychological misconceptions, which leads, in part, to the disintegration of a group whose selection in itself depended upon the actions of others. Maya, also a major character, is initially limited to being a product of her supposed culture and sexuality. Like others, she responds to early narrative stimuli by remaining within the implicit conventionalities of her character, whose rigid definition is effectively used by Robinson as he manipulates her into becoming a force of logical determinism. Only when the narrative allows her to confront events outside the realm of convention (the onset of a deleterious mental condition assists this) does her character begin to display an awareness of choice and its consequences. It is almost as if Robinson wants his characters to write the narrative as if they were real people, even though the authorial design suggests a decision to make them represent certain mindsets and stereotypes. From this perspective, the notion of determinism is paradoxical: Robinson does not really want to force his characters into anything, but he must in order that they may illustrate their function in the narrative and allow the full and final scenario to unfold. Apart from Maya and then Phyllis, there are others (Sax, the archetypal 'boffin', and Ann, the incumbent 'radical') who are likewise designed to illustrate certain roles and attitudes. The text does not permit them much freewill even when they are seen to be exercising it in instances of anger or actions motivated by revenge. Though they may *appear* to want to rebel against the role dictated for them in the text, the novel does not permit this. It needs them as fixed points of reference. There is a fine line here between determination and a convincing plausibility but Robinson's insistence that characters represent only the attitudes allowed them by historical and social precedent strengthens the reader's view of the Martian colony as an archetype and the process of colonialisation as paradigmatic.

Robinson thus presents us with an image of neo-colonialism populated by idiosyncratic but compliant characters, tightly wrapped in historical example and suspended in the ether of the future. The narrative is read on several time levels simultaneously, weaving between Western perceptions of the colonial past, a fashionable contemporary uncertainty and an anxiety of the future. The engagement with all three dimensions is immediate. Before the engine of the *Ares*[7] has cooled, we have already seen that the future of the colony rests in the hands of flawed beings, who are led by an inherent determinism into repetitive patterns of rigidity and folly. Robinson's placement of an inflexible dichotomy between the Mars colony and older modes of thought becomes emphasised. Arcady, a passionate Russian and latter-day Bolshevik, makes a mockingly self-aware acknowledgement of the situation: 'To be twenty-first century scientists on Mars ... but at the same time living within nineteenth century social systems, based on seventeenth century ideologies. It's absurd, it's crazy, it's – it's – it's *unscientific*.'[8] Arcady's speech draws the remnants of a modernist Soviet ideology into the battle between a need for technological reliability and the clinging nostalgias of pre-technological empire.

Arcady's minor tirade is interesting in that it adds weight not only to Robinson's depiction of determinism but also to a certain self-reflexivity in his characters through their views on the restraint of society upon science.

Despite the curb placed on them by the novel, the main protagonists repeatedly protest the perpetuation of historical practices. The Russian's observation touches upon one of the most basic themes of postcolonial theory, as Jonathan Hart submits:

> One of the main recurrent imperial themes is the way in which colonizers, regardless of whether they have been the colonized, identify with earlier empires and create a myth of continuity. The colonized justify their transformation into colonizers by appropriating the political and military culture of earlier regimes.[9]

Arcady's critical announcement of the First Hundred's underlying complicity with the imperial project adds yet another dimension to Robinson's narrative. Though the First Hundred are constrained by conflicting social and scientific demands, they still strive to comply with an often paradoxical set of obligations, even though, led by Arcady, they do revolt in the end. Robinson's text recognises that the need for cultural continuity may often be the reason why history seems compelled to repeat itself. It also indicates that this voluntary acquiescence of the First Hundred with historical precedent *need not take place*. It is with a sense of revelation that we observe the ambiguities of Robinson's experiment in action. While he speaks of what has happened in the past, he is also suggesting what will happen in this future time. Predetermining what will take place on Mars, Robinson points to the alternatives, even though his narrative will not allow the characters to deviate from the 'classical' path of the coloniser. He wants the First Hundred to experience all the ills of an Earthly empire so that the reader understands the importance and validity of their eventual rejection of it. Robinson makes us aware of the pitfalls and identifies the moment of choice, but still returns his characters to the course of inevitable colonial failure. Compressing the cultural baggage of Earth's imperial history into his narrative, Robinson stabs through this dense mass with well founded probabilities, showing us the crucial moments of decision as he moves the experiment first one way, then another. That he chooses to bind the Martian colonists to a predetermined course of planetary exploitation is in itself an act of savage irony, ruthlessly mimicking humanity's imperial blindness and its mismanaged colonial past.

Robinson's deliberate satirisation of colonial failure is often shocking in its clarity. His narrative distinguishes and illuminates the moment and impulse of choice, such as at the beginning of terraforming, where Phyllis calmly announces 'God gave us this planet to make in our image, to create a new Eden'.[10] Though this is not an unexpected statement given the circumstances, Phyllis's character seems oddly ignorant of the acute irony of her position – a pro-industrial Christian on a virgin planet inhabited solely by scientific empiricists – or of her eventual place in the scheme of Robinson's satire – the capitalistic serpent among the innocent idealists. Satire is not the only thing visible in the way the First Hundred anthropomorphise aspects of the topology of the planet, or 'Big Man' as Mars comes to be called. Robinson has recognised how human groups (even rationalist ones) need origin stories and foundation myths. The conflation of American colonial and native American narratives provides an interesting hybridity in itself. Various landscape features are no longer ravines and craters, but 'Big Man's Footprints, Big Man's Bathtub, Big Man's Golf Course'.[11] Robinson not only turns the planet into a satire of Earthly values, by caricaturing the colonial desire for an egocentric taxonomy, or, as Maya puts it, for 'terracentricity',[12] but also simultaneously prods us with our need for such roots. Sara Suleri observes this need, citing British India as 'a tropological repository from which colonial and postcolonial imaginations have drawn – and continue to draw – their most basic figures for the anxiety of empire'.[13]

This 'anxiety of empire' is central to Robinson's experiment. Through a desire to illustrate the fallibility of imperial dominion, he has his colonists acting against their higher intellectual motivations. We become voyeurs as we watch and empathise with the First Hundred's struggles, knowing them made worse by the author's design. In an attempt to bypass the romantic traditions of SF, or, as Neil Lazarus identifies the trope, the 'Utopian rhetoric [which] rests upon an ideal future state, a utopia, a heaven',[14] Robinson remains strictly within the bounds of orthodox colonial evolution. He does not permit the narrative freedom of self-expression and keeps the exoskeleton of his model as one with the imperial doctrine. And while his characters are not aware of the metaphoric responsibilities they assume within this model, they are at least vaguely cognisant that they are controlled, and that there may be alternatives to their actions. Though, as scientists, they might wish to step aside from the past, Robinson has caught them fast in the bindings of a contemporary imagination. Like the author, we cannot hypothesise a flawless humanity and therefore all imaginable future engagements with empire must, on the basis of logical syllogism, be equally flawed. Yet it is not simply the knowledge that all efforts to create the 'perfect' colony must fail which gives Robinson's narrative its intensity, but that, even *knowing* of our failures in this arena, humanity *persists* in the endeavour. Despite their good intent, the Martian colony is condemned to follow the conventions of its forbears. Not until the cycle revolves from colonialism through the uneasy atmosphere of neo-colonialism and beyond does the narrative permit the characters to act outside of the known and to take their places in a genuine postcolonial imagination.

There are two other main themes within the trilogy. The morality of terraforming is much discussed and is combined with the clash of the developing periphery with the centre, with both issues linked through the prophetic visions of technological advance. These themes become critical when scientists on Mars develop a gerontology treatment that effectively greatly extends the average useful human life. Robinson inserts his narrative into a posited scenario where human evolution stands finely balanced. With the ecological and social problems on Earth (the 'old centre'), the terrestrial population needs control of both the home world and its Martian colony in order to survive, but the only way to ensure the valid continuation of either is to relinquish that control. Though the First Hundred are the lauded vanguard of a new human imperialism, their power is gradually usurped by economics, their position regressing into the subaltern. Reflecting all imperial ventures, the *Mars* texts examine the crucial notion of the subaltern as it is deconstructed and its component elements exposed and superimposed upon a futuristic landscape.

Seen in many ways as the new Eden, or at least as a potential utopia, the reality of Mars is almost displaced by a metaphorical goal for which all factions strive. As the First Hundred establish their bases and begin their exploration, Robinson also begins his examination of the problematised motivations that drive them. The First Hundred are scientists and engineers; their express objective is to ready Mars for a wave of migrants and to locate minerals with which to supplement Earth's depleted resources. Their position is a difficult one, since they have a clear directive from Earth's authorities and an equally clear awareness of what will happen to an unspoiled planet if those directives are followed. A divergence between rational purpose and intellectual desire becomes inevitable, and schisms quickly develop. Ann Clayborne, a geologist and head of the aerology team (the Martian equivalent of a geology team), understands that, even if indiscriminate terraforming takes place, the insatiable requirements of Earth can never be fully met. Her stance throughout the narrative represents the ultraminimalist approach to colonial development, which fights for the right of Mars to remain unchanged, to exist for itself. It is Ann the anticolonialist who accepts the mantle of devil's advocate. In debating bitterly with her ideological nemesis, Sax, she declares:

> I think you value consciousness too high and rock too little. We are not lords of the universe. We're one small part of it. We may be its consciousness, but being the consciousness of the universe does not mean turning it all into a mirror image of us.[15]

Offering us the view from the opposing corner, Sax Russell, a brilliant physicist and the philosophical and actual leader of the terraforming effort, utters an apparently provocative, pro-imperial view:

Mars will always be Mars, different from Earth, colder and wilder. But it can be Mars and ours at the same time. And it will be. There is this about the human mind; if it can be done, it will be done. We can transform Mars and build it as you would build a cathedral, a monument to humanity and to the universe. We can do it, so we will do it.[16]

Whether the trilogy is seen as a romance of reconciliation between opposing forces or as a confrontation of ideologies, the narrative poses the same dilemma, although as the series proceeds there is resolution as Mars changes not into an Earth replica but into a new centre. The choice is: to transform Mars into a replica of Earth, repeating practices that resulted in wasted resources and economic and political strangleholds; or to institute a fundamentally experimental but less invasive policy. If the rationale behind colonisation is to improve conditions for the centre, the home world, then Ann's view is inappropriately divergent. Alternatively, if the longevity of both the centre *and* the colony is considered, then it is Sax, representing conventional thought, who is in error, even though it is his argument that eventually dominates. Robinson maintains his strict adherence to imperial convention, his narration of the First Hundred's settlement of Mars very much in keeping with Zeynep Çelik's discourse on the development of Algiers;[17] he avoids setting precedent in this area and treads only in the footsteps of known colonial behaviours. Having already placed the First Hundred into collusion with the conventions of history, it is hardly surprising that Ann's position as the sole (or at least the most vocal) dissident is the least supported. Her logic that all human settlement changes a pristine ecology is correct, but her argument falters when she is pressed to specify the degree of human operation that would be acceptable. Yet hers is still the lone voice of dissent, the one early concession which Robinson makes to a possible, although pessimistic, postcolonial imagination.

Another compelling link between Robinson's colonisation of Mars and colonisation's traditional past is the notion of fiction, artificiality and the legitimacy of narrative.[18] In *Orientalism*, Edward Said speaks of the degeneration of knowledge between perception and textualisation, in that 'knowledge no longer requires application to reality; knowledge is what gets passed on silently, without comment, from one text to another'.[19] If a textual 'knowledge' of a colonial past is information which the coloniser sees fit to record in writing, then that knowledge is implicitly blinkered and, at best, contaminated by the author's cultural conditioning. Dependent upon who is reading it, the text may alternate between a 'known' factual accounting and an apparent work of fabrication. The only redeeming factor is that certain historical facts and dates can assume a relevance for both the coloniser and the colonised, as in the events in Barrackpore, India, on 29 March 1857, when Mangal Pandey, a sepoy of the 34th Bengal Native Infantry, rebelled during a military parade and fired at the officer in command. Narrators of both the Indian National Uprising and the Indian Mutiny agree that this was the first moment of 'official' violence during the turbulence of 1857. Yet despite these occasional synchronous moments, history's ability to legitimise narrative does not make a narrative universally legitimate.

But if historical documents become no more than narratives sprinkled with fixed points of accepted import – dates, incidents, names, places – then Robinson's critical account possesses almost an equal discursive legitimacy, even though it does not yet have history completely on its side.[20] We may even speculate that since Robinson attempts to speak for all sides *before* the event, his narrative is more of a projected political analysis than a work of fiction, and should possibly be judged as such. His postulations of a reasoned series of events, based on historical trends rather than single events, and combined with conventional human behaviour and a moderate extrapolation of contemporary scientific ability, take us not into fiction but into debate. The question most inspired by the *Mars* narrative is not 'What is science fiction?' but 'Where does science fiction begin?' Since Robinson's narrative is set in the future and is liberally strewn with marvellous techno-logical innovation, it may be argued to be entirely artificial, but this would not be the case. The trend of empire and neo-imperialism which Robinson depicts stretches back as far as recorded history itself; the limitations and acknowledged weaknesses of the human animal just as far; and the science in this Martian trilogy is essentially extant.

As we see in numerous passages throughout the text, Robinson moves deeply into realism when he speaks of the science behind the colonisation and terraforming of the planet. In clear and exciting accounts he makes future technology come alive using the metaphors of contemporary narra-tive. Even when he describes something as mundane as a haulage vehicle, he colours his images with absorbing detail:

> The ground stopped trembling. The black leviathan no longer moved. They approached it warily. A Brobdingnagian dump truck, on tracks. Built locally, by Utopia Planitia Machines: a robot built by robots, and as big as an office block.
>
> John stared up at it, feeling the sweat drip down his forehead. They were safe. His pulse slowed. 'Monsters like this are all over the planet,' he said to Nadia wonderingly. 'Cutting, scraping, digging, fill-ing, building. Pretty soon some of them will attach themselves to one of those two-kilometre asteroids, and build a power plant that will use the asteroid itself as fuel to drive it into Martian orbit, at which point other machines will land on it, and begin to transform the rock

into a cable about thirty-seven thousand kilometres long! The *size* of it, Nadia! The size![21]

Whether the technology is real or not is of secondary importance, but it is interesting to note that most of the machines and scientific knowledge incorporated into the narrative by Robinson are genuine. In a recent paper that touches on potential interplanetary commerce, population and even the sale of Martian real estate, Robert Zubrin discusses the economic viability of a Martian colonisation programme in some detail. Currently chairman of the executive committee of the National Space Society, and formerly a senior engineer of Lockheed Martin Astronautics, Zubrin submits in part illustration that:

> If government sponsorship is available, the technological means required for immigration on a significant scale are essentially available today.... A Shuttle-derived heavy lift launch vehicle lifts 145 tonnes (a Saturn V had about this same capacity) to low Earth orbit, then a nuclear thermal rocket (NTR, such as was demonstrated in the USA in the 1960's) stage with an Isp of 900 S hurls a 70-tonne 'habcraft' onto a 7-month trajectory to Mars. Arriving at Mars, the habcraft uses its biconic shell to aerobrake, and then parachutes and lands on its own sets of methane/oxygen engines.[22]

There appears little doubt in Zubrin's mind that, with sufficient monies and appropriate political backing, colonisation of Mars could begin as early as 2030, only four years after Robinson's narrative begins. Additionally, climatologists are currently engaged in research on microbial life in those extreme dry regions of the Earth that most closely approximate the Martian surface.[23] Even the practicalities of terraforming and 'ecopoiesis' – a term derived by Robert Haynes[24] to denote the fabrication of a self-sustaining ecosystem on a lifeless planet, which, when applied to Mars, can be viewed as the creation of a self-regulating biosphere – are undergoing significant investigation. All such current research leads to the seemingly inevitable conclusions not only that Mars can be colonised but also that such a colonisation is inevitable. As Haynes remarks in his foreword to Martyn Fogg's 1995 text *Terraforming: Engineering Planetary Environments*:

> In 1969, astronauts first set foot on the moon. If all goes well, others may arrive on Mars early in the next century. Against this background is it just an idle dream to imagine that people might yet 'slip the surly bonds of Earth' to pioneer new habitats in the sky? Further exploration of Mars may well reveal that ecopoiesis, and even terraforming, are feasible on that planet. Such a discovery would provide our descendants with a tremendous challenge and an exhilarating vision of the

role of humankind as a catalyst in the creation of new worlds. The propagation of life from Earth to other planets may well prove to be the ultimate legacy of our species in the universe.[25]

Robinson has extrapolated current scientific and technological knowledge, and integrated this projection within a realistic, though fictional, discourse. Verging at times upon non-fiction, one of the reasons why his *Mars* trilogy has become such a consequential work is its acute correspondence with a likely reality, where the importance of both survival and moral vision is equally stressed. With this narrative, Robinson has moved SF into new territory: an experimental meta-reality, blending the precision of a mathematical model with the study of ideas, concepts and beliefs into an autonomous matrix capable of evolution and mutation. At the same time, the narrative gives us images both of the ineluctable nature of the imperial drive and of its oblique alternatives: a future which, Robinson suggests, sways between the poles of pessimism and optimism, with the ultimate outcome of a postcolonial functionality.

This being the case, we may assume that at least a proportion of Robinson's postulations are practicable. The First Hundred *could* colonise the planet; terraforming *could* begin; migration and interplanetary commerce *could* be a legitimate aspect of social concern within the next century. If we add to these possibilities the limitations which Robinson has placed around his major characters, in that he permits them only conventional thought and the most minimal freedom of will, then the events which take place during the course of the trilogy take on a new air of plausibility. In fact, by accepting such defensible limitations into his narrative, Robinson is scrupulously upholding that most precious of all SF properties: an experimental ability to enlighten society of an event's possible ramifications before the act itself.

Once we are able to define that which is non-fictional, or at least parafictional, in the area of science and in the development of the narrative's personae, what remains as creative fiction is the plot. Yet even in this Robinson deliberately adheres the narrative to historical and political models of colonisation, populating his scenes with credible characters engaged in fully reasoned activities. He does this because he wants the reader to understand the nature of political determinism and how it influences each step of the First Hundred. His first colonists take the traditional place of the soldiers and cartographers and surveyors, with scientists and technicians as the heralds of the expedition. With no indigenous antagonists to the colonists' activities, Robinson employs subliminal scientific ethics as a replacement, providing his major protagonists with a postcolonial doubling of vision as they deal with the inner demons inspired by the dichotomy between what is 'right' and what is 'determined', where 'nothing bridged the two worlds but the human mind'.[26] Portraying insights conventionally associated with subaltern and hybridised characterisations, the scientists of Mars act out a usually internalised conflict on an externalised platform. At the end of the narrative, Ann 'the coloniser' realises that even she has appropriated a Martian duality:

> She was a new Ann now. Not the counter-Ann, nor even that shadowy third person who had haunted her for so long. A new Ann. A fully Martian Ann at last. On a brown Mars of some new kind, red, green, blue, all swirled together. And if there were a Terran Ann still in there, cowering in a lost quantum closet of her own, that was life. No scar was ever fully lost until death and the final dissolution, and that was perhaps the way it should be; one wouldn't want to lose too much, or it would be trouble of a different kind. A balance had to be kept. And here, now, on Mars, she was the Martian Ann ... a Terran-born yonsei.[27]

Robinson's invocation of emotional hybridisation in his characters is productive in two areas: it illuminates the often conflicting dualism within each personality; and it provides us with an engaging level of intimate detail more normally associated with the realism of Honoré de Balzac and Gustave Flaubert. Renouncing the implicit romance of SF, for instance by making the picturesque and the adventurous appear less romantic than they could be,[28] Robinson instead focuses on presenting an accurate prediction of the life he deduces to be possible. This technique permits his characters to assume a level of reality that renders their situation all the more likely and achieves a comforting degree of plausibility in the text, a necessary credibility if we are to see his narrative as other than fantastic. As Peter Berger and Thomas Luckmann observe: 'Human existence is, *ab initio*, an ongoing externalization. As man externalizes himself, he constructs the world into which he externalizes himself. In the process of exernalization, he projects his own meanings into reality.'[29] As Robinson's characters externalise themselves through science, we are shown glimpses of their internal duality and of the conflicts which rage at them, when even Sax, the most enthusiastic of the terraformists, admits that, 'since they wanted to create a biosphere on Mars in a short time, perhaps 107 times quicker than it had taken on Earth, they would have to intervene continuously in the act of evolution itself.... It was a daunting thought.'[30]

In keeping with his pursuit of realism, Robinson does not use visions of superbeings or nightmarish monsters. Nor does he suggest faster than light space travel, matter transportation or any one of a host of established SF tropes. To aid the flow of people and goods from Earth, Robinson causes a massive 'space elevator' to be constructed on the asteroid 'Clarke'. Phyllis's glib description of this new and incredible technology as 'an extraordinarily elegant piece of engineering'[31] is the zenith of understatement. But is such a technological leap truly SF? Robinson incorporates the recent discovery and early development of what scientists term 'smart' and 'super' materials into his elevator that would make the construction of just such an engineering feat at least theoretically possible. In a 1997 paper in *American Scientist*, Boris I. Yakobson and Richard E. Smalley, materials scientists at the Rice University of Texas, reported on a super-strength substance known as 'crystalline ropes', comprising carbon nanotubes. In discussing the application of the new technology, the authors of the paper suggest:

> Potential applications of carbon nanotubes abound, together forming a highly diversified technology portfolio. The first group includes macro-applications, where armies of nanotube molecules might line up to form a light, strong wire or a composite that could be unbeatable as a material for making lightweight vehicles for space, air and ground. If the costs ever permit, these materials might be used in the elements of bridges, or of tall, earthquake-resistant buildings or towers. Light ammunition and bulletproof vests can be envisaged. All these applications rely on mechanical strength, a property that is essentially straightforward but that requires volume production of the crucial components, defect-free nanotubes of greater length.[32]

Likewise, Robinson's introduction of the longevity/gerontology treatment may appear whimsical. However, even here Robinson does not extend probability beyond the mid-term. Carefully following current scientific thought, he extrapolates the next likely developments, his imagination of human and social consequences (such as the later memory losses caused by extreme old age) serving only to enhance the plausibility of such a treatment. With the notion of extrapolation in mind, how far does Robinson's longevity treatment differ from the introduction of modern antibiotics – of the innovations made by Louis Pasteur, Paul Ehrlich and Alexander Fleming in the nineteenth and early twentieth centuries? The extrapolation of SF need not be restricted to physical journeys in spaceships to other worlds but can also reflect more mundane journeys of science,[33] as Fischer suggests: 'The principle of extrapolation is applied with comparable enthusiasm to patterns of historical progression *and* social structure'.[34]

Thus Robinson's 'treatment' follows the current science of mapping the human genome and those areas of molecular genetics which have been experimented with at the highest level.[35] At the 1996 International Workshop of the NILs (National Institute for Longevity Sciences), which included noted scientists from Harvard Institute of Medicine, the Molecular Physiology and Genetics Section of the Baltimore National Institute on Aging, the University of Texas Department of Cellular and Structural Biology, and the

Department of Molecular Genetics Research at the National Institute for Longevity Sciences (Japan), the analysis and modulation of DNA repair in ageing were examined in detail. It was hypothesised that accumulation of DNA damage in somatic cells results in the inactivation of genes, thereby eventually causing cell death and acting as a basic mechanism of ageing. Given that this level of scientific investigation is under way, it is not outside the bounds of feasibility that some form of practicable longevity treatment (i.e. a treatment which extends the current average life span of a human) may become available within the twenty-first century. In his narrative, Robinson suggests this breakthrough will take place in 2048.

Therefore Robinson's drama is not as speculative as it may appear from an initial reading. Almost every aspect of his trilogy is at least potentially plausible, even if his nominated timeframe may err on the side of optimism. We are presented with a genuine thesis based on a demonstrated historical model, logical characters and plausible science, all of which lend a degree of credibility to the insightfulness of his narrative. Thus when Robinson warns of the dangers approaching the newly formed Martian colony, he does so not from a desire to sensationalise his text but because the warning is prudent and supported in the most part by his research. The dividing line between plausibility and inevitability is clouded at this meeting point. The new Martians have reached the moment not only of a postcolonial realisation but also of a neo-humanism: their unique longevity has taken them beyond all historical markers as they see that 'the meaning of life lay not in the past, but in the present, not in resistance, but in expression'.[36]

With the creation of a longer-living humanity, Robinson has inverted fantasy and subverted realism: all that might be assumed fantastic is potentially real, an act which reinforces the question 'Where does SF begin?' If the science and the scientific thinking in his text are provably legitimate, then little but the characterisations and motivations of his protagonists remain open to question. And his emotionally charged characters, beautifully designed to weave in and out of real science and real situations, provoke the most intense levels of empathy. We *want* them to succeed, even though we recognise Robinson's deliberate irony in the conceptions we hold of ourselves and of our place in a supposedly postcolonial existence. By making us focus upon the evolution of each individual as he or she exchanges an initially inward-looking stereotypicalisation for the freedom of a postmodern externalism, we are shown that a genuine postcoloniality arises only when the desire for its opposite is not only renounced but also made irrelevant. What need has an immortal for a piece of land? Robinson has written a significant piece of SF and, in doing so, has systematically turned the tables on those who see nothing in SF but the fantastic. Wonderland is real: it is Alice whom we must now challenge.

If the only remaining elements of uncertainty in the *Mars* texts lie within the people who populate the red planet, it is essential to examine them closely. If they are not valid representations of reality, what is their purpose? Robinson's choice to render believable all *but* his people indicates a depth of purpose uncommon in the standard tropes of SF. It is through his characters that the author exits the world of realism and returns us to the realm of fantasy. His characters provide *entrée* into a necessary creativity without which the trilogy might be considered a futuristic travelogue. Moving between the fixed points of scientific and technological fact, Robinson's protagonists supply momentum and human interest. The main characters reflect the unsubstantiatable elements of the narrative, and join the emotional and intrinsically incongruous aspects of human life to the cold accounting of science. But why are Robinson's people so often made to seem artificial and their actions so transparent?

One answer is that Robinson does not intend them to be seen as people at all, but more as representations of a specific perception. Throughout the trilogy, each main character acts as the voice for one or a limited subgroup of traditional human values, and which, for the purpose of further exposing the irrelevancy of imperial thinking, finds itself pitted against an ideological opposite. The blond, blue-eyed and attractive John Boone is the adventurer and explorer; his sociable and relatively guileless personality is indicative of the way in which we would like to portray humanity's development. His non-threatening, non-confrontational attitude soothes our worries about the essential wrongness of taking what is not ours to take. John provides a soft, *human* face to the calculated and mechanistic device of imperialism. If he, as the archetype of colonialism, is gentle and intrinsically good, then how could his motives be otherwise?[37]

Frank Chalmers, John's binary opposite, is a very strong work of characterisation. The antithesis to John in virtually every way, his saturnine appearance and frequently Machiavellian intrigues offer up humanity's darker aspects. It is Frank (his very name is an irony) who represents the worldly manipulative form of colonialisation. His motives are selfish, his belief in power for power's sake is breathtaking in its arrogance and his desires are covetous rather than wholesome. These two men are the Cain and Abel of Robinson's narrative: superficially brothers, but radically different in essentials. But Robinson's focus here is not simply on a cultural stereotype, for both men, not one, eventually die. The real importance of the conflict between John and Frank is that neither represents the mindset necessary to herald in a postcolonial future. Robinson is very interested in both these characters because they are able to display so many divergent attitudes, especially in their politics, but even more so because they also stand apart as different from the rest of the group. Whether their natures are pleasing or otherwise to our contemporary thinking is relatively unimportant. Neither is capable of seeing Mars except as an adjunct to Earth, an ideology that must be ruthlessly swept away if Mars is to achieve genuine postcolonial expression.

There are other narrative purposes in the John–Frank relationship. Seen as different sides of a spinning coin, the balance of imperial power fluctuates between them as their values rise and fall according to the tides of political fervour. In the Antarctic training camp on Earth and on the *Ares* it is Frank, the link with capitalism and material things, who is ascendant, but once they have reached Mars it is the mystical idealism of John that sways the group. The power of Earthly (and imperial) influence is perceived to be directly linked to distance from the centre; as the connection attenuates, alternative alliances gather strength. Mars and the colonists begin a reciprocal dance of influence and change. On the rare occasions when both men are striving for the same goal, as in their approach to independent migrants such as an Arab contingent, Frank represents the imperial connection with the home world and the centre, while John represents the challenge of the colony by evoking a quasi-postcolonial awareness, the new in favour of the old. John highlights the positive, the excitement of unique prospects:

> Always talking, talking in public speeches or private conversations, talking to strangers, old friends, new acquaintances, talking almost as fast as Frank did, and all in an attempt to inspire the people on the planet to figure out a way to forget history, to build a functioning society ... fair and just and rational and all those good things. To point the way to a new Mars![38]

In contrast, Frank argues for the maintenance of the status quo by inspiring fear of retribution:

> All life support here is hooked back ultimately to Earth. But they have a number of vast military powers at their disposal, and we don't. You and all your friends are trying to live out a fantasy rebellion, some kind of sci-fi 1776, frontiersmen throwing off the yoke of tyranny, but it isn't like that here! The analogies are wrong, and deceptively wrong because they mask the reality, the true nature of our dependence and their might.[39]

Between them, John and Frank illustrate colonisation on Mars. When the idealistic dreams of John gain popular acclaim, the machinations of the various political power blocs become ever more devious. As John rejects the agenda of Earthly politics, advocating the as yet unimaginable future, Frank instigates a false empathy with factional ethnic groups, cajoling them with visions of the past. In the end, Frank has John murdered, the hero's death an abrupt reminder of the frailty of idealism. It is only in the months and years following Boone's death that Frank comes to realise the necessity of idealism in such a visionary task as the claiming of an entire planet, and here Robinson's erratic humanisation of Frank adds to the power of the novel, the gentling of this passionate and egotistical character once again demonstrating that human imperfections play a vital role in our society. However, we are also shown that, as with John's death, even well meaning intent is sometimes insufficient to create a productive level of change. Frank is swept away just as Mars descends into the quagmire of political bargaining and myopic compromise.

It is the contradictions of Maya which make her such an interesting person; her weaknesses make her a strong protagonist, as her behaviour becomes distanced from the initial limitations of Robinson's fairly rigid representation of her character. Maya also plays an important role as she alternates in her affection between these two men, her ambivalence an interesting gesture in itself as first one then the other of the representations of political power achieves ascendancy. That Maya is depicted as the passionate Russian scientist substantiates Robinson's underlying argument that it is the emotional nature of humankind that offers the only hope of breaking free of determinism and the imperial drive. Indeed, the area most used for an expression of postcolonial thought in the narrative is the unquantifiable domain of the emotions. Robinson uses the nebulous emotional aspects of his characters to balance scientific arguments for and against the imperial project. To free Mars from the landscape of colonial precedent, Robinson relies entirely on those factors which separate humanity from the rest of Earthly life. It is not political intrigue or threat of force or even economic salvation that eventually opens the way to a postcolonial imagination: it is that which we hold within ourselves. Robinson's narrative taps the most basic human impulses of survival and continuance but asserts that, while we may be emotionally 'wired' to continue a human expansion, it is these same emotions that can provide the motivation to take a different path.

While the arrogance of reckless terraforming echoes the historical egotism of European explorers, and the development of the gerontology treatment seems to displace the power of natural science in favour of a new humanism, it is the advent of the space elevator that most critically indentures the possible future to an imperial past. Other than the stereotypical representations of the characters themselves, the space elevator is the most significant image that connects Mars to Earth. Stretching 37,000 kilometres from the moonlet of Clarke down into the bowels of Sheffield, the 'Company' town, the elevator is a massive umbilical cord that ties the colony to the mother world. Though constructed by the colonists from Martian materials and situated on Martian territory, it is there only to serve the imperialism of

Earth and to facilitate the control of that centre over an increasingly rebellious periphery. The words 'The elevator is secured' deliberately echo those
of Neil Armstrong on 20 July 1969 when he told the Earth that 'the *Eagle*
has landed', and that the human desire for expansion had taken a greater
control of its physical realities. As Frank departs Mars for a visit with the
authorities on Clarke, we observe the dawning of his reluctant movement
from colonial to postcolonial thinking. He is beginning to see Earth's control
as a poor thing, the ravages inflicted upon the red planet moving beyond
even his capacity to absolve. 'Mars looked just as blank as it had on their first
approach so long ago, unchanged despite all their meddling', he realises.
'One only had to get far enough away.'[40]

Once more echoing events in Earth's violent colonial past, the elevator is
sabotaged by those no longer willing to tolerate the demands of the home
planet. With birth trauma imagery, the elevator cable is separated from
Clarke and begins its rapid descent to the surface of Mars. The damage
inflicted upon the planet is immense. Whole towns are razed. As one of
the original First Hundred comments, 'this isn't the American Revolution,
or the French or the Russian or the English. It's all the revolutions at once
and everywhere!'[41] The cable wraps itself twice around the equator of the
planet, digging its internal diamond helix deep into the soft regolith as
the new atmosphere of Mars burns its outer sheath away. The destruction
of the elevator speaks volumes, in that Robinson permits it to happen.
His indestructible science is destroyed, his historical model discarded, the
imperial umbilical cord is cut and Mars is temporarily unfettered. But the
birth pangs of a suddenly free world do not come without cost.[42] Frank
Chalmers, for so long the voice of the coloniser, and only now realising the
inherent wrongness in Earth's view of Mars as a peripheral nonentity, is
lost during an attempt to escape from a tsunami of aquifer waters which
rises from the battered surface. In the near biblical flood that follows the
destruction of the elevator, the symbol of all things imperial, the ultimate
silencing punishes Frank's emerging anticolonialism.

With a calculated grace, Robinson uses the flood to leave behind a surface
washed literally clean of such images as hero and anti-hero. John Boone,
the overt idealist 'First Man' of Mars, has succumbed to the rigidity of
entrenched empire, only to be followed by his binary opposite in a fluidic
outpouring of planetary retribution. Robinson's discourse negotiates the
contemporary into the postcolonial as recent Martian history is removed by
the purifying and highly emotive force of events greater than humankind.
Though the First Hundred may have been changed, Mars is no longer the
untouched red planet: it has been replaced by a green, intermediate stage,
where the powers of both empire and colony achieve momentary balance.
A fresh generation of Martians is born, demonstrating the impossibility of

returning home to Earth or of stagnation on Mars, the cry 'You can never go back' appealing once more to the emotional optimism of the reader. The predomination of things Earthly is constantly questioned while hybridisation takes place at every level.

The notion of hybridity is vital in the novel, and Robinson's emphasis on compromise, argument, negotiation and detailed effort constructs the political and social scenario necessary to realise a practical resolution. It is not a physical hybridisation that is important but that the remaining members of the First Hundred are able to see the opportunities of hybridised thought. The only Earthly ideals and concepts that are able to survive are those which meet the needs of both the colony and the home world; all else leads to disaster. Thus Robinson's greening of Mars is not simply a tangible change but an analogy of the imperial passing into an emergent postcoloniality. In the words of Nirgal, the ultimate hybrid, 'there were two worlds, not one – two worlds in the same space, both visible, separate and different but collapsed together, so that they were visible as two only at certain angles'.[43]

Even as political upheaval and the resulting disastrous flood strike Mars, Earth experiences its own inundation. Global warming has increased the overall temperature and the polar ice caps begin to melt, causing massive flooding around the world. The dependence of the centre upon the margin has never been so critical, as increased numbers of longer-living humans are crushed into ever-decreasing spaces. In a pivotal moment, Earth must decide either to negotiate with the new Martian authorities or bring to Mars to heel under the leash of imperial force. As with the example of the British in India, coercion is the preferred option, and Earth dispatches thousands of troops under the auspices of the mega-wealthy multinational corporations. A second elevator is constructed as his Mars-born characters take up Robinson's narrative. It is the generation of subaltern hybrids who now speak as Mars the colony evolves into Mars the emergent free nation.

An increased imperial presence on Mars results in increased resistance from the colony as the stricken centre attempts to re-oppress the colonists, who now speak openly of themselves as Martians, not as humans from Earth. Jackie, a Mars-born character, defends the Martian position: 'Mars is all I know, and all I care about. I was brought up in a culture made of strands from many different Terran predecessors, mixed to a new Martian thing.'[44] Mars is no more interested in the troubles of Earth than Earth concerned itself with the settlement on Mars, or, as Maya noted, 'Nothing mattered to them really, but things Earthly. Mars was interesting in some ways, but not really important.'[45] Jackie is an interesting character. Born an *ex-utero* child of John the hero and Hiroko the militant, Jackie resembles Frank's original character more than either of her parents. It would have been an easy thing to idealise Jackie as the 'new Martian' but Robinson resists the temptation to do so. Instead, Jackie appears to illustrate the weaknesses of her progenitors far more than their combined strengths. The contrast between Jackie and Nirgal repeats several aspects of the John–Frank relationship, as both Martians are seen to represent a similar polarity of politics and ideals, but which this time results in Nirgal's political ascension and Jackie's eventual departure from Mars to a star near Aldebaran, where 'a Marslike planet rolled in an Earthlike orbit around a sunlike sun',[46] leaving Nirgal to care for the developing Martian culture.

Jackie's 'new Martian thing' is the pupal phase of an evolving creature, a time when all forms are transitory and volatile, or, in Sax's words, 'Everything was so temporary now – with so many traditions broken or vanished.'[47] Celebrating an ideological polyvalency that permits his characters to belong simultaneously to more than one culture, Robinson develops the states of marginality and plurality for their (sense of) energy and potential for growth. The central section of his narrative (*Green Mars*) is possibly the most intriguing of all, since it reports and explores the notion of transition and adaptation, of one form moving, through a phased political and cultural change, into another.

The final element of the trilogy (*Blue Mars*) is flowing and placid by comparison, as the powers on both sides of the imperial fence reach a *rapprochement*. In keeping with Robinson's overall theme of circularity, it is only when Mars, now irrigated and terraformed, becomes a 'blue' planet that Earth is finally able to treat its colony as an independent nation. Again, the narrative is charged with a poignant irony as Robinson's characters comment on 'their' world:

> Everything was blue, sky blue, Terran sky blue, drenching everything for most of an hour, flooding their retinas and the nerve pathways in their brains, no doubt long starved for precisely that colour, the home they had left forever.[48]

The position of Earth as the genesis of Robinson's neo-empire has been irrevocably altered. It has become the place where Martians, despite a nostalgic desire for 'the old country', may not easily live – their physiology has been altered by Mars's weaker gravity, which requires that they construct a new centre of their own, their own blue world. Where Earth was once the focus of all desires, Martians are now 'allergic to earth'[49] and, as recent migrants desperately preserve their cultural backgrounds and mores in an unfamiliar setting, native Martians feel 'as if they're letting monsters into their midst'.[50] Mars is not simply *a* new centre: it has seized the designation of nucleus from a weary Earth and has in turn become *the* centre. The cycle of colonial evolution has been completed. The new colony nation is free, its dependence upon the home world virtually removed. In an interesting contrast to the postcolonial situation in the present day, Earth has nothing Mars wants or needs and, far from being the hub of cultural desire, it has become an ageing and barely tolerated parent.

Thus, like Miller in the 1950s, Robinson charts the circularity of the imperial project, although his experiment is led by an extrapolation of 'real' science rather than humanity's moral failure in the face of temptation. Where Miller sees weakness and inevitable cultural decay, Robinson imagines (like Asimov) a humanity that builds stronger towers from the ruins of disaster. Essentially, the *Mars* texts distinguish the paradigm of empire as one of constant forward movement and evolution, each stage leading irresistibly into the next, each syntagmatic sequence of events as predictable as the laws of science. But where empire is inevitable and determined, Robinson offers the view that postempire is not. Akin to the theory of Marxist utopianism, where the getting of socialism would be as ineluctable as any phase of capitalism, Robinson, no doubt hearing the words of his doctoral supervisor, Frederic Jameson, writes of a time when a new kind of history, impossible to specify from our current viewpoint, will begin. By placing his narrative in a future setting, Robinson undermines the universalistic claims of historical colonial precedent and suggests at least one possible perspective on humanity's future. His meticulous reclassification of things fictional advises us that SF cannot be considered wholly fantastic. His narrative's rejection of Terracentric norms and practices extrapolates current postcolonial criticism as the developing population on Mars revisit and eviscerate colonialist ideology until it tumbles to the Martian surface as lifeless as the first elevator.

Using the First Hundred as a binding agent, Robinson constructs a thread of narrative that takes us from the contemporary into postcontemporary images. His employment of an extended life span is essential to maintain the postcolonial 'doubling' of vision experienced by the original colonists as they move transversely across the face of the imperial device. Seeking the intellectual freedoms of a Mars still innocent of empire, the remnants of the original group ironically begin a new diaspora, taking humanity into the first stage of yet another syntagmatic sequence, as they head for more distant stars. Abandoning the contemporary once again, tainted as it is by the early colonial status of Mars, Robinson has the character of Ann maintain her search for a precolonial version of her original home. But she is now coloniser and colonised, and does not understand that the knowledge of both which she carries is her ultimate destiny. Her role in the cycle is tragically limited by the fact that she can never return to innocence. She can never go back. As Maya broods in the café overlooking the corniche in new Odessa, she finally understands the meaning of Frank's ironic comment that 'Empires have long half-lives ... and the idea of empire has the longest half-life of all'.[51]

However, what would happen if we postulate a future so distant that even the idea of empire and imperialism has long been forgotten? If the first empire had never been formed and humans had never learned to think of themselves as belonging to a nation or a nationalistic conglomerate, what form might our desire for expansion and exploration take? To examine the possibility of such a time, we turn now to the vast realm of Iain M. Banks's postcolonial, postimperial and almost post-human 'Culture'. By examining the form and nature of Banks's organism as well as the motivations and behaviours of some of his main characters, it becomes possible to see how one version of our future selves has been extrapolated not from ideas of science but from current cultural mores and ideologies.

9. Beyond Empire:
Meta-empire and Postcoloniality

What happens after an empire is displaced? When an imperial construct is removed, such as the British Raj or the control of the French Caribbean colonies, what fills the vacuum? In the real world, there are various forms of action, from a careful, gradual absence (the British withdrawal from India) to a devastating collapse, with violence accompanying partition (the fall of the Soviet Union). Historically, the removal of an imperium has more often been a gradual process; a new structure of postcolonial governance has usually been able to fill as much as it can or wants of the vacated post-imperial matrix. This new growth has many names. It may reclaim an older nationality or proclaim itself reborn in a different guise. It may become part of a new association or may, as illustrated by events in the demise of the Soviet Union, devolve into small units of varying culture. But in the realm of fiction, and especially of SF, transition between the old regime and the new is often more distinct and abrupt, the requirements of the narrative overriding the realities of slow political exactitude, demanding some more immediate, alternative replacement – an instant fabrication. Political forms can alter radically and without even a partial precedent, especially in the *avant-garde* of SF.

Traditionally, the genre still embraces a certain strain of realism, as the old centre expires and is replaced by something which incorporates a predictable political decay, such as the gradual reformation of the 'old' USA into the economic despond of Philip K. Dick's *Do Androids Dream of Electric Sheep?* (1968) or Isaac Asimov's *Foundation and Empire* (1952). Occasionally the absence of one empire is replaced by some dynamic neo-empire or imperial metaphor, such as the children's developing tyranny in Arthur C. Clarke's *Childhood's End* (1953) or the rise of the Fremen in Frank Herbert's *Dune Messiah* (1969). Occasionally an author will experiment with a completely new concept, offering the reader a new alternative such as Banks's 'Culture'.[1]

There is little room in SF texts for a political hiatus of any kind, as the genre's dynamic demands some explicit alternative, either powerful (neo-empire) or enfeebled (political decay), against which to highlight their futuristic science and technology. Further, this alternative is essential as a background against which to frame the narrative itself and frequently illustrates some consequence of dystopian or violent extreme, such as Robert Bateman's *When the Whites Went* (1963), which has a post-pandemic England inhabited only by non-whites, or György Dalos's *Nineteen Eighty-Five* (1983), a sequel to the characters and classic form of *Nineteen Eighty-Four*, in which Orwell's totalitarian orthodoxy is threatened by the death of 'Big Brother'. Usually associated with technological progress and frequently incorporating a radical movement away from the old centralised authority,[2] the SF alternative is most commonly a reiteration of empire, or form of rebellion against empire, the genre having little taste for the slow realism of political disassociation unless considered in a post-holocaust scenario, for example as described in classic format by Walter M. Miller's *A Canticle for Leibowitz* (1959) (see Chapter 7) and Emma Bull's *Bone Dance: A Fantasy for Technophiles* (1991). Occasionally there are some SF novels which make an effort to move beyond narrative convenience and produce an entirely different background best considered as *meta-empire*: an unknown place where options of both neo-empire and political atrophy are eschewed and a new form of political structure is embraced.

The Culture novels of 'meta-empire' by Iain M. Banks (1954–) stand outside current genre classifications because his texts explore a genuinely new area of SF, where even the concept of 'empire' has passed into myth. No other SF novels, not even Asimov's version of the future, have yet taken us *beyond* an awareness of our own imperial history. Banks does. He writes of time and space so far ahead of us that without his adherence to some elements of known physics we might not even be sure he writes of the same universe. Nor is this new meta-empire a thing of utopian convenience. In many instances it is far from utopian, although it is at the moments when Banks writes of the profound effect technology (or the absence of that technology) has upon his human-like characters that we most see an authentic postcolonial novel that takes us beyond even the conceptual aftermath of empire.

If we consider ourselves familiar with the traditional composition and elements of the political model of empire, then we must be equally aware that such a model is no longer in cultural or ethical favour. Humanity, it seems, has passed by the colonialist stage, relegating its practice to a less enlightened era. We now exist within a time of postcoloniality, in which individuals, societies and entire nations proceed to come to terms with the long-term ramifications of political imperialism, an activity clearly displayed by any examination of our social heritage. However, if we are now beyond empire, grown *outside* of empire, then where exactly are we? Since it is impossible to effect an actual or even an authentically intellectual return to precolonial days, we are left experiencing a different form of personal hybridity: all of us conscious that we, as individuals or as members of a particular society, have been altered by the history of imperialism and colonialisation which surrounds us. It would also be pleasant to imagine we had decided to grow up and leave our youthful games of empire behind, having cast off such tribal impulses. But this is not the case. While the political role and ideologies of empire have been essentially rejected by the beginning of the third millennium, the exoticism of the term 'empire' lingers on in all areas of literature, but particularly in genre SF. Are we humans inherently violent in our reach for control and conquest? Though this is a contentious view, the levels of violence in Banks's non-utopian Culture makes it a logical question. Or is it that the entire possibility of 'postcoloniality' is an unachievable goal? Will we ever really be far enough away from our imperial past to consider ourselves untainted by colonialist history? If the genre is ever to leave the impulses of empire behind, where will it be able to go? What is there after or outside of empire that might appear a logical progression from one state of being to the next? What cultural hybridity is exhibited in contemporary SF? Perhaps instead of trying to locate postcoloniality outside our imperial history, it would be more productive to examine our inner state for its existence, where the problems and issues of nationalism and the sacredness of ethnicity surround the continuing mythology of a nation's past suffering or greatness.

The seductions of empire have never been far from us. The Shang kings of China's first imperial dynasty[3] devised war games in which captives were surrendered in the bloodiest of fashions to the greater glory of the developing Shang sovereignty. Even though the form of Shang authority was eventually superseded, it, like the ancient images of the Mediterranean and Egypt, left an irremovable bookmark in the affairs of our species. Once the early constructs of empire were emplaced, the notion of such a political and cultural supremacy could not be returned to the ether: the path to future empires was already laid down as an achievable and desirable goal, long before the technology to follow the pathway existed. As Rupert Emerson notes:

> Nations, like individuals, are products of heredity and environment, although in the case of nations heredity is to be sought not in the genes but in the social heritage that flows from generation to generation.[4]

As a cultural flow, the possibilities of aggressive imperialism were not limited to the ancient enclaves of dynastic China. Later and much vaster empires have existed and fallen, their methods of evolution self-modifying to accommodate the most effective techniques of the time. Historically, brute force has been the preference for most imperial conquest, since force is the simplest and most immediate of all expansionist methodologies, requiring only superiority in crude physical power and the ability to wield that power in an effective manner. Other cultures are subsumed and silenced both physically and philosophically. Government changes and new laws take hold. Hybridity and polyvancy emerge. The Romans did this with their legions and roads; the Spanish and Portuguese with their gun-ships and missionaries; and the British did it with their Martini–Henry rifles and East India Company. The social heritage spoken of by Emerson may also be described as *power familiarity*, where each subsequent generation of the dominant culture assumes and takes for granted an ever increasing level of cultural precedence; not only does might become 'right', but it becomes 'righteous'.

Cultural development (especially military development) has always been a matter of successive historical advances modifying one another by constant pressure within the crucible of survival and self-governance. In many cases, such pressure has arisen from within a central authority, as the demand for increased territories overcomes natural caution and a desire for a peaceful existence; though empire is not necessarily a primary goal of expansionism it has often been a primary result. But even supposing the absence of an ambition for empire, the *idea* of such a state has remained intact and, in some ways, almost beyond change. Such is the historical authority of the imperial project and, to some, its supremely righteous allure that its immunity to change is no longer questioned, but it is rather viewed as an archetypal yardstick against which many other movements are assessed. The desire of humanity to endlessly recreate variations of this power base is astonishing, and so deeply is this desire hidden within our psyche that often it goes as unobserved. It seems always present, though generally unobserved, always ready to develop, but rarely developed with overt design. Its unseen, unspoken presence guides and manipulates contemporary societies in everything from party politics to international trade agreements and regional educational systems. The very coins in our pocket reflect a lingering allegiance to empires past. Humankind may not always admit its reluctant homage to empire, but neither has it woken fully from the dream and the glories of its myth and archetype.

And just as myth has become one of the most prominent terms in literary analysis as various genres and plot patterns engage with certain ideals and allegorical formulas, so too has the pattern of empire found a home in the texts of SF. Nor should the development of the original notional archetype be viewed in a negative perspective, since the growth of the stereotypical form is often used allegorically, warning us away from the fate of Daniel Dravot in Rudyard Kipling's 'The Man Who Would Be King' (1888). Empire in itself is not an evil thing, yet our histories demonstrate that those who have created empires do not do so in order to produce a state of peace and beauty. From our historical past we have learned that empire is a thing of political imposition, to be avoided by enlightened powers. Alongside our secret acknowledgement of its allure, we currently accept the idea that to concede its seductions is to embrace the notion of tyranny, for surely only a tyrant would wish to return to the ways of war and conquest for gain. Thus the idea of political empire has become shrouded and slightly ominous; and when seriously debated is regarded either as a semi-evil object or as an amusing impossibility in an enlightened society. Yet this makes its presence in our literature an even more powerful motif since, like Kurd Lasswitz's Martian Nume (see Chapter 5), the unsuspected villain is a far greater force of evil against which the powers of good must struggle. The advent of empire has become so unlikely an occurrence in current-day thinking that its existence is usually discussed only in the past tense, although the derogatory term of 'imperialist' has surfaced in contemporary discord between nations.[5] Though there is a reluctance to designate any modern political state as 'imperialist', the economic weight of some of the larger national groups has recently begun to provoke use of the term more frequently.

Rather than invent a 'new' evil, SF often uses an immediately recognisable form of empire – as with Robert A. Heinlein's paralleling of the American War of Independence (see Chapter 6) – and displays such an image in a startling new technological environment, or uses techniques of alienation in a most literal form. We revisit the classical conceptions of imperial evil in terms of the temptations and opportunities of science and the unlimited powers available to those who inhabit space and times outside our own. This is one of the forces behind the immortality of empire. In order to create a suitable foil against which to illustrate both the strategic tenacity and the increasingly technological supremacy of humankind, authors of SF have first been required to construct the appropriate landscape. What could be more convenient an image than a background simultaneously suggestive of the temptations and corruptions of empire?

There are many SF novels that deal with the fall of an empire, the author having constructed one in the text primarily to catalogue and narrate the effects of its decline. Excellent illustrations of this process are provided by Asimov's *Foundation* series based on Edward Gibbon's *The History of the Decline and Fall of the Roman Empire* (1776–88), the modern double-sequence work of Alan Dean Foster in his *Humanx Commonwealth* series (1982–97) and the screenplays of George Lucas's *Star Wars* films. Yet a great deal of even the most recent SF relies upon the reiteration of conventional aspects of empire because it supplies a point in time and space against which to continue the cycle of the periphery's rebellion against the old centre. However, there are also SF narratives that deal with empire in a tangential manner, either moving vastly forward in time or dealing with different concepts encapsulated by the term. Beyond or above the geographical we now have the intellectual possibility of *meta-empire*, one example of which is

William Gibson's *Neuromancer* (1984), which conceives of an imperial model of 'thought',[6] where a person's mind is physically controlled by 'jacking' into the worldwide neural net, a nightmarish concept first characterised in Gibson's story 'Johnny Mnemonic' (1981) though suggested by Winston Smith's torment in George Orwell's *Nineteen Eighty-Four* (1949). Gibson's idea of a mind-abusing technological future is a tangible colonisation not so much of the physical but rather of the non-physical aspects of the brain, harnessed, curbed and abused by a technological society of the future.

In 1971 Donald A. Wollheim wrote *The Universe Makers*, a 'cosmogony of the future',[7] essentially a distillation of the stages of projected empire through history and into the future. Among the eight stages documented by Wollheim, three specify the rise and fall of the galactic empire as it is enshrined as the central myth of SF. Though galactic imperiums are necessarily things of invention, their *potential* permits authors of SF not only to experiment with the implied possibilities of the events and processes of the imperial project but also to examine the various future behaviours of the human species, assuming such processes were technologically feasible. So popular has *future empire* become that contemporary authors often rest on the conventions of the endeavour without explanation. SF empire simply *is*. And one of the reasons why the possibilities of galactic empire have become so essential to SF harkens back to the concept that empire is dormant within numerous, though not all, human actions. This is a vastly unpopular and unfashionable perception that many would decry as untrue but, given the appropriate conditions, there are few who would not feel some positive emotion upon establishing a personal empire. Family businesses do it every day, as do chancellors of universities and leaders of industry. Since the readership of SF has been predominantly educated males, it is understandable why the testosterone-laden adventures of far-flung conquest have proven so addictive. However, the apparently irrepressible urge to empire, even given the psychological and physiological traits of the human male, does not fully explain the attraction of the imperial structure.

The conquest of the unknown and of the unknown Other stems from humanity's basest urges, ably defined by Abraham Maslow's hierarchical theory of human needs (see Chapter 4). Our desire to expand and conquer has deep associations with this theory, especially where it links to the traditional images of the 'heroic' male and 'nurturing' female, both still very much stereotypical icons in SF up until the 1970s and 1980s. This iconography is unsurprising, given SF's early modern masculine demographic readership. SF texts have successfully and logically combined the alluring myth of empire with this wheel of social development and a growing reliance upon technology. Often paralleling the exploitation of the North American 'Wild West', the elementary drama of colonisation in SF texts feeds this subterranean urge to explore and dominate, furthering the social stereotypes and providing a venue where these icons are still permissibly displayed. Thus empire is not intrinsically wrong; it is outward evidence of the social needs of the human species to develop, progress and grow.

Neither is empire as a construct an improper concept, since contemporary societies are quite comfortable with the notion of economic empire – indeed, we laud our commercial entrepreneurs as veritable visionaries and heroes. Therefore it seems that empire as a notion is unfairly castigated while certain elements of its structure are still actively and openly sought. Only the development of political empire appears improper and it is not difficult to observe the paradoxical issues surrounding the imperial ideology. While the ideology of free enterprise and entrepreneurship is not universally appreciated, many of its opponents are prepared to accept certain of its forms rather than embrace radicalism; others may decide that, though they cannot support the negative political model, they may yet see merit in its positive economic results. However, the splitting of the imperial theory in order to isolate its negatives from its positives is an impossible goal: to possess the latter one must embrace the former. This fact is amply illustrated by the advent of capitalism and the importance placed upon gathering of great commercial wealth, another version of 'power familiarity'. To pretend our various societies do not retain some urge to empire is not only transparently foolish but also hypocrisy of the worst order. Individually we may decry the power mongers yet culturally we do nothing to remove an individual's ability to gather power to a new centre. Most industrialised countries have even set legislation in place to protect a specific right to do so. While it is possible to see a genre which writes about empire as serving a form of social absolution, it is far more productive to see SF novels as 'what if' experiments, as they engage with incidents of empire and the results of such cultural forays.

Since much of the impetus of SF depends upon the exploration and settlement of our own and other galaxies, the place and function of the imperial stereotype are understandably exceptionally powerful. Just as the first Shang kings engendered a new level of social order through physical conquest, so too has SF spawned a socially acceptable form of imperialism through intellectual rationalisation and technological possibility. But now authors who have considered the possibilities of *meta-empire* in SF are beginning to look much more closely at the replacement of empire by something other than a newer version of itself. Such are the fascinations of the massive and endlessly various permutations of a postimperial future that Scottish author Iain M. Banks has constructed an extremely successful sequence of texts that portray exactly this attraction, within a vast and interstellar social body known only as the 'Culture'. However, Banks's *Culture* reflects a more complex model than simple replacement, in that his alternative society does not appear affected by an ingrained imperial impulse and therefore his experiment is not motivated by the need to 'replace' but rather by a desire to work from an untainted beginning.

That there is no specific imperium within the Culture, no hierarchical leadership or enclave of all-powerful beings is an anomaly in itself; the underlying essence of Banks's novels is deliberately set against the traditional form of SF empire. In many ways, Banks's Culture books are utopian, freeing their citizens from Maslow's eternal pyramid by simply removing any unfilled needs. Everyone is as physically and intellectually perfect or imperfect as they desire to be. The great 'ship Minds' control all manner of resources and facilities. Nothing is left wanting.[8] Based around the existence of an incomprehensible physical power made possible through highly advanced technological science, the Culture has no unsatisfied needs, no dream it cannot achieve for itself. So omnipotent is its decentralised society that the Culture rarely possesses an identifiable enemy. Banks has looked beyond and outside conventional empire, into a culturally simplified future where our most fundamental wants and desires have been sated, leaving humanity's intellectual and altruistic potential to be continuously explored. His novels postulate a time when imperialism of any form is redundant, not because of any inherent goodness on the part of humanity but because it already has far more than could be gained by embracing such an ideology: in Banks's novels empire has finally become obsolete.

Interestingly not only does Banks posit the obsolescence of imperialism in his texts, but also his logic does away with many of the trappings associated with consumerism, communism and the extremes of both left- and right-wing politics. The Culture advocates an extreme form of libertarianism, in that there is almost a total absence of state intervention[9] in the lives of its citizens. Throughout the series of novels there is an overwhelming argument that private morality is not the state's affair and therefore activities such as drug use and social and sexual practices which would be considered unusual by today's standards are not only perfectly legal but considered the norm.[10] In this respect, Banks's novels share common ground with anarchism and socialism, given that he argues for equal rights and opportunities for all, as well as for a theoretical abolition of all government. The Culture illustrates a utopianist form of anarchy in that it operates extremely fluidly on a voluntary, cooperative basis without (usually) recourse to force or compulsion. Is Banks attempting to recapture the essence of pre-imperialism? Or is he discussing the modus of 'city', in its broadest sense?[11] Given that we cannot actually return to a time before empire was a reality, are the Culture novels advocates not of a highly futuristic and advanced setting but a return to the ancient and idyllic images of island tribalism? This is an immensely powerful objective from a postcolonial perspective, in that the narratives appear to seek voices so far removed from the mood of imperialism that they have reverted to an untainted innocence.

A number of Banks's SF novels thus far have focused loosely on aspects of the Culture's interaction with other galactic societies:[12] *Consider Phlebas* (1987), *The Player of Games* (1988), *Use of Weapons* (1990), *The State of the Art* (1991), *Against a Dark Background* (1993), *Feersum Endjinn* (1994), *Excession* (1996), *Inversions* (1998) and *Look to Windward* (2000). In these, Banks continues his saga of the super-rich anarchistic Culture, where superior artificial intelligences, mega-large artificial environments and an intense desire to associate with other cultures produce the motivation for his characters and plots. In almost all cases these other societies are less technologically advanced, although in his first Culture novel, *Consider Phlebas*, the warlike Idirans violently oppose the Culture, a position highly reminiscent of the Soviet Union and the United States during the Cold War, where the aggressive technology of both sides was frighteningly similar and equally adept at the task of destruction. Horza, the main protagonist in the narrative, muses about the difference between the Idirans, who believe in a god, and the Culture, who do not:

> Maybe the Idirans would have a tougher job than they expected. They were natural warriors, they had the experience and the guts, and their whole society was geared for continual conflict. But the Culture, that seemingly disunited, anarchic, hedonistic, decadent mélange of more or less human species, forever hiving off or absorbing different groups of people, had fought for almost four years without showing any signs of giving up or even coming to a compromise.[13]

Consider Phlebas is a novel about the war between two inimical cultural forces, and readers are placed in a situation where they must confront the fact that Horza, a seemingly rational, sincere and honourable being, sides with a non-human enemy against his own kind. Is Horza simply a race traitor? Through the actions and insights of his character we receive articulate criticisms of the Culture, which is seen as subtly aggrandising and intolerant. It is difficult to see which side is in the 'right' in this novel, a deliberately problematic stance taken by Banks as he probes the nuances of cultural conflict and the desirability (or otherwise) of allocating values to certain cultural stances. Whether the reader considers Horza incorrect in his beliefs is secondary to the fact that the questions Banks raises through him are challenging and difficult to overlook.

Interestingly, the Idirans also seem to mimic the more conventional aspects of traditionally narrated galactic empires in SF, which enables Banks to engage the reader in genre parody and satire, as well as to enthral us with the view from beyond SF's archetypal limitations.

In *The Player of Games*, Banks criticises the traditional construct of empire by literally 'playing' a single Culture citizen against a corrupt and archaic civilisation in which dominion is decided through a monumental game of skill and chance. Through a series of tableaux the author examines first the conventional model – complete with its bastions of physical force, its regimented hierarchy of authorities, its darkness – and then contrasts it with a more utopianist version – where force has become superannuated and obsolete, where a centralised hierarchy no longer exists and where regimentation has given way to a form of civilised anarchy. Though the novel's point of view is provided by a game-player who is himself a pawn in a much larger game, this narrative gives the perspective from the mountain-top: how would humanity, or even human individuals, behave if they could see the much larger view? In the Lesser Magellanic Cloud, the Culture has discovered the Empire of Azad, a brutal and cruel, but surprisingly stable, regime. Jernau Morat Gurgeh, the Culture's best game-player, is seeking new challenges, boredom being a genuine problem when every whim is catered for. The Culture takes it upon itself as one of its acts of semi-selfish altruism to neutralise Azad's threat, and so manipulates Gurgeh into tackling a mission of five years, to literally beat the Azad empire at its own game, where the winner becomes emperor and losers may suffer physical mutilation or even death. The game is used as an integral part of the power system of the empire, where 'Azad' means 'system', the empire even taking its name from the game, equating the playing of its roles with the playing of life itself within the imperial structure.

Analogous to the Culture's decentralised existence, the novel itself possesses several pivotal yet equally decentralised characters, each having an essential role to play within the narrative while being dependent upon other major characters in order to fulfil that role. Banks writes the novel as a game within a game, obliquely equating his alien characters with familiar chess pieces. Primarily there is Gurgeh himself, whom Banks describes as a consummate game-player, almost a politician of games: 'The longest it had taken him to learn any game had been three days; he hadn't forgotten any rule of any game in his life, nor ever had to learn one twice.'[14] Gurgeh is set up to illustrate a prototype of Culture citizenship, in that he has everything he could ever possibly want in terms of material and physical assets. He is intelligent and famous, a noted scholar with a wide circle of lovers and friends. Everything he might need in his life is already available to him. Yet, precisely as Maslow predicted, once all material needs are met, the desire to expand the experience of the mind becomes paramount. In Gurgeh's case the lure of the unknowable and unobtainable – the mysterious and dangerous game of empire – is sufficient to tempt him away from everything, to hazard all he has, even his life, the implication being that even an enlightened and complete individual will entertain curiosity and a desire to develop further, no matter the risks. After an initial resistance, Gurgeh grows increasingly willingly to participate in the game and, indirectly, in the continuance of an imperial structure. His is the tactical position of the white chess queen[15] in both Banks's novel and in the game the Culture elects to play.

The other essential character of the novel is Flere-Imsaho, a tiny library drone[16] which takes the apparently advisory role of bishop to Gurgeh's queen but which, in fact, is a saboteur member of the Culture's secretive 'Contact group', which plans to overthrow Azad because the empire's brutality threatens the periphery of the Culture's (anti-)organisational existence. The drone's role is a cleverly duplicitous one, since it is more aware of the Culture's motives than the game-player himself,[17] yet this bio-mechanoid is deliberately made out to appear small and weak and defenceless, its surmised weakness hiding its true purpose: to provoke a revolution within Azadian society. In the position of Gurgeh's other advisor is the Culture ambassador to Azad, one Shohobohaum Za, who takes it upon himself to keep the unwary Gurgeh out of trouble during his involvement with the empire. The Culture team thus comprises queen, bishop and knight. Taking the role of the black king is the emperor regent of Azad himself, Nicosar, who succeeded to the throne upon the death of the previous emperor, but who has himself never won the complete series of Azad that would legally proclaim him emperor in his own right. Nicosar has much to prove and becomes the figurehead of all things imperial as he strives to overcome the challenges of the game and Gurgeh's increasingly alarming success in it.

It is through the medium and playing of the game that Banks dissects traditional empire and provides a view beyond. From the outset, the reader is given to understand that empire equates with power and the visible show of that power, as Gurgeh experiences his first imperial reception:

> 'What are they standing there for?' Gurgeh whispered to the drone in Eächic, low enough so that Pequil couldn't hear.
> 'Show,' the machine said.
> Gurgeh thought about this. 'Show?'
> 'Yes; to show that the Emperor is rich enough and important enough to have hundreds of flunkeys standing around doing nothing.'
> 'Doesn't everybody know that already?'
> The drone didn't answer for a moment. Then it sighed. 'You haven't really cracked the psychology of wealth and power yet, have you, Jernau Gurgeh?'
> Gurgeh walked on, smiling on the side of his face Flere-Imsaho couldn't see.[18]

It is as if the author is not only writing about a player of games but also playing his own game with the reader as he adroitly satirises matters imperial. Gurgeh understands only too well both the façade and the immediate meanings of Azad, since he has become submerged in the rules of both game and the empire on the two-year journey from his home. The 'show' of Nicosar's court is precisely the same as the 'show' of the boards on which Azad is played – brilliantly superficial, false, metaphoric and easily altered by the skilful player. Moreover, Gurgeh is very skilful, his ability enabling him to take risks in the game because he has nothing to risk, other than a temporary risking of his own reputation and safety. Unlike Nicosar, Gurgeh is the perfectly objective player, able to look at the game/empire from a viewpoint outside its enticements and to act accordingly. The regent emperor, however, has his entire life and position at stake: he cannot possibly see this as a game but as the official and public workings of his sovereignty. Gurgeh's role provides the 'big picture' perspective as Banks examines and skilfully unravels the structure of both contest and empire. As seen in the tumultuous endgame, the empire cannot be divorced from the game itself, Azad's essential weakness and strength being the combination of the two elements. When the game is strong and well played, the empire is also strong, with powerful leaders. But when it is weakened by either internal or, in the case of Gurgeh's involvement, *external* forces, the emperor-player is forced into dangerous tactics and gambits, as encapsulated in his final violent moves, the death throes of his game, his empire and, finally, his own life. This novel, by making a game of empire, explores and criticises each element of the structure and the extremities of conventional power play, and shows the weaknesses of traditional empires as well as their vulnerability to the shady machinations of an anarchic force. The unchanging, isolated and unique model of Azad cannot stand against a power that seeks only to disrupt rather than conquer.

Two characters who act both as supporters to Nicosar and as suitably placed 'opponents' to Flere-Imsaho and ambassador Za, are Lo Pequil, a liaison official with Azad's Alien Affairs Bureau, and Hamin, rector of Candsev College, where the 'great game' is officially taught. Throughout the novel, these six main pieces weave a complex game among themselves, just as Gurgeh and Nicosar represent the opposing forces of the carefully non-imperial Culture and the meticulously sculpted metaphor of Azad.[19] As the narrative progresses, Banks defines several moments where the two sides conflict, offering the reader moments of insight between the conflict of empire and postempire, where first one then the other side appears to gain an upper hand. Finally, Gurgeh and Nicosar meet in the climax of competition, an acid test of ideologies, where all extraneous detail is removed, leaving only the bare bones of political structure and the deployment of power inherent in each structure. By this time the reader is fully informed as to the nature of Azad, but what of the Culture's moral standing? Does the Culture's use of Machiavellian tactics render it morally reprehensible: a shell of techno-sophistication surrounding a vacuum of pure anarchy and cynicism? Or is Banks giving us another taste of authentic postcolonialism, by showing us that imperial behaviour does not require the frame of empire in order to accomplish its ends, but that imperialism is as much a single act as it is a mode of thought or philosophy? Is the real postcolonial form one that can recognise and use aspects of an imperial mindset to its advantage without taking on the actual shape of empire?

Poised at the edge of the novel, the reader is almost convinced that empire will prevail as Nicosar grasps the full centralised power of Azad and changes the rules. This is a typical response of empire, in that at the last moment, when all else fails, it will become violently self-cannibalistic, destroying its own centre rather than permit its overthrow by an outside force. The reader witnesses Azad's enraged descent into madness and anarchy as its leading player – Nicosar – destroys everything around him to avoid losing it to the Culture. The Culture does not win because there is nothing left *to* win, but neither does it lose, since the empire cannot continue, leaving the Culture (in the figure of Gurgeh) as the last ideology standing. Given that the Culture is held together by the great ship Minds, is this battle of ideologies simply for their vast amusement, a game, or is the eventual destruction of all potentially threatening non-Culture ideologies the real and more sinister objective?

In *The Player of Games*, Banks has produced a novel of postcolonial signifi-cance in that he describes not the fall but the very obsolescence of empire, and provides an insight into what might next be studied in place of empire in current postcolonial critical theory. Looking through the paradigm of his Culture, the author stands beyond contemporary attitudes, where political empire is still a matter of recent history, and stares into the far future of one particular cultural group, where all thought of an imperium has long been removed from everyday living. Beginning with *Consider Phlebas*, Banks has taken the reader into a time so far distant from today that the work of the Shang has been removed not only from memory but from conceptual thought. It is as if he has recreated humanity in the moment before the devising of the first imperial structure, so that, in *The Player of Games*, we are able to compare and contrast the mechanisms of both empire and the game of Azad as if they were something foreign to us, regaining an objectivity that is precluded by our own familiarity with the notion of empire. It does not matter that this novel is fictional since, just as did Thomas More's *Utopia* (1516), it deals with specific ideologies set in a deliberately nebulous and fictionalised place. The reader's ability to examine those ideologies in an uncontextualised scenario renders *The Player of Games* a brilliant experiment in cultural and theoretical objectivity.

In a similar vein and published two years later, *Use of Weapons* is also an exercise in objectivity, offering another view from the high moral ground of enormous distance. Again there is one main character, but one who forms part of a linked triad and echoes in micro the Culture proper. Banks's novels are full of such scenarios, where the great mass of the macro-environment is subtly influenced and directed by the events and situational responses of small groups, each forming, in themselves, an offshoot of the Culture in the perceived atmosphere of externally imposed barbarism. In this manner, Banks tells us that the Culture is strong not only as a whole but also in its parts and subsidiary elements. It has transcended the need for grand outward displays of power, although the presence of the great ship Minds and of the marvellous technologies implies a certain understandable smugness. It requires no physical, centralised mass to achieve success in its goals, although this is primarily because it holds such incredible technological advantage over nearly every other extant culture. The very use of the epithet *Culture* is a massive irony on the part of the author, since it posits almost an exact opposite of the term's contemporary meaning.

An image of Banks's future hegemony may be gained by looking at it from an external viewpoint, to define the Culture by examining how it defines those things not of itself, from the perspective of an extra-Culture event. In *Excession*, we have:

> You were a tribe on a largish, fertile island; you'd tamed the land, invented the wheel or writing or whatever, the neighbours were co-operative or enslaved but at any rate peaceful and you were busy raising temples to yourself with all the excess productive capacity you had, you were in a position of near-absolute power and control which your hallowed ancestors could hardly have dreamed of and the whole situation was just running along nicely like a canoe on wet grass … when suddenly this bristling lump of iron appears sailless and trailing steam into the bay and these guys carrying long funny-looking sticks come ashore and announce you've just been discovered, you're all subjects of the Emperor now, he's keen on presents called *tax* and these bright-eyed holy men would like a word with your priests. That was an Outside Context Problem.[20]

Most ironically, Banks's satirisation of empire means that the overwhelming powers of the Culture do not *seek* control. The ship Minds look only for a peaceful continuation of the status quo, except when their gentle peregrinations bring them into contact with forms such as Azad. The Culture advocates no deliberate political expansion of any configuration other than the movement of peaceful relationships throughout the galaxy and the devising of suitable non-planetary habitats for its citizens. It takes great pains not to interfere with external societies other than to attempt to prevent conflict and destruction. And here we observe indications that even the peace of the Culture is not without cost. To maintain the super-economics and non-political balances within a non-imperial space, there will occasionally be times where violence and force may be used during confrontations with those races and cultures who still cling to the archaic architecture of power and violence. Those outside the Culture who choose to live by the sword will be defeated by their weapon of choice.

In order to maintain the relatively harmonious social conditions within the Culture and to support its balance of politics and policies, most individual leanings in opposing thought have become obsolescent or irrelevant, or have been removed in some manner. The average Culture citizen no longer knows how to deal effectively with violence and overt political power because they lack importance. The Culture's citizens have become largely as children in interstellar politics, hence the need for an organisation such as Special Circumstances and, in turn, the recruitment of such unusual or violent individuals as Cheradenine Zakalwe (on both of which, see below) and indeed Gurgeh. We see that even utopia possesses thorns when we realise the cultural form created by Banks must, at some point, support an outermost periphery, even though it is a vague and hazy version of its ancient ancestors.

It is along this intangible periphery that disruptive confrontation will be experienced no matter how much the Culture seeks to avoid it, although there is equally an argument that, if is it so all powerful, will the Culture ever develop a true periphery? While there will, at some point, come the Idirans or an Azad, and during those moments of friction the secular evangelism of the Culture meets and possibly conflicts with the ideology of the Other, does the term 'periphery' hold the same sense of absolute in Banks's meta-empire, or are we now required to re-examine the basis of postcolonial literary theory? Though the author has removed evidence of any obvious centre, he still speaks of the 'volume' of space currently occupied by the Culture: 'The Culture was able to use almost the entire galaxy to hide in. Its whole existence was mobile in essence; even Orbitals could be shifted, or simply abandoned, populations moved.'[21] This would argue for some definition of what constitutes 'inside' and 'outside' Culture space, and some terminology to describe the outer perimeter of that 'volume' (Banks's term for the Culture's galactic spread). But is this the new periphery? In *Use of Weapons* Banks takes the reader even further away from traditional notions of hegemony, along a theoretical sublime to a precise event and back again since, without definable frontiers, there can be no definable interior, the body of the Culture illustrated only by what it is and does *now*, and not by its historical past. This means that, to succeed, Banks's model of meta-empire must not only stand apart from most political extremes but also be able to move between states, to alter its behaviours in certain parts in order to deal with localised threats. The Culture is better defined as a living organism than as a political structure.

In *Use of Weapons*, the first and most exposed of the main characters is Cheradenine Zakalwe, a mercenary and relatively secret agent of the Culture group known only as Special Circumstances, an organisation whose task is to infiltrate outsider societies and carry out whatever task is deemed likely to pacify or render a society less adverse to the Culture's own philosophy. His violence and blunt physical response often forms the cutting edge (the 'precise event') and most un-Culture-like part of the action, yet it is exactly this odd, peripheral behaviour which is most open to peril, another indication that non-Culture behaviours are dangerous and unhealthy. Although there are a few select members of the Culture involved in the dirty work of intercultural peace-keeping,[22] Banks's deployment of mercenaries like Zakalwe at the front line of the Culture's various conflicts is interesting: does this mean that the Culture's hedonistic pursuits have rendered the great majority of the citizenry unable or unwilling to risk themselves at a time of crisis?[23] But Zakalwe's often overtly antagonistic attention does not mean that the external civilisation under his temporary focus will be absorbed by the Culture; rather, it will be simply rendered less of a physical threat to Culture citizens. We are also reminded that Zakalwe is not Culture-born, but Other, co-opted to perform certain duties for Special Circumstances.

Since very few actual members of the Culture are willing to act effectively in situations so far outside their usual mindset, it falls to individuals adopted into the ranks and who retain some vestige of barbarianism to do the actual dirty work. This suggests that while the Culture has advanced beyond things of empire, it has also become effete and ineffective by contemporary standards (this was the Idiran assumption and the cause of their eventual undoing). Banks writes of hedonists and sybarites, much as did H. G. Wells when he described the lotos-eating innocence of the Eloi in *The Time Machine* (1895), yet Culture members seem to fight all the more effectively for having reached beyond primitive notions of nationalism and individual courage. But since the Culture novels are set in a time so distant from the need or use of force, do these terms maintain useful meanings in themselves? What does the word 'mercenary' mean in the far future when wars themselves are barely remembered? In Banks's mechanised and smoothly oiled society, the term 'mercenary' is more easily equated with the word 'tool'. Zakalwe is the most logical agency to use on the extreme perimeter. He is a practical tool in a society that is able to identify and then act upon the most rational course of action.

Zakalwe is a fascinating character. He is a violent man, an assassin-poet, a lover and a soldier; despite his chilling ability to take life, he is portrayed as a humanitarian and an individual who dislikes causing unnecessary distress or pain. Although we understand he must possess an intriguing past, in a narrative where irony piles onto irony Banks gives us no explanation other than exposing elements of Zakalwe's tormented and jagged memory. As the narrative is explored, certain events cause spontaneous and deeply disturbing moments of recall, and these permit both the protagonist and the reader to glimpse fragments of Zakalwe's earlier self. As his memory becomes more complete, his darkly Freudian problems of jealousy, sibling rivalry and guilt intensify, and the obsession with the completion of his current assignment grows. It is not until the completion (successful for the Culture) of his task that Zakalwe finally meets the one person who can shed light on the images which plague him. He is driven to this meeting by his lack of identity, yet it is this very lack that makes him such a perfect operative for Special Circumstances. Once the mission has been completed, Zakalwe receives his 'reward', which both completes and destroys him. The Culture, through the guise of Special Circumstance, manipulates Zakalwe, whose history is profoundly and destructively imperialist, into a narrative that sees him identify and eliminate not only the enemy without but also the enemy within.

The second member of the central triad is Diziet Sma, a senior representative of Special Circumstances whose main role is to locate, indoctrinate and control members of this specialised internal group. Sma is the liaison, the interface between the smooth world of the Culture and the rough, brutal world of the outside. As with her peers in Special Circumstances, she is neither soldier nor spy, but is effective and highly competent in a variety of roles. Her main responsibility in this novel is to be a buffer between the Culture proper and the potentially offensive incursions of all that is Other. The third persona is the artificial life form, or drone, Skaffen-Amtiskaw, whose vast abilities extend across the range of abstract human thought and into the mechanical.

Use of Weapons is an important novel in SF's genre of future empire in that it transcends all prior conventions of the form. Banks writes about a social body which has itself transcended the need or desire to create a centre since such a construct would only serve to delineate and encapsulate a thing that has passed beyond any ability to be so enclosed. The text is also exquisite in its ability to focus upon certain distinctive aspects of traditional imperial thought, as it physically positions Zakalwe at pivotal moments of activity in external societies. Zakalwe is the smoking gun of the Culture's activities, guided by Special Circumstances through the human aspect of

Sma, who is herself linked to the larger body of the decentralised whole via Skaffen-Amtiskaw. Though each of the three plays a distinct and separate role, their combined efforts translate the design of the Culture into specific and accurate operations.

In addition to portraying certain aspects of their own characters, each member of the trio is representative of a cultural and social stereotype. Zakalwe is the archetypal 'alpha male': supremely masculine and forceful; brutal yet intelligent; emotionally callused yet capable of vast sympathies for those whom he is instructed to betray. Sma is the beautiful woman, able to be the angel of the hearth as well as the angel of death, her final scene in the novel generating an extreme ambiguity as she recruits yet another operative. Hers is perhaps the broadest of the three roles, in that she is required to produce the requisite emotions and arguments with which to channel the soft human core of Zakalwe, as well as the coldest and most calculating of objectivities as she conforms to the necessities of Special Circumstances. Skaffen-Amtiskaw intrigues the reader as he (although drones are essentially genderless, the voice of this drone is male) mediates between the larger Culture and the two other characters. Seemingly capable of whatever task is asked of him, the drone both meets the human fear of the invasive robot as it mercilessly slaughters a handful of Sma's attackers and portrays, at times, the most delicate emotional and moral aesthetics:

> 'They also,' Skaffen-Amtiskaw said, 'refuse to acknowledge machine sentience fully; they exploit proto-conscious computers and claim only human subjective experience has any intrinsic value; carbon fascists.'[24]

The words of the drone echo loud in postcolonial terms, as they suggest that only outside the Culture are subjective values and judgements of the individual considered important, a suggestion continued throughout his series of novels. Banks makes widespread use of the bizarre and the vaguely shocking: parties where people queue up for temporary physical mutilations; the absence of 'ownership' of anything except one's mind; casual sex changes; pregnancies deliberately extended into decades. Through these references to the eccentric, the author is able to suggest both the vastly tolerant nature of the society that accepts such activities and the virtually complete absence of any form of social judgementalism compared with the *outside*. No matter how unsettling such activities might be in *other* societies, Banks uses potentially offensive images to further illustrate Culture members' acceptance of themselves and their dependence upon no other morality or expediency than their own. Banks paints a bigger picture of the utopian aspects of the Culture by focusing on small details and anticipating the reader's extrapolation of the larger philosophies present.

Banks's narrative is written at several intersecting levels. The first level consists of the actions of Zakalwe: mercenary, assassin and soldier. His is the story of past betrayals and the bitter loss of family and home through war and revenge. This life-weary character is recruited by Sma into Special Circumstances to act as an on-site operative and to undertake whatever task deemed necessary at the time. From beginning a war to rescuing an advocate of peace, Zakalwe moves from one operation to the next, assuming whatever guise is required of him as he follows the unfathomable dictates of Diziet Sma. His entire role is one of flexibility and transition as he undertakes assignments along the periphery, although this semi-constant violence is not without an emotional or psychic toll. Zakalwe's despondency after accidentally crushing a bird's nest full of eggs while on a sabbatical to write poetry echoes the later revelations of his deeper crime and loss, and which in turn suggest that his use as a weapon by the Culture was a more deliberate act than even Sma might imagine.

Sma herself is as much a puppet as Zakalwe, in that she does not choose where or why to send in her various activists. Under the vague and faintly overwhelming auspices of the Culture, she too demonstrates a flexibility of purpose; though seeming more autonomous than Zakalwe, Sma takes on a variety of attitudes, dependent upon the work in hand. She is the ultimate power broker of the decentralised centre, even though she views her position as nothing more than a facilitator of operations: "'Zakalwe,' Diziet Sma said, 'we diverted twenty-eight million people and a trillion tons of spaceship two months off course to get you to Voerenhutz on time; I'd appreciate it if you'd wait until the job is done before you blow your brains out.'"[25]

Just as her story relates her actions to Zakalwe, it also describes another level of complex interactivity that is her place in the will of the Culture. In addition, seemingly working in conjunction with Sma, yet clearly at an intrinsically higher level still, is the drone Skaffen-Amtiskaw. Possessing an artificial intelligence of profound ability, the drone provides a link with the even greater Minds of the colossal galactic ships that at times appear to form the Culture proper. This triad are themselves guided by the collective will of the ship's Minds, who, Banks's narrative suggests, are capable of perceiving the larger and most objective of all views of the current state of the galaxy. But in all the interaction of these characters we see an absence of elitism and a signatory flexibility, an ability to change rapidly in response to immediate needs. This flexibility is yet another difference between a central-ised imperium and a decentralised meta-empire: the former is rigid and constrained, bound by visibly hierarchical methodologies and paradigms; the latter is loosely connected both physically and philosophically, so more able to adapt and thus survive.

An observation can be made at this point in the development of empire within SF: to survive, the imperial form has necessarily evolved from the strictly conventional historical model, as written by Asimov and Poul Anderson, into a less immediately recognisable form, as in the novels of Banks and Gibson. There is now more extant power and a greater variety of forces than might ever have been previously imagined by either ancient or recent colonial empires. Not only has the nationality of empire become an irrelevancy, but the force of contemporary globalisation and the power of postmodernity have rendered even the imaginings of such archaic philosophies superfluous. Banks is asking us to hypothesise what may happen in the space *beyond* empire, as new generations of readers demand an end to the imposition of a social heritage no longer theirs in fact or ideology.

Banks offers us a wholly new form of society, one that does not rise, phoenix-like, from the warm ashes of its recently deceased parent, but one which dispenses with the idea of 'parent' altogether. Regardless of how much Banks plays with conventional SF tropes and clichés, his novels look far beyond traditional identifiers of empire, as his Culture narratives compare and contrast the weaknesses and strengths of familiar and innovative structures, allowing the reader to decide which is the stronger. By doing this, Banks has also opened a new door into critical literary theory because there is now something beyond the extant, something to inform our thinking in a forward rather than a backward direction. That the Culture does not yet exist is of moot significance for, as in More's *Utopia*, we are dealing with theoretical structures of both political and cultural intent, and SF's unique forum has long been a place where both areas have received widespread examination and criticism.

Conclusion

We are all products of the historical imperial project, though not necessarily artefacts of a deterministic history. Since almost every extant society today can look back at moments in time when it was subject to empire in one form or another, it would be foolish to assume our imaginations have not been conditioned, in some manner, by this experience. We are the products of our societies; our deepest and most private values have been informed by a historical presence or absence of political and economic power. We are not required to be proud of our societies or even to like them very much, but it is essential we become aware of who we are and *why* we are this way in order to ensure our future does not repeat the past mistakes of abusive power manipulation.

But to be consciously aware of and continually to remain objective in relation to all social development, even within our own small part of the global culture, is an impossible task. We are too close to the picture and can see only details, when what we really need to examine are the more general design and frame of the image. And to do this we require an inverse telescope: a tool with the ability to capture the quantum image and locate it within the greater representation, and with the additional ability to transpose images at will. There are many such mechanisms in current use: everything from divergent political systems and educational philosophies to the world of the arts and even the daily news reports. But these devices are restrained by the human ability (or inability) to embrace the contemporary and initiate change. The smallest elements of the image, such as minor legislation or the regulation of a banking system, may evolve comparatively quickly, but the more complex aspects of social development can take years, decades, to develop, as has been witnessed with the fall of the Soviet Union and the decentralised emergence of the former Soviet states. And even these developments, major though they are in relation to our current perception of global society, are still only references of the contemporary or, at best, the near future. Clairvoyance is not an attribute our species enjoys and therefore all we can extrapolate from the near past and today is what is probable tomorrow or next year. To explore and investigate what might be of importance to us in fifty, one hundred or even one thousand years hence, we have only our imaginations as a guide, and often the best of these futuristic imaginations are given voice through the experiments of SF.

As this text has discussed, many SF narratives deal with the purely fabulous: worlds where dragons become domesticated,[1] or where an expanding humanity encounters weird creatures[2] only to discover the fantasy of the Other is reduced to political realities once again. These are works that liberate our imaginations, which enable us to play with power and the results of that power and which permit us the extravagances of Homer and Lewis Carroll. These narratives are fiction in one of its unalloyed forms, exceeding even the magical realism of Voltaire and Gabriel García Márquez, as perfect utopia is created and the hero is always victorious. Then there is the other side of SF: narratives that look back into the past of our various cultures and define a differing *Weltanschauung*, from which a single potential future is extrapolated and investigated. Though many SF texts bear a similarity to others, each of these literary investigations is sufficiently different to effect a slightly different result, and it is through the intellectual amalgam of these results that we may see something of the possible far future here and now in the contemporary. Isaac Asimov's vision of cities encased in steel, the *Dune* novels of Frank Herbert, the 'spindizzy'-powered cities of James Blish, Ken MacLeod's *The Stone Canal* (1996), George Orwell's *Animal Farm* (1945) and Robert A. Heinlein's *Red Planet* (1949) are all examples of experiments in the purely imaginative.

Nor does SF's inescapable intertextuality diminish the function of a single text, for just as scientific development builds upon the discoveries and innovations of earlier generations, so too does SF incorporate and adapt worthy elements from preceding narratives. An example of this is Mary Shelley's monstrous creation of 1818, where both her monster and her science inspired numerous related works about the dangers of the Promethean impulse. In more modern works we see a reiterated concern with the creation of both biological and non-biological life, such as Edmond Hamilton's 'The Metal Giants' (1926), in which an artificial brain goes mad and turns against its creator, and Ursula Le Guin's 'Nine Lives' (1969), which explores the existence of clones on a mining planet. In turn, Arthur C. Clarke's *Imperial Earth* (1975) and Robert Dick's *Do Androids Dream of Electric Sheep?* (1968) invoke a more socially 'acceptable' approach to cloning or artificially conceived life as they engage with narratives of imperial exclusivity and the human biological imperative to maintain both bloodline and the notion of 'home'. Iain M. Banks extrapolates this concept still further and incorporates the design of artificial life into his multi-sentient Culture. The clear intertextual inheritance in SF is not only useful in the genre: it becomes essential if authors are to explore concepts to their fullest. And as Shelley's prototype continues to evolve into the ambiguous potential of artificial life, so too have authors of

SF taken the basic precepts of an archaic political system and dissected its possible nuances for the generations ahead, taking the classically moulded shape of ancient empire and evolving it into the form of meta-empire.

It is almost impossible to ascertain when writers first began incorporating the idea and ideals of power and imperialism into SF. Was it Cyrano de Bergerac's *Histoire comique des états et empires de la lune* of 1656, or perhaps Jean-Baptiste Cousin de Grainville's *Le Dernier homme* of 1805? Certainly George T. Chesney's 'The Battle of Dorking' (1871) established the notion of the 'future war' at a time when Britain's own empire was about to destabilise and two of the world's greatest SF writers, H. G. Wells and Jules Verne, were only beginning to explore the different uses and abuses of power in such dystopian works as *The Time Machine* (1895) and *Maître du monde* (1904). However, it must be remembered that these early authors lived in imperial times. Secure in their Western lifestyles, their respective countries holding massive colonial dominions, it would seem only natural for them to manifest aspects of imperialism in their narratives. US writer Jack London's most formidable work, *The Iron Heel* (1907), speaks even further of political dystopia as his twenty-seventh-century scholars unearth a twentieth-century fascist oligarchy and an account of the proletariat's epic revolutionary struggle against the state.

It is on these early beginnings that more modern writers such as Asimov and Heinlein lay the foundation of increasingly ambitious empires. In Asimov's case, the definitive version of the galactic empire is produced: an enormously complex organisation which, thanks to his innovative philosophy of 'psychohistory', spans years in terms of time as well as distance. But whereas the Asimovean experiments entirely escape the realism of physics, Heinlein makes use of known science to posit an extrapolation of peripheral theoretical physics and allows his characters to explore not only different dimensions but also how their cultural and political mores might be adapted in these new and uncharted regions.

Thus the role of empire in SF is in itself multidimensional. It provides a primary doorway into the potential future from the past: a figurative trope by which a contemporary reader may locate the framework of a modern narrative. The mass of intertextuality is vital in this sense, since it is only through an iteration of similar models that the reader may construct an immediate intellectual image, and it is upon this construct that new authors, such as Banks and MacLeod, create their works. The trope of empire is now an archetype of fictional form. Like the Other, and the notion of centre and periphery, it has become one of the basic blocks of SF creativity, still popular and still a matter of fascination, as may be seen in the latest SF publications.

Yet with the potential of neo-imperialism, be it geo-political or economic, there is also the potential for the development of a new subalternity. When power raises one society it automatically means that another is seen as lesser. How the future generations of humanity will coexist with the binary opposites of power and parity is precisely the type of interrogation performed by SF. Therefore power and imperialism are not concepts we may assume have been left behind us: such ideologies are as strong now as they ever were for the Roman caesars, the Soviet premiers or the American presidents. The best way to understand empire as it has been treated in SF is to consider that it does *not* describe a Western cultural bias, as has often been assumed, but that it stems from a many-sided impulse to which any one of us might be prone. In the final analysis, empire in SF, with its globally expanding market and with humanity's increasing affinity with the world of science, is a positive tool for social awareness. We have not left empire behind us for the simple reason that it still has a role to play in our cultural productions and, until we achieve a global existence where power is no longer sought after or lauded, we still need our fictional imperialisms with which to seek out and identify its most problematic issues.

Therefore empire in SF is a fundamental theme by which a vast number of SF texts are shaped, for, like the water we drink, we need it, if only to complain about its taste. Empire's intellectual presence is neither good nor bad, but neutral. Its fictional peculiarities are dependent upon those actions by which the narrative defines its boundaries and policies. And it is this constant work of definition and redefinition that marks SF as a place of intellectual activity and hope. It is the genre of anticipation and discovery, extrapolating all areas of a human existence into an increasingly scientific future. By shining a series of lights on the imperial iniquities of our past, SF removes all shadows and allows us to see objective variations of our past selves projected into the future. If the sight of such images permits us to avoid a repetition of ancient mistakes, then the genre is possessed of greater power than some might suspect.

The theme of empire, with the complexities and ramifications that post-colonial and other recent criticisms have brought to our attention (treatment of the Other, of the exotic, of matters of power), is so ingrained in SF that to discuss empire in SF is also to investigate the fundamental purposes and attributes of the genre itself. That it is necessarily intertextual, despite the often solitary journey of the author's imagination, equips the genre with the power of its own history, as successive experiments progress from and beyond the boundaries of earlier narratives. It works by extrapolation, reasoning from what is already known (in the case of contemporary science) into a multitude of technological tomorrows, or from historical empire in order that we might hypothesise the advent of future political powers. It is tied to the ideology and time of writing (of nineteenth-century imperialism, of scientific diaspora), yet, because of its orientation towards imagined futures and experimentation with those futures, it is not completely determined by the ideology and culture of the time of writing. It is both connected and free. And as the experimentation of SF continues into a new century, it is possible to endow the closing lines of Kim Stanley Robinson's *Icehenge* with even greater significance: 'We dream, we wake on a cold hillside, we pursue the dream again. In the beginning was the dream, and the work of disenchantment never ends.'[3]

Notes

Introduction

1. The following texts (detailed information is listed in the bibliography) have influenced my sense of the history and prehistory of SF (more widely than the context of empire considered in this book) and have introduced me to the debate as to how the genre may be defined: the novels of Aldiss, Asimov, Banks, Blish, Clarke, Dick, Heinlein, Le Guin, Robinson, Wells and Verne; Alkon's *Science Fiction Before 1900: Imagination Discovers Technology*; Fischer's *The Empire Strikes Out: Kurd Lasswitz, Hans Dominik, and the Development of German Science Fiction*; Knight's *A Century of Science Fiction*; Mendlesohn's 'Science Fiction in the Academies of History and Literature'; Parrinder's *Shadows of the Future: H. G. Wells, Science Fiction and Prophecy*; Scholes' *Structural Fabulation: An Essay on Fiction of the Future*; Slusser and Rabkin's *Mindscapes: The Geographies of Imagined Worlds*; Slusser *et al.*'s *Storm Warnings: Science Fiction Confronts the Future*; Suvin's *Metamorphoses of Science Fiction: On the Poetics and History of a Literary Genre*; Wolfe's *The Known and the Unknown: The Iconography of Science Fiction*.

2. H. G. Wells, *The Time Machine, The Island of Dr. Moreau, The Invisible Man, The First Men in the Moon, The Food of the Gods, The War of the Worlds* (anthology), Heinemann/Octopus, London (1977). This preface originally appeared in an earlier collection: *The Scientific Romances of H. G. Wells*, Gollancz, London (1933).

3. Terry Eagleton, *Literary Theory: An Introduction* (2nd edition), Blackwell, Oxford (1983), p. 190.

4. Samuel Taylor Coleridge, in *Biographia Literaria* (1817), wrote 'transfer from our inward nature a human interest and a semblance of truth sufficient to procure for these shadows of imagination that willing suspension of disbelief for the moment, which constitutes poetic faith'. See H. J. Jackson (ed.) *Samuel Taylor Coleridge*, Oxford University Press, Oxford (1985), p. 314.

Chapter 1

1. Edward W. Said, *Orientalism: Western Conceptions of the Orient*, Vintage, London (1978), p. 93.

2. Ibid., p. 67.

3. Said, *Orientalism*, p. 63.

4. Bernhard Waldenfels, 'Response to the Other', in Gisela Brinker-Gabler (ed), *Encountering the Other(s): Studies in Literature, History and Culture*, State University of New York, Albany (1995), p. 39.

5. Ted Krulik, 'Bounded by Metal', in Robert E. Myers (ed), *The Intersection of Science Fiction and Philosophy*, Greenwood Press, Westport (1983), p. 121.

6. Konstanze Streese, 'Writing the Other's Language', in Gisela Brinker-Gabler (ed.), *Encountering the Other(s): Studies in Literature, History and Culture*, State University of New York, Albany (1995), p. 286.

7. Heinlein's 'Black Hats' represented all the negative values of the alien Other: conspicuously inhuman, visually revolting, evil but relatively easy to overcome.

8. Larry Niven, *A Gift From Earth*, Sphere Books, London (1968).

9. Kim Stanley Robinson, *Blue Mars*, Voyager, London (1996), p. 189.

10. Robert A. Heinlein, *Red Planet: A Colonial Boy on Mars*, Schribner, New York (1990), p. 12.

11. Gary K. Wolfe, *The Known and the Unknown: The Iconography of Science Fiction*, Kent State University Press, Ohio (1979), p. 187.

12. Ibid., p. 200.

13. Philip K. Dick, *Do Androids Dream of Electric Sheep?*, Orion Books, London (1968). The book was filmed as *Blade Runner* (1982).

14. The work of Boris and Arkady Strugatsky, a Soviet writing duo published from the late 1950s onwards, dwelt in the world of social SF, rejecting past Stalinistic conformity and examining how technology and the future might affect the lives of people in the Eastern bloc nations. Their best-known novel, *Piknik na obochine* (1972), translated as *Roadside Picnic*, Macmillan, New York (1977), was filmed as *Stalker* (1979).

15. As in the case of Dervley Linter, who has himself biologically altered in order to live with humans in Iain M. Banks's novella *The State of the Art*, Orbit Books, London (1991).

16. Such as the offer Kurd Lasswitz has the Nume make to the Earthlings in *Two Planets* (see Chapter 5) or the false perception of the Dune Fremen created by the House Harkonnen in Frank Herbert's early *Dune* novels.

17. Peter Barry, *Beginning Theory: An Introduction to Literary and Cultural Theory*, Manchester University Press, Manchester (1995), p. 193.

18. Wolfe, *The Known and the Unknown*, p. 151.

19. H. G. Wells, *The War of the Worlds*, William Heinemann, London (1898).

20. The differences, though often monstrous, may equally be divine, as in such works as C. S. Lewis's *Out of the Silent Planet*, Bodley Head, London (1938) and Paul J. McAuley's *Eternal Light*, Gollancz, London (1991).

21. Kim Stanley Robinson, *Red Mars*, Grafton Books, London (1993), p. 15.

22. Leo Spitzer, 'Andean Waltz', in Gisela Brinker-Gabler (ed.), *Encountering the Other(s): Studies in Literature, History and Culture*, State University of New York, Albany (1995), p. 217.

23. Waldenfels, 'Response to the Other', p. 36.

24. Said, *Orientalism*, p. 63.

25. Angelika Bammer, 'Xenophobia, Xenophilia, and No Place to Rest', in Gisela Brinker-Gabler (ed.), *Encountering the Other(s): Studies in Literature, History and Culture*, State University of New York, Albany (1995), p. 47.

26. Stephen David Ross, 'What of the Others? Whose Subjection?', in Gisela Brinker-Gabler (ed.), *Encountering the Other(s): Studies in Literature, History and Culture*, State University of New York, Albany (1995), p. 19.

27. Brian Ash, *Faces of the Future: The Lessons of Science Fiction*, Taplinger, London (1975), p. 73.

28. Consider such films as *Starship Troopers* (1997) and *Enemy Mine* (1985).

29. Waldenfels, 'Response to the Other', p. 42.

30. Emmanuel Levinas, 'Die Spur des Anderen', translated by Elizabeth Naylor Endres, 'The Trace of the Other', in Gisela Brinker-Gabler (ed.), *Encountering the Other(s): Studies in Literature, History and Culture*, State University of New York, Albany (1995), p. 11.

31. Edward W. Said, *Culture and Imperialism*, Vintage, London (1994), p. 121.

32. Bammer, ''Xenophobia, Xenophilia, and No Place to Rest', p. 51.

33. Robinson, *Red Mars*, p. 204.

34. Ibid., p. 56.

35. Ibid., p. 205.

36. Robinson, *Blue Mars*, p. 3.

37. Ash, *Faces of the Future*, p. 74.

Chapter 2

1. Damien Broderick, *Reading by Starlight: Postmodern Science Fiction*, Routledge, London (1995), p. 68.

2. There has been much excellent critical discussion of Dick's novel as well as Ridley Scott's film version, *Blade Runner* (1982), notably Judith B. Kerman (ed.), *Retrofitting Blade Runner: Issues in Ridley Scott's Blade Runner and Philip K. Dick's Do Androids Dream of Electric Sheep?*, Bowling Green State University Popular Press, Ohio (1991).

3. David Seed (ed.), *Anticipations: Essays on Early Science Fiction and Its Precursors*, Syracuse University Press, New York (1995), p. 185.

4. Brian Stableford, 'Philip Kindred Dick', in John Clute and Peter Nicholls (eds), *The Encyclopaedia of Science Fiction* (2nd edition), Orbit Books, London (1999), pp. 328–30.

5. Dick, *Do Androids Dream of Electric Sheep?*, p. 8.

6. Ibid., p. 4.

7. A 'Chickenhead' is one who does not have sufficient intelligence to pass the minimum mental faculties test. Isidore's radioactively mutated genes gave him an ability to restore dead animals to life. Isidore was 'treated' for this mutation, but the treatment rendered him mentally incompetent and a 'Special': a non-person, unable to emigrate off-world and given only the most menial of work to perform. Following World War Terminus, all residents of Earth are required to undergo a yearly mental faculties test.

8. Dick, *Do Androids Dream of Electric Sheep?*, p. 28.

9. Wells's Martians are 'natural' in that they come from a race of creature we may assume to be self-replicating in a more or less normal biological sense. To humans, this entire race of Martians would be 'monstrous'. Where the Other can be clearly perceived as such, there is a different type of fear – one which permits an outward and almost acceptable expression of conflict. The Other within is the most difficult to detect and therefore inspires a colder and deeper sense of disquiet. Wells's Martians are frightening because we can see a monstrous difference between them and humanity. Dick's androids are frightening because we cannot see any difference at all. These are two separate forms of fear and are treated differently by the two authors.

10. George Orwell, *Animal Farm*, Secker & Warburg, London (1945), quote from Penguin edition, p. 109.

11. Dick, *Do Androids Dream of Electric Sheep?*, p. 157.

12. Jean-François Lyotard, *The Inhuman: Reflections on Time*, translated by Geoffrey Bennington and Rachel Bowlby, Stanford University Press, Stanford (1991), pp. 3–4.

13. It is interesting to note that in several of Dick's other fictions the victims are children, for example Manfred Steiner in *Martian Time-Slip*, Ballantine Books, New York (1964).

14. John Wyndham, *The Midwich Cuckoos*, Michael Joseph, London (1957), p. 24.

15. Ibid., p. 59. Ferrelyn's situation also provides a suggestive allusion to the Virgin birth and the coming of Christ. Are these children the spawn of gods?

16. Aaron Perkus, 'The Instincts of Race and Text', in Gisela Brinker-Gabler (ed.), *Encountering the Other(s): Studies in Literature, History and Culture*, State University of New York, Albany (1995), p. 74.

17. An entire segment of John Clute and Peter Nicholls, *The Encyclopaedia of Science Fiction* (2nd edition), Orbit Books, London (1999) is devoted to children in SF. Apart from Wyndham's previous novel, *The Chrysalids*, Michael Joseph, London (1955), which deals with the advent of mutant telepathic children after an atomic war, another notable text dealing with children as Other is by British author Arthur C. Clarke, whose *Childhood's End* (1953) tells of the growth of a new generation of children with enormous mental powers, who not only render their parents' generation obsolete, but whose destiny is as an unknowable force among the stars. It is not an optimistic novel for parents to read. The short stories 'Mimsy Were the Borogroves', by Henry Kuttner (writing as Lewis Padgett) and Catherine L. Moore (*Astounding*, February 1943) and 'Zero Hour' by Ray Bradbury (*Planet Stories*, autumn 1947) both dwell on the subject of children either working in concert with aliens or using alien technology in order to achieve their own ends, regardless of parental restriction. Unquestionably, the immediate postwar years witnessed a significant alteration in the Western perception of children.

18. Salman Rushdie, *Shame*, Adventura Books, New York (1984), p. 85.

19. Karl Marx, Introduction to *Contribution to the Critique of Hegel's Philosophy of Law*, in *Deutsch Französische Jahrbücher* (1844). Available online at http://www.marxists.org/archive/marx/works/1843/critique-hpr/intro.htm (last accessed February 2007).

20. Wyndham, *The Midwich Cuckoos*, p. 93.

Chapter 3

1. U. A. Fanthorpe, 'Tomorrow and', in *Selected Poems*, King Penguin, London (1984), p. 90.

2. Isaac Asimov, *Nightfall*, Grafton Books, London (1991), p. 11.

3. George Lakoff and Mark Turner (eds), *More Than Cool Reason*, University of Chicago Press, Chicago (1989), p. 89.

4. Joanna Russ maintains that 'In a sense, science fiction includes (or is parasitic on, depending on your point of view) non-science fiction'. Joanna Russ, 'Towards an Aesthetic of Science Fiction', *Science Fiction Studies*, 2 (July 1975). Available online at http://www.depauw.edu/sfs/backissues/6/russ6art.htm (last accessed February 2007).

5. Wells, *The War of the Worlds*, p. 717.

6. Jacques Derrida believed the inevitable clash of metaphors in all writing demonstrated how language may subvert or exceed an author's intended meaning.

7. Asimov's first robot story, 'Robot AL-76 Goes Astray', appeared in the magazine *Amazing Stories* in February 1942.

8. Isaac Asimov, 'Three Laws of Robotics', in *The Rest of the Robots*, Panther Science Fiction, London (1981). The three laws are:

    (1) A robot may not injure a human being or, through inaction, allow a human being to come to harm.

    (2) A robot must obey the orders given it by human beings except where such orders would conflict with the First Law.

    (3) A robot must protect its own existence as long as such protection does not conflict with the First or Second Law.

9. Iain M. Banks, *The Player of Games*, Orbit Books, London (1988), p. 41.

10. Gerard Steen, 'Analyzing Metaphor in Literature', *Poetics Today*, 20 (1999), p. 508.

11. Sara Suleri, *The Rhetoric of English India*, University of Chicago Press, Chicago (1992), p. 16.

12. Leela Gandhi, *Postcolonial Theory: A Critical Introduction*, Allen & Unwin, St Leonards (1998), p. 3.

13. Ibid., p. 14.

14. Denis Judd, *Empire: The British Imperial Experience from 1765 to the Present*, HarperCollins, London (1996); Isaac Asimov, *Foundation and Empire*, Panther Books, St Albans (1952), p. 14.

15. George Lakoff and Mark Johnson, 'Conceptual Metaphor in Everyday Language', *Journal of Philosophy*, 77 (1980), p. 484.

16. Ursula K. Le Guin, *The Dispossessed*, Avon Books, New York (1974), p. 1.

17. Shakespeare was perhaps the most well known proponent of a metaphoric idea of 'wall', in *A Midsummer Night's Dream*, through a chink in which the lovers Pyramus and Thisby are required to converse. 'Some man or other must present wall; and let him have some plaster, or some loam, or some rough-cast about him, to signify wall' (Act III, Scene I). Le Guin presents the wall on the planet Annares in almost the same tone; a metaphoric barrier existing most powerfully in the minds of the indigenous culture. To those inside the wall, it is merely an inconsequential barrier, a common form of division, theirs to control and therefore insignificant. For those on the outside, it is the entrance to a different world and assumes vast symbolism. A similar contributor to a division between ideologies was the Berlin Wall, which became even more metaphorical in structure by its fall and eventual absence in 1989 than it ever was during its existence.

18. Le Guin, *The Dispossessed*, p. 2.

19. Ibid., p. 7.

20. Le Guin's 1974 text holds strong echoes of the politics of the times. In 1972, US President Richard Nixon visited China and Russia, and Britain imposed direct rule over Northern Ireland. In 1973, one year before the novel's publication, the peace accord between North and South Vietnam was signed (though fighting continued); East and West Germany established diplomatic relations, formally acknowledging, for the first time, their post-World War II separation; the Soviet leader Leonid Brezhnev visited the United States; and Henry Kissinger and Le Duc Tho were awarded the Nobel Peace Prize for their negotiations over Vietnam.

21. Le Guin, *The Dispossessed*, p. 7.

22. Odo, the spiritual leader of the Annaresti, bears similarities with Bunyan, both having been prisoners of conscience.

23. The incident in which Shevek attempts to rape one of his hosts (p. 185) is particularly interesting in this regard.

24. Arthur C. Clarke, *Imperial Earth*, Pan Books, London (1975), p. 15.

25. Laurence Sterne, *The Life and Opinions of Tristram Shandy, Gentleman (1759–69)*, online version prepared by Masaru Uchida (1997), http://www1.gifu-u.ac.jp/~masaru/TS/contents.html (last accessed February 2007), volume 2, chapter XI.

26. Robinson's elevator is a fascinating political metaphor of control and power which makes its later destruction far more meaningful than might the removal of a straightforward architectural construct (see also Chapter 8).

27. Arthur C. Clarke, *2001: A Space Odyssey*, Arrow Books, London (1968), p. 47.

28. These marvellous machines may be found in Robert A. Heinlein's *The Number of the Beast*, Fawcett Columbine, New York (1980) and H. G. Wells's *The Time Machine*, William Heinemann, London (1895).

29. The Death Star is huge and 'unnatural', and radiates evil as it mocks all things of nature, including the planets themselves. The pre-cogs are enclosed in a womb-like watery bed which is all the more noticeable when one of them is released and behaves as a vulnerable infant. *Minority Report* is based on a short story of the same name by Philip K. Dick (*Fantastic Universe*, January 1956).

30. Daniel Ust, 'Communication Breakdown: The Novels of Stanislaw Lem' (2001), http://uweb.superlink.net/neptune/Lem.html (last accessed February 2007).

31. Mark Rose, 'Filling the Void: Verne, Wells and Lem', *Science Fiction Studies*, 8 (July 1981), p. 134.

32. Stanislaw Lem, *Solaris* (1961), quotes here (p. 26) and below from King Penguin edition (1981).

33. Ibid., p. 134.

34. Ibid., p. 4.

35. Ibid., p. 6.

36. Ibid.

37. Ibid.

38. Ibid., p. 172.

39. Ibid., p. 54.

40. Ibid., p. 31.

41. Said, *Culture and Imperialism*, p. xiii.

42. The textual 'over-description' through metaphor often translates poorly into film. The critically acclaimed 1972 film version of *Solaris* (directed by Andrei Tarkovsky) is regarded by some as tediously long winded. It spends much of its 132 minutes of running time in flashbacks to Kelvin's childhood, with 'meaningful' attempts to illustrate Lem's remarkable metaphor through imagery of water and troubling technology. *Solaris* was remade in 2002, with George Clooney starring.

43. Lem, *Solaris*, p. 76.

44. Le Guin, *The Dispossessed*, p. 16.

45. Ibid., p. 18. The word itself has metaphorical weight as it contrasts Shevek's perception of Urrasti 'brightness' against the drab utilitarianism of Annares.

46. Ibid., p. 19.

47. Ibid., p. 20.

48. As with the punishment of Prometheus, so does the image of Rheya renew itself even after Kelvin has ensured the ghost's initial destruction. The metaphor of ceaseless punishment continues in an inverted form as Rheya herself learns of her genesis and attempts to end her ghostly incarnation just as she did her corporeal one. And yet, just as Dick argued for the humanity of his androids, so too does Lem consider the dreadful sadness of Rhea's involuntary existence and its eventual end.

49. Lem, *Solaris*, p. 142.

50. Ibid., p. 156.

51. Ibid., p. 148.

52. Ibid., p. 166.

53. Ibid., p. 203.

54. Le Guin, *The Dispossessed*, p. 307.

Chapter 4

1. Clarke, *Imperial Earth*, p. 86.

2. Around 186,300 miles per second, or 1,000,000,000 kilometres per hour.

3. The problem of distance was experienced in the early nineteenth century, when news of wars or peace treaties could take months to reach distant colonies. The Battle of New Orleans

(1815) was fought some two weeks *after* the signing of the Treaty of Ghent, which ended the War of 1812 between the USA and Great Britain.

4. Perkus, 'The Instincts of Race and Text', p. 73.

5. Allen Steele, 'Hard Again', *New York Review of Science Fiction*, 46 (June 1992), p. 1, defines 'hard' SF as being a form of imaginative literature that uses either established or carefully extrapolated science as its backbone. Clute and Nicholls, *The Encyclopaedia of Science Fiction*, p. 542, further suggest that this style of SF should 'respect the scientific spirit; it should seek to provide natural rather than supernatural or transcendental explanations for the events and phenomena it describes'. Some of the more noted of the many exponents of this style are Arthur C. Clarke, Larry Niven and Boris Strugatsky.

6. Interestingly, the link between 'hard' and 'soft' SF often appears to reflect similar demarcations between the 'hard' and 'soft' sciences (i.e. 'soft' sciences being social sciences and those which study human affairs).

7. Daniel R. Headrick, *The Tools of Empire: Technology and European Imperialism in the Nineteenth Century*, Oxford University Press, New York (1981), p. 4.

8. Wylie Sypher, *Literature and Technology: The Alien Vision*, Random House, New York (1968), p. 247.

9. Headrick, *The Tools of Empire*, p. 10.

10. James Blish, *Cities in Flight* (compendium edition), Millennium Books, London (1999), p. 269.

11. Joe Haldeman, *The Forever War*, Orion Books, London (1974), offers an excellent illustration of this notion of 'distance' as time; because of relativity, time passes differently for those who travel the galaxy to fight and those who remain on Earth. A soldier may have only served for two years, but twenty-five years may have passed for those whom he has left behind.

12. Clarke, *Imperial Earth*, p. 37.

13. See http://spaceflight.nasa.gov/shuttle/support/researching/aspl/index.html (last accessed February 2007).

14. Judy Pearsall and Bill Trumble (eds), *The Oxford English Reference Dictionary*, Oxford University Press, Oxford (1995).

15. Judd, *Empire*, p. 18.

16. Elleke Boehmer, *Colonial and Postcolonial Literature: Migrant Metaphors*, Oxford University Press, Oxford (1995), p. 2.

17. Banks, *The Player of Games*, p. 74.

18. Clarke, *Imperial Earth*, p. 37.

19. Ali A. Mazrui, 'The "Other" as the "Self" Under Cultural Dependency: The Impact of the Cultural University', in Gisela Brinker-Gabler (ed.), *Encountering the Other(s): Studies in Literature, History and Culture*, State University of New York, Albany (1995), pp. 333–62.

20. Robert Scholes, *Structural Fabulation: An Essay on Fiction of the Future*, University of Notre Dame Press, New York (1975), p. 24.

21. Susan A. George, 'Space for Resistance: The Disruption of the American Frontier Myth in 1950s Science Fiction Films', in Gary Westfahl (ed.), *Space and Beyond: The Frontier Theme in Science Fiction*, Greenwood Press, Westport (2000), p. 77.

22. Jack Williamson, 'On the Final Frontier', in Gary Westfahl (ed.), *Space and Beyond: The Frontier Theme in Science Fiction*, Greenwood Press, Westport (2000), p. 52.

23. Richard Wilson, 'Honor', in Allen DeGraeff (ed.), *Human and Other Beings*, Collier Books, New York (1963), p. 11.

24. Ibid.

25. Poul Anderson, 'Laws and Surprises', in George S. Slusser and Eric S. Rabkin (eds), *Mindscapes: The Geographies of Imagined Worlds*, Southern Illinois University Press, Carbondale (1989), p. 4.

26. Patrick Parrinder, *Shadows of the Future: H. G. Wells, Science Fiction and Prophecy*, Syracuse University Press, New York (1995), p. 65.

27. Maslow posited the 'hierarchy of human need': once the basic requirements of biological and physiological needs have been met, issues of safety, security and then social demands are next to be satisfied, followed by self-actualisation.

28. Similar to the colonisation of Louisiana and Texas by slave-holding cotton-growers, the land in the eastern South of the USA having been 'cottoned out'.

29. Paul Carter, 'Spatial History', in Bill Ashcroft *et al.* (eds), *The Post-colonial Studies Reader*, Routledge, London (1995), p. 376.

30. See James White, *The Dream Millennium*, Ballantine Books, New York (1974); and Don Wilcox, 'The Voyage That Lasted 600 Years', *Amazing Stories* (October 1940).

31. Kurt Vonnegut Jr, 'The Big Space Fuck', in Harlan Ellison (ed.), *Again, Dangerous Visions*, Doubleday, New York (1972), is an interesting text (short story) written in this mode, in which only germ cells are sent out to colonise a new planet.

Chapter 5

1. Jane M. Jacobs, *Edge of Empire: Postcolonialism and the City*, Routledge, London (1996), p. 4.

2. Bill Ashcroft *et al.*, *The Empire Writes Back: Theory and Practice in Post-colonial Literatures*, Routledge, London (1989), p. 7.

3. Said, *Culture and Imperialism*, p. 269.

4. It should be noted that Wells did author some speculative pieces for the *Science School's Journal* in 1893, as well as a textbook on biology, and acted as co-author on a text of physiography at the University Correspondence College in the same year. At his death in 1946, he had written 110 novels and over 500 articles.

5. 'Radio Play Upsets Americans: "Martian Invasion" of United States Taken Seriously', *Manchester Guardian*, 1 November 1938, p. 11.

6. Kurd Lasswitz, *Two Planets* (1897), translated by Hans Rudnick, Southern Illinois University Press, Carbondale (1971), p. 61.

7. Wells, *The War of the Worlds*. Quotations here (p. 718) and below are taken from the 1977 Heinemann/Octopus anthology *The Time Machine....*

8. Though, of course, Wells also uses the term quite literally.

9. Lasswitz, *Two Planets*, p. 25.

10. Grunthe to Saltner and Torm. Ibid., p. 8.

11. Frantz Fanon was, despite his short life, a distinctive voice in the anticolonial argument in the early twentieth century.

12. Lasswitz, *Two Planets*, pp. 61–62.

13. Wells, *The War of the Worlds*, p. 717.

14. Ibid., p. 726.

15. For example, George T. Chesney, 'The Battle of Dorking', *Blackwood's Magazine* (1871); William Le Queux, *The Great War in England in 1897*, Tower Publishing, London (1894). See also I. F. Clarke, *Voices Prophesying War 1763–1984*, Oxford University Press, London (1966).

16. This fear of 'unseen evil' is clearly evident in other fictions of the period, such as Robert Louis Stevenson's *The Strange Case of Dr Jekyll and Mr Hyde*, Longmans, Green, London (1886) and Oscar Wilde's *The Picture of Dorian Gray*, Ward, Lock, London (1891), as well as in the perceptions of 'unnatural' people, notably the 'new women' who purportedly abandoned their femininity.

17. Lasswitz, *Two Planets*, p. 61.

18. Wells, *The War of the Worlds*, p. 814.

19. Frederik Pohl, 'Ninth Galaxy Reader', in Brian Ash (ed.), *Faces of the Future: The Lessons of Science Fiction*, Elek/Pemberton, London (1975), p. 11.

20. Despite Wells's choice of England, the heart of the great empire, as the site for a Martian landing, it is interesting to note that empire here is almost invisible. Surrey is a place of suburban villas, pubs and front gardens – and the sublime blandness of the background provides a superb backdrop to the terrifying menace and savagery of the invaders.

21. Gandhi, *Postcolonial Theory*, p. 14.

22. Ibid., p. 15.

23. It is interesting to note that Lasswitz has *both* parties displaying flags during the conflict with the English destroyer *Prevention* (p. 166).

24. Wells, *The War of the Worlds*, p. 745.

25. Lasswitz, *Two Planets*, p. 48.

26. Gandhi, *Postcolonial Theory*, p. 29.

27. Wolfe, *The Known and the Unknown*, p. 217.

28. Eagleton, *Literary Theory*, p. 205.

29. Wells, *The War of the Worlds*, p. 805.

30. Bammer, 'Xenophobia, Xenophilia, and No Place to Rest', p. 47.

31. Jonathan Hart, 'Translating and Resisting Empire: Cultural Appropriation and Postcolonial Studies', in Bruce Zif and Pratima V. Rao (eds), *Borrowed Power: Essays on Cultural Appropriation*, Rutgers University Press, Piscataway (1997), p. 137.

32. Ell, the image of a peaceful integration reduced to absurdity, may also be seen in the light of the 'inferior hybrid', a creature of both races but belonging to neither.

33. Lasswitz, *Two Planets*, p. 208.

34. Wells, *The War of the Worlds*, p. 810.

35. Ash, *Faces of the Future*, p. 12.

36. W. B. Yeats, 'The Second Coming' (1920), in *W. B. Yeats: Selected Poetry*, Macmillan, London (1990), p. 99.

Chapter 6

1. Frances Yates, *Giordano Bruno and the Hermetic Tradition*, University of Chicago Press, Chicago (1964).

2. William Gibson, *Neuromancer*, Ace Books, New York (1984),

3. Dates of the 'golden age' defined by Clute and Nichols, *The Encyclopedia of Science Fiction*.

4. Not all these innovations sprang from the North Americas, yet futuristic technology was most fully embraced by American writers, whereas British and continental European writers often concentrated on social alterations, such as Aldous Huxley's *Brave New World*, Chatto & Windus, London (1932), Eden Phillpotts' *Saurus*, John Murray, London (1938) and the various later social commentaries of the Strugatsky brothers, such as *Roadside Picnic* and *Ponedel'nik nachinaetsia v Subbotu* (1966), translated as *Monday Begins on Saturday*, Daw Books, New York (1977).

5. The development of the ram-scoop process is under practical exploration at several facilities in the United States such as the Hanson Research Group at Stanford and the Marshall Space Flight Centre in Alabama.

6. Robert A. Heinlein (under the pseudonym Anson MacDonald), 'Waldo', *Astounding* (August 1942). Reprinted in *Waldo and Magic Inc.*, Del Rey Books, New York (1986).

7. Andrew Feenberg, 'An End to History: Science Fiction in the Nuclear Age', *Johns Hopkins Magazine* (March 1977), pp. 12–22.

8. Tonya Browning speaks of the traditional male readership, saying 'Hard SF was associated with the traditional male writer: soft, of course, was what the women were: Sex, Sub-atomic Particles and Sociology'. Tonya Browning, 'Protohistories and Protofeminists: Women and Science Fiction', *Hugo Gernback's Forecast* e-zine (November 1997).

9. Although there were writers who admired the Other, such as Eric Frank Russell in such works as 'Dear Devil', *Other Worlds* (May 1950) and 'And Then There Were None', *Astounding* (June 1951).

10. Julia Witner, 'The Best of Both Worlds: On Star Trek's Borg', in Gabriel Brahm Jr and Mark Driscol (eds), *Prosthetic Territories: Politics and Hypertechnologies*, Westview Press, Boulder (1995), pp. 270–71.

11. Wolfe, *The Known and the Unknown*, p. 226.

12. Darko Suvin, *Metamorphoses of Science Fiction: On the Poetics and History of a Literary Genre*, Yale University Press, New Haven (1979), p. 115.

13. Roger Luckhurst, *The Angle Between Two Walls: The Fiction of J. G. Ballard*, St Martin's Press, New York (1997), p. 41.

14. Brian W. Aldiss, *New Arrivals, Old Encounters*, Harper & Row, New York (1979), pp. 12–13.

15. Interestingly, Asimov's attempts to produce a rational, positive picture of the future were often undermined by an apparently unconscious reflection of old atavisms. He made his robots sentient and intelligent, but they were still required, as part of their very existence, to serve 'real' people.

16. An interesting question is whether Asimov and Heinlein were basing 'perfection' on the human scale, that is, whether robot perfection would be the achievement of humanity itself. Or were they implying that there is yet another level of perfection, to which both robot and humanity might aspire? Metahumanity, perhaps?

17. Heinlein incorporates the notion of a sentient computer in many of his texts, especially those involving the Howard Families.

18. Robert A. Heinlein, *The Moon Is a Harsh Mistress*, Putnam, New York (1966), quotes here (p. 87) and below from New English Library edition.

19. Mike's activities are another example of Heinlein's maintenance of the status quo, since all that Mike does is to destroy the old, externally imposed authority, so that it may be replaced with a new, internally imposed one.

20. Examples in the novel include: extending one's power over less powerful nations through trade or influence; policies generating dependence in less developed cultures; formation of a sovereign state.

21. Heinlein, *The Moon Is a Harsh Mistress*, p. 155.

22. Andrew Feenberg, *Alternative Modernity: The Technical Turn in Philosophy and Social Theory*, University of California Press, Berkeley (1995), p. 47.

23. There are moments in the novel where Olivaw outwits the Three Laws, using sophisticated reasoning to do so. At these times Asimov is permitting him the only licence possible, in effect allowing Olivaw to transcend his mechanical form only by thinking 'more like a human'. Again we see suggestions of the author's superior attitude towards beings deemed 'lesser' than human.

24. Isaac Asimov, *The Caves of Steel*, Doubleday, New York (1954); quote taken from HarperCollins edition, London (1997), p. 205.

25. Wolfe, *The Known and the Unknown*, p. 15.

26. Feenberg, *Alternative Modernity*, p. 47.

27. Isaac Asimov, *The Naked Sun*, Doubleday, New York (1957); quote taken from Panther Books edition, St Albans (1960), p. 202.

Chapter 7

1. Neil Easterbrook, 'State, Heterotopia: The Political Imagination in Heinlein, Le Guin and Delany', in Donald M. Hassler and Clyde Wilcox (eds), *Political Science Fiction*, University of South Carolina Press, Columbia (1997), p. 44.

2. 'Inhibitors' seeded the universe with machines designed to detect life and then suppress it, but after hundreds of millions of years the machines started to fail and intelligent cultures begin to emerge.

3. Humankind is strung out across a region of interstellar space inherited from an ancient civilisation discovered on Mars. Colonies are linked by an occasional sub-light colony ship and by hyperspatial datacasting; human consciousness is digitally freighted between the stars and downloaded into bodies as a matter of course.

4. Three stories intertwine in this complex narrative. In the *now* is Michael Kearney, who is destined to take part in a discovery which will make possible interstellar travel, but who is currently tormented by a strange and possibly alien entity known as the Shrander. In the future there is Seria-Mau Genlicher, a spaceship pilot surgically and biologically modified to interact directly with her ship the *White Cat*; and there is Ed Chianese, drifter and sensation seeker, down and out in Venusport.

5. In MacLeod's far-future trilogy, the empire of Nova Babylonia is in decline. The expected alien invaders never arrived and the regime has fallen.

6. Protagonist Lou is autistic. One of his skills is an ability to find patterns in data: complex patterns that not even the most powerful computers can comprehend. Those for whom he works and has made money now want him to change, to become 'normal'.

7. Set against a backdrop of plausible events, Steele's novel tells the story of Earth's first interstellar colonists – and the mysterious planet that becomes their home.

8. Weber advises us that no one wanted another war. Baron High Ridge certainly didn't. The Prime Minister of Manticore was happy with the war he had. No one was shooting anyone else, and as long as he could spin out negotiations on the formal treaty of peace, his government could continue to milk all those 'hostilities only' tax measures for their own partisan projects.

9. Ingrid's two-book series tells the story of an Earth divided by genetics. Some are determined to return the human race to its original form. But others believe the world belongs to those who have been genetically engineered.

10. Darko Suvin, 'SF and the Novum', in Teresa Lauretis *et al.* (eds), *The Technological Imagination: Theories and Fictions*, Coda Press, Madison (1980), p. 142.

11. Consider the ordinary openings of such novels as E. E. 'Doc' Smith's, *Triplanetary* (first published in parts in *Amazing Stories*, January–April 1934, and first published in book form by Fantasy Press, Reading, 1948) or Greg Bear's *Vitals*, Del Rey Books, New York (2002). The latter begins: 'The last time I talked to Rob, I was checking my luggage at Lindbergh Field to fly to Seattle...'. It is not just the initial scenario in the narrative but also the act of contextual historical placement for the reader – the link and doorway between the reality of *now* and the fiction of the future – that is often ordinary. Indeed, many novels begin with a form of chronology, as with *The Mote in God's Eye* by Larry Niven and Jerry Pournelle, Simon & Schuster, New York (1975), where the authors provide a summary of history up to the point of the narrative's opening, thus bringing the reader 'up to speed'.

12. Suvin, *Metamorphoses of Science Fiction*, p. viii.

13. Wolfe, *The Known and the Unknown*, p. xiii.

14. And specifically to his remark 'There are no facts, only interpretations' (from Nietzsche's *Nachlass*).

15. Wells, *The Time Machine*.

16. This also takes the reader into the land of religious allegory and parable, which, though potentially confusing, may alert said reader to the possible presence of multilevel intertexualities.

17. Haldeman, *The Forever War*, p. 8.

18. Einstein's special theory of relativity states that time does not flow at a set rate, an example being that moving clocks seem to tick more slowly relative to stationary ones. This effect becomes significant only at speeds approaching that of light.

19. Serving, as it does, as an analogy for the Vietnam conflict and as a practical link between contemporary physics and tomorrow's treatment of physics.

20. See for instance Frederik Pohl and C. M. Kornbluth, *The Space Merchants*, Ballantine Books, New York (1953).

21. Dawn Duncan, 'A Flexible Foundation: Constructing a Postcolonial Dialogue', in David Theo Goldberg and Ato Quayson (eds), *Relocating Postcolonialism*, Blackwell, Oxford (2002), p. 332.

22. Robert A. Heinlein, *The Green Hills of Earth*, Signet Books, New York (1951), p. 13.

23. Walter M. Miller Jr, *A Canticle for Leibowitz*, Lippincott, Philadelphia (1959), quotations here (pp. 22–23) and below from Orbit Books edition (1993).

24. Iain M. Banks, *Look To Windward*, Orbit Books, London (2000), p. 57.

25. Though these social occasions or conversations are not difficult to place, Banks dislocates the reader's assumed familiarity by placing such occasions inside a completely unfamiliar setting. The decadent party is set inside an old nuclear power-plant; the drunks are in an exquisitely ornate antique palace wearing generals' insignia, yet they are not generals and the palace explodes; the soldiers are in the foxhole awaiting transport to another planet.

26. James Romm, 'Belief and Other Worlds: Ktesias and the Founding of the Indian Wonders', in George S. Slusser and Eric S. Rabkin (eds), *Mindscapes: The Geographies of Imagined Worlds*, Southern Illinois University Press, Carbondale (1989), p. 121.

27. William B. Fischer, *The Empire Strikes Out: Kurd Lasswitz, Hans Dominik, and the Development of German Science Fiction*, Bowling Green State University Popular Press, Ohio (1984), p. 33.

28. Maslow's hierarchical theory argues that once humanity has procured all necessary things for the comfort of the body, things pertinent to the comfort of the mind – moral comfort – are likely next. For example, as soon as we have discovered a way to provide an adequate and replenishable source of timber, the old forests will cease to be logged.

29. Françoise Verges, 'Post-scriptum', in David Theo Goldberg and Ato Quayson (eds), *Relocating Postcolonialism*, Blackwell, Oxford (2002), p. 351.

30. 'Let There Be Man', 'Let There Be Light', with allusion to the (Latin) Genesis, and 'May Thy Will Be Done', Mary's response at the Annunciation, hence the Marian allusions in the last part of the novel with the two-headed woman.

31. Miller dedicates the novel saying 'a dedication is only a scratch where it itches'.

32. Miller's Leibowitz abbey is replicating the work undertaken by the Irish monks of the Dark Ages.

33. The Brothers of Leibowitz are also called 'Bookleggers' and 'Memorizers', as they spread an oral history by committing to memory entire volumes of sacred writings, literature and science. This form of an orally transmitted underground of knowledge may also be seen in Ray Bradbury's *Fahrenheit 451*, Ballantine Books, New York (1953), where people have memorised literary works so that someday, when it is safe to do so, they can again print books. When bombs destroy their society, the people begin to construct a place where books and the free thought they inspire can flourish.

34. Miller, *A Canticle for Leibowitz*, p. 75.

35. The current debate surrounding cloning is an excellent example of the scientific community's preference to stand outside the pressure of localised authorities.

36. Miller, *A Canticle for Leibowitz*, pp. 228–29.

37. Ibid., p. 258.

38. A novel of initiation and education.

39. George E. Slusser, Colin Greenland and Eric S. Rabkin (eds), *Storm Warnings: Science Fiction Confronts the Future*, Southern Illinois University Press, Carbondale (1987), p. 3.

40. Jean Pfaelzer, *The Utopian Novel in America, 1886–1896: The Politics of Form*, University of Pittsburgh Press, Pittsburgh (1984), p. 80.

41. Ken MacLeod, *The Stone Canal*, Legend Books, London (1996), p. 138.

42. Susan Wood (ed.), *The Language of the Night: Essays on Fantasy and Science Fiction by Ursula K. Le Guin*, Putnam, New York (1979), p. 163.

Chapter 8

1. See Gerald Jones, 'Science Fiction', *New York Times* (30 June 1996) (see http://query.nytimes.com/gst/fullpage.html?res=9C07EEDF1339F933A05755C0A960958260&sec (last accessed February 2007).

2. The physical transformation of a non-habitable extraterrestrial environment into an approximation of Earth, and which extends postcolonial theory into a geographical Othering of Mars.

3. Wolfe, *The Known and the Unknown*, p. xiii.

4. Robinson, *Red Mars*, p. 42.

5. Ibid., p. 41.

6. Wolfe, *The Known and the Unknown*, p. 224.

7. The ship in which the First Hundred travelled to Mars.

8. Robinson, *Red Mars*, p. 113.

9. Hart, 'Translating and Resisting Empire', p. 146.

10. Robinson, *Red Mars*, p. 205.

11. Ibid., p. 227.

12. Robinson, *Blue Mars*, p. 189.

13. Suleri, *The Rhetoric of English India*, pp. 4–5.

14. Neil Lazarus, *Resistance in Postcolonial African Fiction*, Yale University Press, New Haven (1990), p. ix.

15. Robinson, *Red Mars*, pp. 213–14.

16. Ibid., p. 213.

17. Zeynep Çelik, *Urban Forms and Colonial Confrontations: Algiers Under French Rule*, University of California Press, Berkeley (1997). Çelik discusses the 'trial and error' model of French colonial urbanism, including the fragmentation of the kasbah, ambitious 'beaux arts' schemes to create European forms of housing, master plans inspired by high modernism and comprehensive regional plans.

18. A notion Robinson partially explored in *Icehenge*, Ace Books, New York (1984).

19. Said, *Orientalism*, p. 116.

20. Again, see *Icehenge*, where Robinson explores the unknowability of past histories.

21. Robinson, *Red Mars*, p. 380.

22. Robert Zubrin, 'The Economic Viability of Mars Colonisation', *Journal of the British Interplanetary Society*, 48 (1995), pp. 407–14, available at http://www.aleph.se/Trans/Tech/Space/mars.html (last accessed February 2007).

23. See http://cmex.ihmc.us/ExtremeEnvironments/index.html (last accessed February 2007).

24. Robert H. Haynes, 'Ethics and Planetary Engineering. 1. Ecce. Ecoposis: Playing God on Mars', in D. Macniven (ed.), *Moral Expertise*, Routledge, London (1990), pp. 161–83.

25. Robert H. Haynes, 'Foreword', in Martyn Fogg, *Terraforming: Engineering Planetary Environments*, SAE International, Pennsylvania (1995).

26. Robinson, *Blue Mars*, p. 237.

27. Ibid., p. 779.

28. For example, Nadia does not launch into a politically rousing speech when stepping onto the Martian surface for the first time: she 'hits the ground with both feet solid' (*Red Mars*, p. 123). Robinson does not glorify the wonders of science but speaks of the fascination of chemical engineering operations such as dehumidification, liquefaction, fractional distillation, electrolysis, electrosynthesis, of the seductions of the Sabatier process, the Raschig process, the Oswald process etc. (*Red Mars*, p. 139).

29. Peter Berger and Thomas Luckmann, *The Social Construction of Reality*, Doubleday, Garden City (1967), p. 104.

30. Kim Stanley Robinson, *Green Mars*, HarperCollins, London (1994), p. 237.

31. Robinson, *Red Mars*, p. 521. The elevator combines an extrapolation of current science as well as the same type of metaphor invoked by Ursula Le Guin's 'ansible' and Stanislaw Lem's 'Solaris station', since all three things represent far more in the narrative than their actuality (see Chapter 3).

32. Boris I. Yakobson and Richard E. Smalley, 'Fullerene Nanotubes: $C_{1,000,000}$ and Beyond', *American Scientist* (July–August 1997). Available at http://www.americanscientist.org/template/AssetDetail/assetid/28780/page/9 (last accessed February 2007).

33. In Robinson's case, the special heated quilting on Nadia's suit is but a further example.

34. Fischer, *The Empire Strikes Out*, p. 21.

35. The First International NILS Workshop on Longevity Sciences, 'The Role of Molecular Genetics in Longevity Sciences', National Chubu Hospital, 36-3, Gengo, Morioka-cho, Obu-shi, Aichi, Japan, 29 November 1996.

36. Robinson, *Blue Mars*, p. 368.

37. This use of Boone to portray a specific theme echoes Asimov's use of the detective Elijah Baley (see Chapter 6).

38. Robinson, *Red Mars*, p. 335.

39. Ibid., p. 543.

40. Ibid., p. 519.

41. Ibid., p. 599.

42. Heinlein's vision of independence (a new form of domination – see Chapter 6) does not seem to apply to the *Mars* novels.

43. Robinson, *Green Mars*, p. 19.

44. Ibid., p. 457.

45. Robinson, *Blue Mars*, p. 189.

46. Ibid., p. 653.

47. Ibid., p. 64.

48. Ibid., p. 673.

49. Ibid., p. 224.

50. Ibid., p. 613.

51. Robinson, *Green Mars*, p. 638.

Chapter 9

1. The Culture is not necessarily offered as a 'replacement' for anything, however, given that Banks provides us with no sense of what preceded it.

2. Norman Spinrad's *The Iron Dream* (1972) suggests that if Hitler had become an SF writer instead of a dictator his sublimated dreams would have been readily accommodated within the great traditions of space opera and heroic fantasy. See Clute and Nicholls, *The Encyclopaedia of Science Fiction*, p. 946.

3. *Circa* 1523–1027 BC. The Shang dynasty is the first imperium of which there is both documented and archaeological evidence.

4. Rupert Emerson, *From Empire to Nation: The Rise to Self-assertion of Asian and African Peoples,* Beacon Press, Boston (1960), p. 60.

5. The involvement of the USA in Iraq is an example.

6. Gibson's stories take the reader to a different plane of experience, where power and the manipulation of that power exist within the confines of the 'Net'. Though his narratives are not discussing the formal aspects of empire, he does seem to be illustrating a form of control over the minds of a population. In this sense, Gibson's novels are 'beyond' an empire.

7. Clute and Nicholls, *The Encyclopedia of Science Fiction,* p. 461.

8. Interestingly, this state of unlimited resources is echoed in Kim Stanley Robinson's *Mars* trilogy (see Chapter 8) and, indeed, in early settlement narratives, such as Daniel Defoe's *The Life and Strange Surprising Adventures of Robinson Crusoe* (1719). Does the human colonisation fantasy become more satisfying when the colonisers are seen to have all the facilities they need or want? So that they can make a 'proper' job of it?

9. There being no 'state' to intervene, only the fabulous 'Minds', which secure personal safety and which supply all physical needs.

10. Culture citizens are born with built-in drug glands in order to manufacture drugs of choice on reaching physical maturity.

11. The Culture is not pastoral but more closely resembles an immeasurable cosmopolis.

12. *State of the Art* is a collection of short stories, and neither *Feersum Endjinn* nor *Against a Dark Background* are explicitly Culture novels.

13. Iain M. Banks, *Consider Phlebas,* Orbit Books, London (1987), p. 35.

14. Banks, *The Player of Games,* p. 33.

15. The queen being not the 'chief' piece, but the most powerful one.

16. 'Flere-Imsaho kept itself to itself most of the time, only calling on Gurgeh once a day or so, and not staying onboard the *Limiting Factor.* Gurgeh was glad of that; the young machine – it said it was only thirteen – could be trying at times. The ship reassured Gurgeh that the little drone would be up to the task of preventing social gaffes and keeping him informed on the finer linguistic points by the time they arrived at the Empire ...' Ibid., pp. 110–11.

17. This use of a pawn in a game within a larger game is even more clearly observed in *Use of Weapons,* where the main protagonist's ability to do violence is used in a deliberately inflammatory manner as a means of distraction and false strategy.

18. Banks, *The Player of Games,* p. 127.

19. Banks's Azad is both an actual activity and a metaphor, not only a symbol of Azad itself but also an anti-metaphor for the way the Culture organises itself in order to experience the most enjoyment in life. This use of metaphor places Banks's writings beside the work of Ursula Le Guin and Stanislaw Lem, in that they, too, incorporate this most effective resource of SF in their literary experiments, as discussed in Chapter 3.

20. Iain M. Banks, *Excession,* Orbit Books, London (1997), pp. 71–72.

21. Banks, *Consider Phlebas,* p. 461.

22. See the roles of Balveda and Fal in *Consider Phlebas.*

23. It should be noted that in *Consider Phlebas,* the Idirans went to war on the assumption that the Culture was an effete conglomerate, a strategic misjudgement demonstrated by the fact of Culture tenacity and its ability to withstand both massive attack and loss.

24. Iain M. Banks, *Use of Weapons,* Orbit Books, London (1990), p. 101.

25. Ibid., p. 121.

Conclusion

1. See Anne McCaffrey's *Pern* series.

2. See the 'Moties' in Niven and Pournelle's *The Mote in God's Eye.*

3. Robinson, *Icehenge,* p. 262.

Bibliography

Achebe, Chinua, *Things Fall Apart*, London, Heinemann (1958), edition illustrated by Uche Okeke, Heinemann Educational Books, London (1967).

Aldiss, Brian, *The Primal Urge*, Ballantine Books, New York (1961).

——, *Frankenstein Unbound*, Jonathan Cape, London (1973).

——, *New Arrivals, Old Encounters*, Harper & Row, New York (1979).

——, *Helliconia Spring*, Atheneum, New York (1982).

——, *Helliconia Summer*, Atheneum, New York (1983).

——, *Helliconia Winter*, Atheneum, New York (1985).

—— (ed.), *Common Clay: 20-Odd Stories*, St Martin's Press, New York (1996).

—— and Harry Harrison (eds), *Decade: The 1960s*, Macmillan, London (1977).

—— and Harry Harrison (eds), *Decade: The 1950s*, St Martin's Press, New York (1978).

—— and Harry Harrison (eds), *Decade: The 1940s*, St Martin's Press, New York (1978).

Alexander, Meena, *The Shock of Arrival: Reflections on the Postcolonial Experience*, South End Press, Boston (1996).

Alkon, Paul K., *Science Fiction Before 1900: Imagination Discovers Technology*, Twayne, New York (1994).

Allen, Dick (ed.), *Science Fiction: The Future*, Harcourt Brace Jovanovich, New York (1971).

Anderson, Poul, *Orbit Unlimited*, Ace Books, New York (1961).

——, 'Laws and Surprises', in George S. Slusser and Eric S. Rabkin (eds), *Mindscapes: The Geographies of Imagined Worlds*, Southern Illinois University Press, Carbondale (1989).

Ash, Brian, *Faces of the Future: The Lessons of Science Fiction*, Taplinger, London (1975).

Ashcroft, Bill, *et al.*, *The Empire Writes Back: Theory and Practice in Post-colonial Literatures*, Routledge, London (1989).

Asimov, Isaac, 'Marooned Off Vesta', *Amazing Stories* (1939).

——, 'Robot AL-76 Goes Astray', *Amazing Stories* (February 1942).

——, *I, Robot*, Grafton, London (1950).

——, *Foundation*, Gnome Press, New York (1951).

——, *Foundation and Empire*, Panther Books, St Albans (1952).

——, *The Caves of Steel*, Doubleday, New York (1954).

——, *The Naked Sun*, Doubleday, New York (1957).

—— (ed.), *Where Do We Go From Here?*, Fawcett Crest Books, Greenwich (1971).

——, 'Three Laws of Robotics', in *The Rest of the Robots*, Panther Science Fiction, London (1981).

——, *Foundation and Earth*, Grafton, London (1986).

——, *Nightfall*, Grafton Books, London (1991).

——, Martin H. Greenberg and Charles G. Waugh (eds), *Intergalactic Empires*, Signet Books, New York (1983).

Atwood, Margaret, *The Handmaid's Tale*, McClelland and Stewart, Toronto (1985).

Bacon, Francis, *Novum Organum* (1620), translated by R. Ellis and James Spedding, with preface and notes, G. Routledge, London (n.d.).

Baker, Victor R., *The Channels of Mars*, University of Texas Press, Austin (1982).

Balmer, Edwin, *The Achievements of Luther Trant*, Small, Maynard, Boston (1910).

Bammer, Angelika, 'Xenophobia, Xenophilia, and No Place to Rest', in Gisela Brinker-Gabler (ed.), *Encountering the Other(s): Studies in Literature, History and Culture*, State University of New York, Albany (1995).

Banks, Iain M., *Consider Phlebas*, Orbit Books, London (1987).

——, *The Player of Games*, Orbit Books, London (1988).

——, *Use of Weapons*, Orbit Books, London (1990).

——, *The State of the Art*, Orbit Books, London (1991).

——, *Against a Dark Background*, Orbit Books, London (1993).

——, *Feersum Endjinn*, Orbit Books, London (1994).

——, *Excession*, Orbit Books, London (1997).

——, *Inversions*, Orbit Books, London (1998).

——, *Look To Windward*, Orbit Books, London (2000).

Barry, Peter, *Beginning Theory: An Introduction to Literary and Cultural Theory*, Manchester University Press, Manchester (1995).

Bateman, Robert, *When the Whites Went*, Walker, New York (1963).

Bates, Harry, 'Farewell to the Master', *Astounding* (October 1940).

Baum, L. Frank, *The Wonderful Wizard of Oz*, G. M. Hill, Chicago (1900).

Bear, Greg, *Vitals*, Del Rey Books, New York (2002).

Berger, Peter and Thomas Luckmann, *The Social Construction of Reality*, Doubleday, Garden City (1967).

Bishop, Michael (ed.), *Light Years and Dark: Science Fiction and Fantasy of and for Our Time*, Berkley Books, New York (1984).

Blish, James, *Cities in Flight*, Doubleday, New York (1970).

Boardman, Tom (ed.), *An ABC of Science Fiction*, Four Square Books, London (1966).

Boehmer, Elleke, *Colonial and Postcolonial Literature: Migrant Metaphors*, Oxford University Press, Oxford (1995).

Booker, M. Keith (ed.), *Dystopian Literature: A Theory and Research Guide*, Greenwood Press, Westport (1994).

Bradbury, Ray, 'Zero Hour', *Planet Stories* (autumn 1947).

——, *The Martian Chronicles*, Doubleday, New York (1950).

——, *Fahrenheit 451*, Ballantine Books, New York (1953).

Brahm, Gabriel Jr and Mark Driscol (eds), *Prosthetic Territories: Politics and Hypertechnologies*, Westview Press, Boulder (1995).

Breuer, Miles J. and Williamson, Jack, 'The Birth of a New Republic', *Amazing Stories Quarterly* (winter 1931).

Brinker-Gabler, Gisela (ed.), *Encountering the Other(s): Studies in Literature, History and Culture*, State University of New York, Albany (1995)

Broderick, Damien, *Reading by Starlight: Postmodern Science Fiction*, Routledge, London (1995).

Browning, Tonya, 'Protohistories and Protofeminists: Women and Science Fiction', *Hugo Gernback's Forecast* e-zine (November 1997).

Bruno, Giordano, *De l'Infinito universo e mondi*, Rome (1584).

Bull, Emma, *Bone Dance: A Fantasy for Technophiles*, Ace Books, New York (1991).

Bunyan, John, *The Pilgrim's Progress from This World to That Which Is to Come: Delivered Under the Similitude of a Dream* (1678, 1684).

Caidin, Martin, *Destination Mars*, Doubleday, New York (1972).

Campanella, Tommaso, *Civitas Solis* (1623), edited and translated by Daniel J. Donno, University of California Press, Berkeley (1981).

Campbell, John W. Jr, *The Mightiest Machine*, Ace Books, New York (1934).

Camus, Albert, *L'Étranger*, Libraire Gallimard, Paris (1942).

Capek, Karel, *R.U.R.* (*Rossumovi Univerzální Roboti*) (written 1920, premiered in Prague 1921), translated by P. Selver as *Rossum's Universal Robots*, Oxford University Press, London (1923).

Carr, Terry, 'The Dance of the Changer and the Three', in Joseph Elder (ed.), *The Farthest Reaches*, Trident Press, New York (1968).

—— (ed.), *Creatures From Beyond*, Thomas Nelson, New York (1975).

Carter, Paul, 'Spatial History', in Bill Ashcroft *et al.* (eds), *The Post-colonial Studies Reader*, Routledge, London (1995).

Çelik, Zeynep, *Urban Forms and Colonial Confrontations: Algiers Under French Rule*, University of California Press, Berkeley (1997).

Chesney, George T., 'The Battle of Dorking', *Blackwood's Magazine* (1871).

Clareson, Thomas D. (ed.), *A Spectrum of Worlds*, Doubleday, New York (1972).

——, *Science Fiction in America 1870s–1930s: An Annotated Bibliography of Primary Sources*, Greenwood Press, Westport (1984).

Clarke, Arthur C., *Childhood's End*, Ballantine Books, New York (1953).

——, *2001: A Space Odyssey*, Arrow Books, London (1968).

——, *Imperial Earth*, Pan Books, London (1975).

——, *The Fountains of Paradise*, Gollancz, London (1979).

——, *The Songs of Distant Earth*, Grafton, London (1986).

——, *Reach for Tomorrow*, Ballantine Books, New York (1998).

——, *Expedition to Earth*, Ballantine Books, New York (1998).

Clarke, I. F., *Voices Prophesying War 1763–1984*, Oxford University Press, London (1966).

Clute, John and Peter Nicholls, *The Encyclopedia of Science Fiction* (2nd edition), Orbit Books, London (1999).

Cornell, John (ed.), *No Place Like Earth*, Jarrod & Sons, Norwich (1952).

Cortiel, Jeanne, *Demand My Writing: Joanna Russ, Feminism, Science Fiction*, Liverpool University Press, Liverpool (1999).

Crichton, Michael, *Timeline*, Random House, New York (1999).

Currey, L. W. and David Hartwell (eds), *A Bibliography of First Printings of Their Fiction and Selected Non-fiction*, G. K. Hall, Boston (1987).

Dalos, György, *Nineteen Eighty-Five*, Pantheon, New York (1983).

Davin, Eric L., *Pioneers of Wonder: Conversations with the Founders of Science Fiction*, Prometheus Books, New York (1999).

de Bergerac, Cyrano, *Histoire comique des états et empires de la lune*, Garnier, Paris (1656).

——, *Histoire comique des états et empires de la soleil*, Garnier, Paris (1662).

de Camp, L. Sprague, 'Lest Darkness Fall', *Unknown*, 10 (December 1939).

Defoe, Daniel, *The Life and Strange Surprising Adventures of Robinson Crusoe* (1719).

DeGraeff, Allen (ed.), *Human and Other Beings*, Collier Books, New York (1963).

de Grainville, Jean-Baptiste Cousin, *Le Dernier homme* (1805).

Dick, Philip K., 'The Minority Report', *Fantastic Universe* (January 1956).

——, *Martian Time-Slip*, Ballantine Books, New York (1964).

——, *Do Androids Dream of Electric Sheep?*, Orion Books, London (1968).

Dickson, Gordon R., *Delusion World*, Ace Double, New York (1961).

Disch, Thomas M. (ed.), *The New Improved Sun: An Anthology of Utopian SF*, Harper & Row, New York (1975).

Duncan, Dawn, 'A Flexible Foundation: Constructing a Postcolonial Dialogue', in David Theo Goldberg and Ato Quayson (eds), *Relocating Postcolonialism*, Blackwell, Oxford (2002).

Dvorkin, David, *Time for Sherlock Holmes*, Dodd Mead, New York (1983).

Eagleton, Terry, *Literary Theory: An Introduction* (2nd edition), Blackwell, Oxford (1983).

Easterbrook, Neil, 'State, Heterotopia: The Political Imagination in Heinlein, Le Guin and Delany', in Donald M. Hassler and Clyde Wilcox (eds), *Political Science Fiction*, University of South Carolina Press, Columbia (1997).

Ellison, Harlan (ed.), *Again, Dangerous Visions*, Berkley Books, New York (1983).

Emerson, Rupert, *From Empire to Nation: The Rise to Self-assertion of Asian and African Peoples*, Beacon Press, Boston (1960).

Erlich, Richard D. and Thomas P. Dunn (eds), *Clockwork Worlds: Mechanised Environments in SF*, Greenwood Press, Westport (1983).

Fanthorpe, U. A., 'Tomorrow and', in *Selected Poems*, King Penguin, London (1984), p. 90.

Feenberg, Andrew, 'An End to History: Science Fiction in the Nuclear Age', *Johns Hopkins Magazine* (March 1977), pp. 12–22.

——, *Alternative Modernity: The Technical Turn in Philosophy and Social Theory*, University of California Press, Berkeley (1995).

Fischer, William B., *The Empire Strikes Out: Kurd Lasswitz, Hans Dominik, and the Development of German Science Fiction*, Bowling Green State University Popular Press, Ohio (1984).

Gandhi, Leela, *Postcolonial Theory: A Critical Introduction*, Allen & Unwin, St Leonards (1998).

George, Susan A., 'Space for Resistance: The Disruption of the American Frontier Myth in 1950s Science Fiction Films', in Gary Westfahl (ed.), *Space and Beyond: The Frontier Theme in Science Fiction*, Greenwood Press, Westport (2000).

Gernsback, Hugo, 'Ralph 124C 41+', *Modern Electrics* (1911–12). The twelve-part serial was later published in book form by Straford, Boston (1925).

Gibbon, Edward, *The History of the Decline and Fall of the Roman Empire* (1776–88).

Gibson, William, 'Johnny Mnemonic', *Omni* (1981)

——, *Neuromancer*, Ace Books, New York (1984).

Goffi, Frank Louis, *Genesis of a Genre: American Science Fiction of the Nineteen-Thirties*, PhD dissertation, University Microfilms International, London (1980).

Graves, Robert, *I, Claudius*, Arthur Barker, London (1934).

Greenberg, Martin (ed.), *All About the Future*, Gnome Press, New York (1955).

Griffin, Brian and David Wingrove, *A Study of the Writings of Brian W. Aldiss*, Greenwood Press, Westport (1984).

Haldeman, Joe, *The Forever War*, Orion Books, London (1974).

Hamilton, Edmond, 'The Metal Giants', *Weird Tales* (December 1926).

——, 'Conquest of Two Worlds', *Wonder Stories* (February 1932).

Harrison, M. John, *Light*, Orion Publishing, London (2002).

Hart, Jonathan, 'Translating and Resisting Empire: Cultural Appropriation and Postcolonial Studies', in Bruce Zif and Pratima V. Rao (eds), *Borrowed Power: Essays on Cultural Appropriation*, Rutgers University Press, Piscataway (1997).

Haynes, Robert H., 'Ethics and Planetary Engineering. 1. Ecce. Ecoposis: Playing God on Mars', in D. Macniven (ed.), *Moral Expertise*, Routledge, London (1990).

——, 'Foreword', in Martyn Fogg, *Terraforming: Engineering Planetary Environments*, SAE International, Pennsylvania (1995).

Headrick, Daniel R., *The Tools of Empire: Technology and European Imperialism in the Nineteenth Century*, Oxford University Press, New York (1981).

Heinlein, Robert A., 'Lifeline', *Astounding* (1939).

——, 'Logic of Empire', *Astounding* (March 1941).

——(under the pseudonym Anson MacDonald), 'Waldo', *Astounding* (August 1942). Reprinted in *Waldo and Magic Inc.*, Del Rey Books, New York (1986).

——, *Red Planet: A Colonial Boy on Mars*, Schribner, New York (1949).

——, *The Man Who Sold the Moon*, Shasta, Chicago (1950).

——, *The Green Hills of Earth*, Signet Books, New York (1951).

——, *Stranger in a Strange Land*, Putnam, New York (1961).

——, *The Moon Is a Harsh Mistress*, Putnam, New York (1966).

——, *Time Enough for Love*, Putnam, New York (1973).

——, *The Number of the Beast*, Fawcett Columbine, New York (1980).

Herbert, Frank, *Dune*, Chilton Books, Philadelphia (1965).

——, 'Dune Messiah', *Galaxy Science Fiction* (July–November 1969). The five-part serial was later published in book form by Berkley Books, New York (1970).

Hoskins, Robert (ed.), *First Step Outward*, Dell, New York (1969).

Huxley, Aldous, *Brave New World*, Chatto & Windus, London (1932).

Ingrid, Charles, *The Marked Man Omnibus*, Daw Books, New York (2002).

Jackson, H. J. (ed.), *Samuel Taylor Coleridge*, Oxford University Press, Oxford (1985).

Jacobs, Jane M., *Edge of Empire: Postcolonialism and the City*, Routledge, London (1996).

Jones, Gerald, 'Science Fiction', *New York Times* (30 June 1996).

Judd, Denis, *Empire: The British Imperial Experience from 1765 to the Present*, HarperCollins, London (1996).

Kerman, Judith B. (ed.), *Retrofitting Blade Runner: Issues in Ridley Scott's Blade Runner and Philip K. Dick's Do Androids Dream of Electric Sheep?*, Bowling Green State University Popular Press, Ohio (1991).

King, Betty, *Women of the Future: The Female Main Character in Science Fiction*, Scarecrow Press, London (1984).

Kipling, Rudyard, 'The Man Who Would Be King', in *The Phantom Rickshaw and Other Eerie Tales* (volume 5 of the *Indian Railway Library*), Wheelers, Allahabad (1888).

——, 'The White Man's Burden', *McClure's Magazine* (1899).

Knight, Damon (ed.), *A Century of Science Fiction*, Simon & Schuster, New York (1962).

——(ed.), *First Flight: Maiden Voyages in Space and Time*, Lancer Books, New York (1963).

——, *First Contact*, Pinnacle Books, New York (1971).

Kornbluth, C. M., 'Two Dooms', *Venture Science Fiction Magazine* (July 1958).

Krulik, Ted, 'Bounded by Metal', in Robert E. Myers (ed.), *The Intersection of Science Fiction and Philosophy*, Greenwood Press, Westport (1983).

Kuttner, Henry, *Fury*, Lancer, New York (1947).

Lakoff, George and Mark Johnson, 'Conceptual Metaphor in Everyday Language', *Journal of Philosophy*, 77 (1980), pp. 453–86.

—— and Mark Turner (eds), *More Than Cool Reason*, University of Chicago Press, Chicago (1989).

Large, E. C., *Sugar in the Air*, Jonathon Cape, London (1937).

Lasswitz, Kurd, *Auf zwei Planeten* (1897), translated as *Two Planets* by Hans Rudnick, Southern Illinois University Press, Carbondale (1971).

Lauretis, Teresa, Andreas Huyssen and Kathleen Woodward (eds), *The Technological Imagination: Theories and Fictions*, Coda Press, Madison (1980).

Lazarus, Neil, *Resistance in Postcolonial African Fiction*, Yale University Press, New Haven (1990).

Le Guin, Ursula K., 'Nine Lives' (1969), published in *The Wind's Twelve Quarters* (collection of short stories by Ursula K. Le Guin), Harper & Row, New York (1975).

——, *The Dispossessed*, Avon Books, New York (1974).

Lem, Stanislaw, *Solaris* (1961).

Le Queux, William, *The Great War in England in 1897*, Tower Publishing, London (1894).

Levinas, Emmanuel, 'Die Spur des Anderen', translated by Elizabeth Naylor Endres, 'The Trace of the Other', in Gisela Brinker-Gabler (ed.), *Encountering the Other(s): Studies in Literature, History and Culture*, State University of New York, Albany (1995).

Lewis, C. S., *Out of the Silent Planet*, Bodley Head, London (1938).

——, *Perelandra*, Bodley Head, London (1943).

London, Jack, *The Iron Heel*, Macmillan, New York (1907).

Lowell, Percival, *Mars*, Houghton-Mifflin, New York (1895).

Luckhurst, Roger, *The Angle Between Two Walls: The Fiction of J. G. Ballard*, St Martin's Press, New York (1997).

Lyotard, Jean-François, *The Inhuman: Reflections on Time*, translated by Geoffrey Bennington and Rachel Bowlby, Stanford University Press, Stanford (1991).

MacLeod, Ken, *The Stone Canal*, Legend Books, London (1996).

——, *Engine City*, Orbit Books, London (2002).

Macniven, D. (ed.), *Moral Expertise*, Routledge, London (1990).

Manlove, C. N. (ed.), *Science Fiction: Ten Explorations*, Kent State University Press, Ohio (1986).

Marx, Karl, Introduction to *Contribution to the Critique of Hegel's Philosophy of Law*, in *Deutsch-Französische Jahrbücher* (1844).

Mazrui, Ali A., 'The "Other" as the "Self" Under Cultural Dependency: The Impact of the Cultural University', in Gisela Brinker-Gabler (ed.), *Encountering the Other(s): Studies in Literature, History and Culture*, State University of New York Press, Albany (1995).

McAuley, Paul J., *Eternal Light*, Gollancz, London (1991).

McNelly, Willis E. and Stover, Leon E. (eds), *Above the Human Landscape: A Social Science Fiction Anthology*, Goodyear, Santa Monica (1987).

Melville, Douglas and Reginald, R. (eds), *Ancestral Voices: An Anthology of Early Science Fiction*, Arno Press, New York (1975).

Mendlesohn, Farah, 'Science Fiction in the Academies of History and Literature; Or, History and the Use of Science Fiction', in Gary Westfahl and George Slusser (eds), *Science Fiction, Canonization, Marginalization and the Academy*, Greenwood Press, Westport (2002).

Merril, Judith, *Shadow on the Hearth*, Sidgwick & Jackson, London (1950).

Miller, Walter M. Jr, 'The Darfsteller', *Astounding* (January 1955).

——, *A Canticle for Leibowitz*, Lippincott, Philadelphia (1959).

Mogen, David, *Wilderness Visions: Science Fiction Westerns*, Borgo Press, San Bernadino (1982).

Moon, Elizabeth, *Speed of Dark*, Orbit Books, London (2002).

Moorcock, Michael (ed.), *England Invaded: A Collection of Fantasy Fiction*, Allen, London (1977).

——, *Mother London*, Secker & Warburg, London (1988).

More, Thomas, *Utopia* (1516), edited by George M. Logan and Robert M. Adams, translated by R. M. Adams, Cambridge Texts in the History of Political Thought, Cambridge University Press, Cambridge (1989).

Morgan, Richard, *Altered Carbon*, Orion Books, London (2002).

Murray, Stuart (ed.), *Not on Any Map: Essays on Postcoloniality and Cultural Nationalism*, University of Exeter Press, Exeter (1997).

Myers, Robert E. (ed.), *The Intersection of Science Fiction and Philosophy*, Greenwood Press, Westport (1983).

Niven, Larry, *A Gift From Earth*, Sphere Books, London (1968).

—— and Pournelle, Jerry, *The Mote in God's Eye*, Simon & Schuster, New York (1975).

Orbe, Mark P., *Constructing Co-cultural Theory: An Explication of Culture, Power and Communication*, Sage, Thousand Oaks (1998).

Orwell, George, *Animal Farm*, Secker & Warburg, London (1945).

——, *Nineteen Eighty-Four*, Secker & Warburg, London (1949).

Padgett, Lewis (Henry Kuttner) and Catherine L. Moore, 'Mimsy Were the Borogroves', *Astounding Stories* (February 1943).

Palmer, Chris, 'Galactic Empires and the Contemporary Extravaganza: Dan Simmons and Iain M. Banks', *Science-Fiction Studies*, 26 (1999), pp. 73–90.

Panshin, Alexei, *Rite of Passage*, Sphere, London (1968).

Parrinder, Patrick, *Shadows of the Future: H. G. Wells, Science Fiction and Prophecy*, Syracuse University Press, New York (1995).

Pearsall, Judy and Bill Trumble (eds), *The Oxford English Reference Dictionary*, Oxford University Press, Oxford (1995).

Perkus, Aaron, 'The Instincts of Race and Text', in Gisela Brinker-Gabler (ed.), *Encountering the Other(s): Studies in Literature, History and Culture*, State University of New York Press, Albany (1995).

Pfaelzer, Jean, *The Utopian Novel in America, 1886–1896: The Politics of Form*, University of Pittsburgh Press, Pittsburgh (1984).

Phillpotts, Eden, *Saurus*, John Murray, London (1938).

Philmus, Robert M., *Into the Unknown: The Evolution of Science Fiction from Francis Godwin to H. G. Wells*, University of California Press, Berkeley (1970).

Pohl, Frederik, 'Ninth Galaxy Reader', in Brian Ash (ed.), *Faces of the Future: The Lessons of Science Fiction*, Elek/Pemberton, London (1975).

—— and Kornbluth, C. M., *The Space Merchants*, Ballantine Books, New York (1953).

Pringle, David, *Science Fiction: The Best 100 Novels: An English Language Selection 1949–1984*, Xanadu, London (1985).

Rémusat, Abel, *Mélanges Posthumes* (1843), in R. Schwab (ed.), *The Oriental Renaissance: Europe's Rediscovery of India and the East, 1680–1880*, Columbia University Press, New York (1984).

Reynolds, Alastair, *Redemption Ark*, Orion Books, London (2002).

Robinson, Kim Stanley, *Icehenge*, Ace Books, New York (1984).

——, *Red Mars*, HarperCollins, London (1993).

——, *Green Mars*, HarperCollins, London (1994).

——, *Blue Mars*, Voyager, London (1996).

Romm, James, 'Belief and Other Worlds: Ktesias and the Founding of the Indian Wonders', in George S. Slusser and Eric S. Rabkin (eds), *Mindscapes: The Geographies of Imagined Worlds*, Southern Illinois University Press, Carbondale (1989).

Rose, Mark (ed.), *On the Poetics of the Science Fiction Genre*, Prentice-Hall, Upper Saddle River (1976).

——, *Alien Encounters: Anatomy of Science Fiction*, Harvard University Press, Cambridge (1981).

——, 'Filling the Void: Verne, Wells and Lem', *Science Fiction Studies*, 8 (July 1981), p. 134.

Roshwald, Mordecai, *Level 7*, Heinemann, London (1959).

Ross, Stephen David, 'What of the Others? Whose Subjection?', in Gisela Brinker-Gabler (ed.), *Encountering the Other(s): Studies in Literature, History and Culture*, State University of New York, Albany (1995).

Rotsler, William (ed.), *Science Fictionisms*, Gibbs Smith, Salt Lake City (1995).

Rousseau, Victor, *The Messiah of the Cylinder*, Curtis Brown, London (1917).

Ruddick, Nicholas, *Ultimate Island: On the Nature of British Science Fiction*, Greenwood Press, Westport (1993).

Rushdie, Salman, *Shame*, Adventura Books, New York (1984).

Russ, Joanna, 'Towards an Aesthetic of Science Fiction', *Science Fiction Studies*, 2 (July 1975), pp. 112–19.

Russell, Eric Frank, 'Dear Devil', *Other Worlds* (May 1950).

——, 'And Then There Were None', *Astounding* (June 1951).

Said, Edward W., *Orientalism: Western Conceptions of the Orient*, Vintage, London (1978).

——, *Culture and Imperialism*, Vintage, London (1994).

Santesson, Hans Steffan (ed.), *The Day After Tomorrow: Science Fiction Stories*, Little, Brown, Boston (1969).

Sargent, Lyman T., *British and American Utopian Literature 1516–1985*, Garland, New York (1988).

Savage, Robert L., *et al.* (eds), *The Orwellian Moment: Hindsight and Foresight in the Post-1984 World*, University of Arkansas Press, Fayetteville (1989).

Scholes, Robert, *Structural Fabulation: An Essay on Fiction of the Future*, University of Notre Dame Press, New York (1975).

Seed, David (ed.), *Anticipations: Essays on Early Science Fiction and Its Precursors*, Syracuse University Press, New York (1995).

—— (ed.), *Imagining Apocalypse: Studies in Cultural Crisis*, Macmillan, London (2000).

Sheffield, Charles (ed.), *How To Save the World*, Tom Doherty, New York (1995).

Shelley, Mary, *Frankenstein; or, The Modern Prometheus*, Lackington, Hughes, Harding, Mavor & Jones, London (1818).

Silverberg, Robert, *Invaders from Earth*, Ace Books, New York (1958)

—— (ed.), *Earthmen and Strangers: Nine Stories of Science Fiction*, Rey Dell Books, New York (1968).

—— (ed.), *To the Stars: Eight Stories of Science Fiction*, Hawthorn Books, New York (1971).

—— (ed.), *Beyond Control: Seven Stories of Science Fiction*, Rey Dell Books, New York (1972).

—— (ed.), *Invaders from Space: Ten Stories of Science Fiction*, Hawthorn Books, New York (1972).

——, *Earth Is the Strangest Planet*, Thomas Nelson, Nashville (1974).

—— (ed.), *Galactic Dreamers*, Random House, New York (1977).

Simak, Clifford D., *Cosmic Engineers*, Smith and Street, New York (1939).

Slusser, George E. and Eric S. Rabkin (eds), *Mindscapes: The Geographies of Imagined Worlds*, Southern Illinois University Press, Carbondale (1989).

——, Colin Greenland and Eric S. Rabkin (eds), *Storm Warnings: Science Fiction Confronts the Future*, Southern Illinois University Press, Carbondale (1987).

Smith, E. E., 'Doc', 'Triplanetary', *Amazing Stories* (January–April 1934).

Spinrad, Norman, *The Iron Dream*, Avon Books, New York (1972).

Spitzer, Leo, 'Andean Waltz', in Gisela Brinker-Gabler (ed.), *Encountering the Other(s): Studies in Literature, History and Culture*, State University of New York, Albany (1995).

Spivak, Gayatri, 'Can the Subaltern Speak?', in *Marxist Interpretations of Culture*, Cary Nelson and Lawrence Grossberg (eds), Macmillan Education, Basingstoke (1985).

——, *In Other Worlds: Essays in Cultural Politics*, Oxford University Press, London (1996).

Stableford, Brian, 'Philip Kindred Dick', in John Clute and Peter Nicholls (eds), *The Encyclopaedia of Science Fiction* (2nd edition), Orbit Books, London (1999), pp. 328–30

Staicar, Tom (ed.), *Critical Encounters II: Writers and Themes in Science Fiction*, Frederick Ungar, New York (1982).

Steele, Allen, 'Hard Again', *New York Review of Science Fiction*, 46 (June 1992), p. 1.

——, *Coyote: A Novel of Interstellar Exploration*, Baen Books, New York (2002).

Steen, Gerard, 'Analyzing Metaphor in Literature', *Poetics Today*, 20 (1999), pp. 499–522.

Sterne, Laurence, *The Life and Opinions of Tristram Shandy, Gentleman* (1759–69).

Stevenson, Robert Louis, *The Strange Case of Dr Jekyll and Mr Hyde*, Longmans, Green, London (1886).

Stoker, Carol A. and Emmart, Carter (eds), *Strategies for Mars: A Guide to Human Exploration*, Univelt, San Diego (1996).

Streese, Konstanze, 'Writing the Other's Language', in Gisela Brinker-Gabler (ed.), *Encountering the Other(s): Studies in Literature, History and Culture*, State University of New York, Albany (1995).

Strugatsky, Arkady and Strugatsky, Boris, *Polden: Dvadcat vtoroy vek* (1961), translated as *Noon: 22nd Century*, Macmillan, New York (1978).

—— and Strugatsky, Boris, *Stazhory* (1962), translated as *Space Apprentice*, Macmillan, New York (1981).

—— and Strugatsky, Boris, *Ponedel'nik nachinaetsia v Subbotu* (1966), translated as *Monday Begins on Saturday*, Daw Books, New York (1977).

—— and Strugatsky, Boris, *Piknik na obochine* (1972), translated as *Roadside Picnic*, Macmillan, New York (1977).

Suleri, Sara, *The Rhetoric of English India*, University of Chicago Press, Chicago (1992).

Suvin, Darko, *Metamorphoses of Science Fiction: On the Poetics and History of a Literary Genre*, Yale University Press, New Haven (1979).

——, 'SF and the Novum', in Teresa Lauretis, Andreas Huyssen and Kathleen Woodward (eds), *The Technological Imagination: Theories and Fictions*, Coda Press, Madison (1980).

Swift, Jonathan, *Travels into Several Remote Nations of the World*, Benjamin Motte, London (1726).

Sypher, Wylie, *Literature and Technology: The Alien Vision*, Random House, New York (1968).

Teunissen, John J. (ed.), *Other Worlds: Fantasy and Science Fiction since 1939*, University of Manitoba, Winnipeg (1980).

Thompson, Amy, *The Color of Distance*, Ace Books, New York (1999).

Tsiolkovsky, Konstantin E., *Reflections on Earth and Heaven and the Effects of Universal Gravitation*, Izdanie A. N. Goncarova, Moscow (1895).

Tubb, E. C., *Alien Dust*, Boardman, London (1955).

Ust, Daniel, 'Communication Breakdown: The Novels of Stanislaw Lem' (2001), http://uweb.superlink.net/neptune/Lem.html (last accessed February 2007).

Van Vogt, A. E.,'Recruiting Station', *Astounding* (March 1942).

——, *The Voyage of the Space Beagle*, Simon & Schuster, New York (1950).

Verges, Françoise, 'Post-scriptum', in David Theo Goldberg and Ato Quayson (eds), *Relocating Postcolonialism*, Blackwell, Oxford (2002).

Verne, Jules, *Maître du monde* (1904).

Vinge, Vernor, *A Deepness in the Sky*, Orion Books, London (1999).

Voltaire, *Micromégas* (1752).

Vonnegut, Kurt Jr, 'The Big Space Fuck', in Harlan Ellison (ed.), *Again, Dangerous Visions*, Doubleday, New York (1972).

Waldenfels, Bernhard, 'Response to the Other', in Gisela Brinker-Gabler (ed.), *Encountering the Other(s): Studies in Literature, History and Culture*, State University of New York, Albany (1995).

Weber, David, *War of Honor*, Baen Books, New York (2003).

Wells, Herbert G., *The Time Machine*, William Heinemann, London (1895).

——, *The War of the Worlds*, William Heinemann, London (1898).

——, *When the Sleeper Wakes*, George Bell, London (1899).

Westfahl, Gary (ed.), *Space and Beyond: The Frontier Theme in Science Fiction*, Greenwood Press, Westport (2000).

White, James, *The Dream Millennium*, Ballantine Books, New York (1974).

Wilcox, Clyde, 'Governing the Alien Nation: The Comparative Politics of Extraterrestrials', in Gary Westfahl and George Slusser (eds), *Science Fiction, Canonization, Marginalization and the Academy*, Greenwood Press, Westport (2002).

Wilcox, Don, 'The Voyage That Lasted 600 Years', *Amazing* (October 1940).

Wilde, Oscar, *The Picture of Dorian Gray*, Ward, Lock, London (1891).

Williamson, Jack, 'The Equalizer', *Astounding* (March 1947).

——, 'On the Final Frontier', in Gary Westfahl (ed.), *Space and Beyond: The Frontier Theme in Science Fiction*, Greenwood Press, Westport (2000).

Wilson, Richard, 'Honor', in Allen DeGraeff (ed.), *Human and Other Beings*, Collier Books, New York (1963).

Witner, Julia, 'The Best of Both Worlds: On Star Trek's Borg', in Gabriel Brahm Jr and Mark Driscol (eds), *Prosthetic Territories: Politics and Hypertechnologies*, Westview Press, Boulder (1995).

Wolfe, Gary K., *The Known and the Unknown: The Iconography of Science Fiction*, Kent State University Press, Ohio (1979).

Wollheim, Donald A., *The Universe Makers*, Gollancz, London (1971).

Wolmark, Jenny, *Aliens and Others: Science Fiction, Feminism and Postmodernism*, University of Iowa Press, Iowa City (1994).

Wood, Susan (ed.), *The Language of the Night: Essays on Fantasy and Science Fiction by Ursula K. Le Guin*, Putnam, New York (1979).

Wymer, Thomas L., *et al.* (eds), *Intersections: The Elements of Fiction in Science Fiction*, Popular Press, Bowling Green State University, Ohio (1978).

Wyndham, John, *The Chrysalids*, Michael Joseph, London (1955).

——, *The Midwich Cuckoos*, Michael Joseph, London (1957).

——, *Chocky*, Michael Joseph, London (1968).

——, *The Man From Beyond and Other Stories*, Michael Joseph, London (1975).

Yakobson, Boris I. and Richard E. Smalley, 'Fullerene Nanotubes: $C_{1,000,000}$ and Beyond', *American Scientist* (July–August 1997), pp. 324–37.

Yates, Frances, *Giordano Bruno and the Hermetic Tradition*, University of Chicago Press, Chicago (1964).

Yeats, W. B., 'The Second Coming' (1920), in *W. B. Yeats: Selected Poetry*, Macmillan, London (1990).

Zif, Bruce and Pratima V. Rao (eds), *Borrowed Power: Essays on Cultural Appropriation*, Rutgers University Press, Piscataway (1997).

Zubrin, Robert, 'The Economic Viability of Mars Colonisation', *Journal of the British Interplanetary Society*, 48 (1995), pp. 407–14.

—— and Wagner, Richard (eds), *The Case for Mars: The Plan to Settle the Red Planet and Why*, Free Press, New York (1996).

Index

Achebe, Chinua 14, 15
Aldiss, Brian 25, 79, 80, 129, 193
American War of Independence 6, 22, 112, 172
Anderson, Poul 77, 78, 187, 199
android 4, 13, 27, 30–36, 40–41, 78, 80, 111, 195
    see also drone, robot
anthropomorphisation 12, 13, 30, 44, 51, 151
appropriation 38, 98, 99, 100, 101, 103
archetype 57, 93, 121, 129, 149, 160, 171, 190
Ash, Brian 18, 23, 102
Asimov, Isaac 6, 43, 44, 47, 64, 78, 106, 107, 110, 111, 115, 118, 119, 120–32, 135, 136, 138, 139, 141, 145, 166, 168, 169, 172, 187, 189, 190, 193

Bacon, Francis 8
Bammer, Angelika 18, 22, 98
Banks, Iain M. 4, 7, 24, 25, 45, 70, 129, 132–36, 143, 167, 168–70, 174–90, 193
barbarism 45, 46, 100, 181
Barry, Peter 15
Berger, Peter 157
Bildungsroman 15, 67, 128, 143
Blish, James 68, 128, 136, 189, 193
Boehmer, Elleke 70
Brecht, Bertholt 3, 129
British empire 47, 70, 100, 103
British Raj 5, 20, 75, 168

Camus, Albert 9
Capek, Karel 44
capitalism 11, 13, 33, 138, 147, 148, 161, 166, 174

Carr, Terry 21
Carroll, Lewis 189
Carter, Paul 79
Çelik, Zeynep 153
characterisation 160
chauvinism 98, 100
Chesney, George T. 26, 190
Clarke, Arthur C. 5, 21, 43, 50, 62, 63, 67, 71, 74, 80, 81, 107, 115, 157, 162, 163, 168, 189, 193
colonialism 11, 46, 67, 75, 76, 85, 103, 115, 121–24, 149, 151, 160
communism 13, 175

derangement 74, 103
determinism 27, 28, 54, 126, 138, 145, 147, 148, 149, 156, 162
diaspora 33, 74, 77, 115, 116, 124, 166, 191
Dick, Philip K. 4, 13, 27–36, 40–42, 78, 88, 111, 168, 189, 193
differentiation 9, 16, 45, 53, 89, 143
drone 178, 184–86
    see also android, robot
Duncan, Dawn 63, 67, 69, 74, 81, 133
dystopia/dystopian 6, 10, 14, 46, 77, 79, 85, 105, 126, 131, 132, 143, 169, 190

Eagleton, Terry 2, 96
Easterbrook, Neil 127
ecopoiesis 155
Eden 12, 22, 114, 150, 152, 201
Einstein, Albert 66, 67, 68, 69, 71, 79, 111, 131, 134, 145, 203
Emerson, Rupert 170, 171
Eurocentrism 15, 18
exoticism 18, 19, 59, 123, 125, 170
expansionism 66, 99, 115, 122, 171

extraterrestrial 4, 15, 20, 28, 29, 38, 78, 94, 204

fantasy 1, 3, 6, 10, 27, 33, 50, 62, 63, 76, 77, 81, 82, 110, 112, 127, 138, 159, 160, 161, 189, 205, 206
Fanthorpe, U. A. 43
fascism 46, 99, 112
Feenberg, Andrew 107, 120, 123
fin de siècle 89
Fischer, William B. 136, 158, 193
Fogg, Martyn 155
Frankenstein 9, 25, 45, 52, 58, 92

Gandhi, Leela 46, 92, 93, 94
George, Susan 76
Gibbon, Edward, *Decline and Fall of the Roman Empire* 128, 136, 172
Gibson, William 106, 172, 173, 187
Gilgamesh 19
golden age of SF 6, 82, 106, 107, 108, 125, 201

Haldeman, Joe 126, 130, 131, 134, 135
Hart, Jonathan 98, 150
Haynes, Robert 155
Headrick, Daniel R. 65, 68
Hegel, Georg Wilhelm Friedrich/Hegelian 11
Heinlein, Robert A. 6, 11–13, 26, 50, 76, 79, 106, 107, 110–25, 129, 133–39, 145, 172, 189–97, 201–5
Heisenberg, Werner 17
Herbert, Frank 109, 115, 128, 130, 138, 168, 189
humanism 159, 162
Huxley, Aldous 10, 46, 91, 108
hybridisation 157, 164
hybridity 4, 6, 11, 41, 99, 151, 164, 169, 170

imperialism 3–8, 22, 24, 26, 29, 40, 42, 49, 54–55, 62–66, 71, 74, 75, 77, 83, 87, 103, 106, 112–22, 131, 136–44, 152, 154, 160, 162, 167–76, 180, 190, 191
implied reader 129
intertextuality 6, 25, 27, 54, 94, 129, 134, 189, 190

irony 26, 29, 33, 44, 46, 48, 84, 85, 123, 134, 137, 150, 159, 160, 165, 181, 184

Jacobs, Jane M. 83
Judd, Denis 46, 70

Kipling, Rudyard 20, 89, 110, 171
Krulik, Ted 10

Lakoff, George 4, 43, 47
Lasswitz, Kurd 4, 5, 83–92, 94–104, 147, 172
Lazarus, Neil 151
Le Guin, Ursula K. 4, 5, 42, 47–51, 55–61, 77, 125, 127, 144, 189
leitmotif 10, 47, 51, 143
Lem, Stanislaw 4, 5, 35, 42, 51–61, 77, 198
Leninism 13
Levinas, Emmanuel 21
Lewis, C. S. 8, 21, 189
libertarian 110, 114–17, 133
libertarianism 175
longevity 1, 130, 153, 158, 159
Lowell, Percival 84
Lucas, George 131, 136, 172
Luckhurst, Roger 109
Luckmann, Thomas 157
Lyotard, Jean-François 36

MacLeod, Ken 24, 77, 127, 144, 189, 190
Malthus, Thomas/Malthus 23, 106, 118, 119, 147
marginalisation 4, 8, 11, 13, 20, 41, 74
Marx, Karl 39
Marxism 13
Maslow, Abraham 78, 140, 173, 175, 177, 199, 203
Mazrui, Ali 75, 199
meta-empire 7, 169, 172, 174, 182, 183, 186, 190
Miller, Walter M. 6, 125, 133–35, 138–45, 166, 169
modernist 149
Moorcock, Michael 79
myth 20, 52, 76, 134, 135, 148, 150, 169, 171, 173

NASA 68, 69
neo-colonialism 124, 149, 151
Nietzsche, Friedrich 130
Niven, Larry 12, 66
non-Western 11, 13
nostalgia 17, 28, 80, 83, 132
novum 6, 129, 130

orientalism 4, 13, 45
Orwell, George 10, 46, 132, 169, 173, 189
Othering 4, 10, 13, 14, 17, 204

Parrinder, Patrick 78
patriarchal 107, 111, 113
Perkus, Aaron 38, 63
Pfaelzer, Jean 144
Pinocchio 14, 32
Pohl, Frederick 91, 138
polyvalency 4, 11, 41, 165
postcolonialism 3, 8, 11, 64, 180
postmodern 13, 26, 30, 64, 81, 130, 135, 143, 144, 159
Prometheus 51–52, 198
prototype 93, 177, 189

Raj see British Raj
Rand, Ayn 114
relativity 63, 66, 67, 68, 71, 131, 136, 198, 203
revolution 6, 22, 49, 80, 101, 112–15, 120, 163, 178, 190
Robinson, Kim Stanley 6, 7, 12, 16, 17, 20, 22, 23, 49, 50, 66, 74, 75, 78, 80, 84, 108, 115, 126, 128, 145, 146–66, 192
robot 119–25, 185
Romm, James 135
Roshwald, Mordecai 79
Ross, Stephen David 18
Rushdie, Salman 39, 110
Russia 14, 100
    see also Soviet Union

Said, Edward W. 4, 5, 8, 9, 13, 15, 16, 18, 20, 21, 45, 53, 54, 84, 87, 89, 153
satire 26, 36, 112, 151, 176
Scholes, Robert 75

scientific romance 1
Seed, David 29
sentience 36, 54, 59, 185
Shakespeare, William 4, 27, 58, 196
Shelley, Mary 16, 52, 58, 59, 92, 127, 189
silencing 4, 11, 25, 28, 31, 37, 38, 40, 74, 163
Silverberg, Robert 116, 125
Slusser, George E. 143
Smalley, Richard E. 158
social Darwinism 38, 44, 91, 94, 112
Soviet Union 168, 176, 188
    see also Russia
space opera 108, 205
speculative fiction 105, 112, 113
Spengler, Oswald 128, 136
Spinrad, Norman 205
Spitzer, Leo 17
Spivak, Gayatri 4
Stableford, Brian 30
Star Trek 46, 62, 107, 130, 132, 201
Star Wars 20, 50, 131, 136, 172
Steen, Gerard 46
Sterne, Lawrence 50, 51, 197
Streese, Konstanze 11
Strugatsky, Arkady 13, 14, 194
Strugatsky, Boris 13, 14, 194
subaltern 4, 11, 20, 34, 35, 36, 38, 41, 48, 49, 56, 57, 84, 94, 152, 157, 164
Suleri, Sara 46, 151
super-economics 182
Suvin, Darko 6, 109, 129, 130
Swift, Jonathan 2, 14
symbolism 70, 196
Sypher, Wylie 65, 198

terracentricity 12, 151
terracentrism 12
terraforming 3, 6, 26, 146, 150, 151–56, 162
Turner, Mark 4, 43, 196

utopia/utopian 14, 84, 85, 105, 112, 132, 137, 143, 145, 151, 152, 169, 170, 175, 185, 182, 189

Verges, Françoise 137

Verne, Jules 64, 105, 106, 190, 193
Voltaire (Francois Marie Arouet) 2, 14, 64, 105, 189

Waldenfels, Bernard 9, 17, 20
Wells, H. G. 2, 4, 5, 14, 16, 18, 26, 33, 37, 38, 44, 50, 64, 81, 83–97, 100–6, 183, 190, 193, 195, 199
Western 4, 5, 10–15, 18, 21, 26, 38, 40, 42, 46, 56, 57, 59, 63, 79, 83, 111, 117, 139, 146, 149, 190, 191, 193, 196
Westernised 84, 113
Williamson, Jack 76, 108, 116
Wilson, Richard 77
Witner, Julia 108
Wolfe, Gary K. 13, 16, 95, 109, 123, 130, 147, 148, 193

Wollheim, Donald A. 173
World War I 45, 79, 95
World War II 37, 39, 79, 107, 138, 197
World War III (Terminus) 33, 79, 195
Wyndham, John 4, 14, 26, 27, 28, 29, 32, 36–42, 84

xenophilia 18, 22
xenophobia 18

Yakobson, Boris I. 158
Yeats, W. B. 103

Zubrin, Robert 155

Printed and bound by CPI Group (UK) Ltd, Croydon, CR0 4YY

13/04/2025

14656594-0004